Government and Politics in Sri Lanka

The island of Sri Lanka (formerly Ceylon) was one of the few Asian colonies in which the British Empire experimented with liberal state-building in the nineteenth century, and where many British colonial officials predicted that the independent state would become a liberal democratic success story. Sri Lanka has held on to much of the liberal democratic state-institutions left behind by the British Empire, including periodic elections. At the same time, the UN's Office of the High Commissioner for Human Rights concluded in September 2015 that there are reasonable grounds to believe that Sri Lanka committed serious international crimes against the Tamils. Such accusations are usually levelled against authoritarian states; it is unusual for a democracy to face such charges.

This book analyses where Sri Lanka stands as a state that has in place liberal democratic state-institutions but exhibits the characteristics of an authoritarian state. Using Michel Foucault's concept of biopolitics, the author argues that Sri Lanka enacted racist legislations and perpetrated mass-atrocities on the Tamils as part of its biopolitics of institutionalising and securing a Sinhala-Buddhist ethnocratic state-order. The book also explores the ways that, apart from military action, power relations produce the effects of battle, and thus the way that peace can often become a means of waging war. The author provides fresh insights into Sri Lanka's postcolonial policies and the system of government that it has in place.

A novel approach to analysing Sri Lanka's postcolonial policies and the system of government, this book will be of interests to researchers in the field of Political Science, Asian Politics and International Relations.

A. R. Sriskanda Rajah received his PhD from Brunel University, UK, where he has also worked as Module Convenor/Associate Lecturer in International Relations.

Routledge Studies in South Asian Politics

For a full list of titles in this series, please visit www.routledge.com

3 **Refugees and Borders in South Asia**
   The Great Exodus of 1971
   Antara Datta

4 **India's Human Security**
   Lost Debates, Forgotten People, Intractable Challenges
   Edited by Jason Miklian and Ashild Kolas

5 **Poverty and Governance in South Asia**
   Syeda Parnini

6 **US-Pakistan Relations**
   Pakistan's Strategic Choices in the 1990s
   Nasra Talat Farooq

7 **Public Policy and Governance in Bangladesh**
   Forty Years of Experience
   Nizam Ahmed

8 **Separatist Violence in South Asia**
   A Comparative Study
   Matthew J. Webb

9 **Pakistan's Democratic Transition**
   Change and Persistence
   Edited by Ishtiaq Ahmad and Adnan Rafiq

10 **Localizing Governance in India**
   Bidyut Chakrabarty

11 **Government and Politics in Sri Lanka**
   Biopolitics and Security
   A. R. Sriskanda Rajah

Government and Politics in Sri Lanka
Biopolitics and Security

A. R. Sriskanda Rajah

LONDON AND NEW YORK

First published 2017
by Routledge
2 Park Square, Milton Park, Abingdon, Oxon OX14 4RN

and by Routledge
711 Third Avenue, New York, NY 10017

Routledge is an imprint of the Taylor & Francis Group, an informa business

© 2017 A. R. Sriskanda Rajah

The right of A. R. Sriskanda Rajah to be identified as author of this work has been asserted by him in accordance with sections 77 and 78 of the Copyright, Designs and Patents Act 1988.

All rights reserved. No part of this book may be reprinted or reproduced or utilised in any form or by any electronic, mechanical, or other means, now known or hereafter invented, including photocopying and recording, or in any information storage or retrieval system, without permission in writing from the publishers.

Trademark notice: Product or corporate names may be trademarks or registered trademarks, and are used only for identification and explanation without intent to infringe.

British Library Cataloguing-in-Publication Data
A catalogue record for this book is available from the British Library

Library of Congress Cataloging-in-Publication Data
A catalog record for this book has been requested

ISBN: 978-1-138-29097-6 (hbk)
ISBN: 978-1-315-26571-1 (ebk)

Typeset in Times New Roman
by Apex CoVantage, LLC

For my eldest sister, Mala

Contents

Acknowledgements ix
Abbreviations x

Introduction 1

1 Biopolitics as war 11

2 Constructing an ethnocracy 27

3 In defence of the race/species 48

4 Unleashing Jihadism and starving the 'enemy' 74

5 War through 'peace' 102

6 Managing life in pain 138

Conclusion 158

Index 163

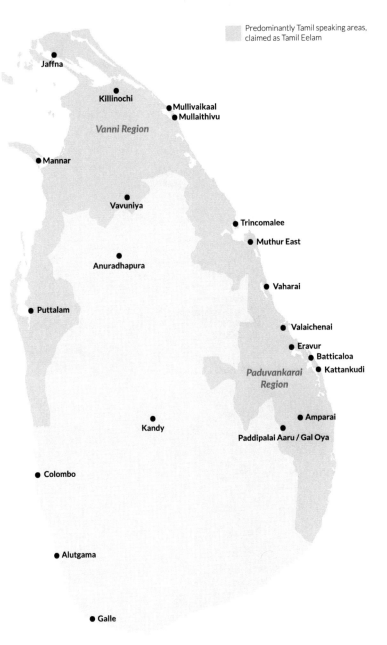

Acknowledgements

I thank Dorothea Schaefter, the senior editor (Central, South and Southeast Asia) at Routledge, for the interest she has shown in publishing this book. I also thank the anonymous independent reviewer for his invaluable comments.

I am greatly indebted to Professor Mark Neocleous and Dr. David Scott. It was their unwavering support, wise advice and guidance during my PhD research at Brunel University London that shaped-up the theoretical framework used in this book and, to a greater extent, the book's empirical findings. I especially thank Professor Neocleous for his advice and support even after my PhD. I also thank Dr. Suthaharan Nadarajah of SOAS University of London for some of his advice on Foucault's work and politics in Sri Lanka.

I am very grateful to Dr. A. Stanislaus for reviewing my book manuscript and providing me with invaluable advice, support and encouragement.

I thank my good friend Parthipan for developing an adapted version of the map of Sri Lanka, highlighting the areas of conflict and towns/cities mentioned in the book. I also thank Mr. Daniel Dalet, the webmaster of d-maps.com, for granting permission to adapt the map.

Most importantly, I thank my eldest sister, Mala, for her support and encouragement, without which I would not have been able to write this book. I dedicate this book to her. I also thank my elder sister, Divya and all of my family members and friends who have supported me.

Abbreviations

ACTC	All Ceylon Tamil Congress
BBC	British Broadcasting Corporation
BBS	*Bodhu Bala Sena*
CIC	Ceylon Indian Congress
CNN	Cable News Network
CPA	Centre for Policy Alternatives
ER 2005	*Emergency (Miscellaneous Provisions and Powers) Regulations* No.1 of 2005
EU	European Union
FBI	Federal Bureau of Investigation
GWoT	Global War on Terror
HRCSL	Human Rights Commission of Sri Lanka
ICEP	International Crimes Evidence Project
ICRC	International Committee of the Red Cross
IDP	Internally displaced person
IPKF	Indian Peace Keeping Force
ITAK	*Ilankai Thamil Arasu Katchi*
IUF	Islamic Unity Foundation
JHU	*Jathika Hela Urumaya*
JVP	*Janatha Vimukthi Peramuna*
LTTE	Liberation Tigers of Tamil Eelam
MBRL	Multi-barrelled rocket launcher
MULF	Muslim United Liberation Front
NDTV	New Delhi Television
NFZ	No fire zone
OHCHR	Office of the High Commissioner for Human Rights
PFLT	People's Front of Liberation Tigers
PLO	Palestinian Liberation Organisation
PSO	*Public Security Ordinance* No.25 of 1947
PTA	*Prevention of Terrorism Act* No.48 of 1979
RAW	Research and Analysis Wing
RPG	Rocket propelled grenade
SAS	Special Air Service

SLMC	Sri Lanka Muslim Congress
STF	Special Task Force
TNA	Tamil National Alliance
TULF	Tamil United Liberation Front
UK	United Kingdom
UN	United Nations
US/USA	United States/United States of America
UTHR-J	University Teachers for Human Rights – Jaffna
WFP	World Food Programme

Introduction

The presidential election of 8 January 2015 made the island-state of Sri Lanka (formerly Ceylon) the centre of much international attention. Since attaining independence in 1948, Sri Lanka has held periodic elections; it was also one of the first few Asian colonies in which the British Empire experimented with liberal state-building and introduced universal franchise. Yet, the presidential election of 8 January 2015 was seen to be a watershed moment. This was because it marked the end of the 9-year rule of the anti-Western, statist regime of Mahinda Rajapaksa, and heralded into power a pro-Western coalition led by President Maithripala Sirisena and Prime Minister Ranil Wickremesinghe, both favourable to open market economic policies.

The then-US-President Barack Obama (2015) hailed the regime change as 'a symbol of hope for those who support democracy all around the world'. Nisha Desai Biswal (2016), the US Assistant Secretary of State for South and Central Asia during Obama's presidency, went a step further and called Sri Lanka a resilient democracy. Similar remarks have also been made in the past by other Western leaders when Sri Lanka had in place pro-Western, pro-market governments (see, for example Reagan, 1984; Thatcher, 1985). The former-US-President George W. Bush (2005) once claimed that 'the United States and Sri Lanka have enjoyed close relations based on common support for the values of democracy, the rule of law, human rights and free trade'. But can Sri Lanka be called a democracy?

In September 2015, after undertaking an investigation into the conduct of the Sri Lankan state in the final years of the armed conflict with the Liberation Tigers of Tamil Eelam (LTTE), the organisation that waged an armed struggle to establish a Tamil state on the island, the United Nations (UN) (2015: 219) concluded that there are 'reasonable grounds to believe' that Sri Lanka committed 'gross violations of international human rights law, serious violations of international humanitarian law and international crimes' against its Tamil population. Such accusations are frequently levelled against authoritarian states. It is unusual for a democracy to face such charges (the UN has also accused the LTTE of violating international law and committing international crimes). Two of the key defining features of a democracy in a contemporary sense are respect for civil liberties and human rights (Doyle, 1986: 1152; Mandelbaum, 2002: 268–269; Paris, 2009: 5).

2 Introduction

Where does Sri Lanka stand as a state that has held periodic elections as other democracies do, but at the same time remains accused of perpetrating mass atrocities on a population whose lives, rights and liberties it should have protected, as all democracies are expected to do? Using Michel Foucault's concept of 'biopolitics', this book provides fresh insights into Sri Lanka's policies and the system of government that it has in place.

In his philosophical works and lectures of the 1970s, Foucault (2004: 255; 2009: 1) used the concept of 'biopolitics', a system of power that treats populations as a political problem, to analyse power relations through the matrix of war. Drawing on this concept of Foucault, in this book I argue that Sri Lanka perpetrated mass atrocities on the Tamils as part of its biopolitics of institutionalising and securing a Sinhala Buddhist ethnocratic state order. In doing so, I explore the ways that, apart from military action, other power relations produce the effects of battle, and thus the way that 'peace' can often become a means of waging war.

Until the British began governing Sri Lanka as a single administrative unit in 1833, it had existed as an island of kingdoms and principalities ruled by two linguistically distinct nations, the Tamils and the Sinhalese (see Ribeiro, 1909: 3–4; HC Deb 21 November 1947; Kemper, 1991: 144; Chilcott, 2006). Whilst the Tamil kingdoms and principalities existed in the northern (at times extending to the northwestern parts) and eastern parts of the island, the Sinhala ones existed in the southern and central parts (Ribeiro, 1909: 3–4; HC Deb 21 November 1947; Kemper, 1991: 144; Chilcott, 2006). The Portuguese and the Dutch ruled some of those kingdoms and principalities and governed them as separate colonies, before the British took control of them at the end of the eighteenth century. When the British created the island-state in 1948, they gave it the colonial name Ceylon. The name Sri Lanka came into existence only in 1972 when the island-state became a republic (in this book, I use 'Ceylon' and 'Sri Lanka' interchangeably, depending on the historical periods).

As we will see in Chapter 2, this renaming was done to signify the island-state's transition to a Sinhala Buddhist ethnocracy.

Oren Yiftachel (1999), in his critique of Israel's policy of Judaising the Palestinian territories, defines 'ethnocracy' as 'a non-democratic regime that attempts to extend or preserve disproportional ethnic control over contested multi-ethnic territory' (1999: 368). Though Sri Lanka has regularly held elections, on the basis that its election process allows the Tamils to be excluded from the state's 'decision-making circles', Yiftachel sees fit to call it an 'ethnocracy' (1999: 368). Neil DeVotta also suggests that a state can be called an ethnocracy 'when the dominant ethnic group' within its borders 'eschews accommodation, conciliation, and compromise with the state's minorities and instead seeks to institutionalize its preferences so that it alone controls the levers of power' (2007: 56). In light of the Sri Lankan state's discriminatory policies that adversely impact on the Tamils, and the fact that it has accorded in its two republican constitutions the 'foremost place' to Buddhism and the 'pre-eminent position' to the Sinhala language, the main religion and the language of the island's numerically majority Sinhalese, DeVotta finds it fitting to refer to it as an 'ethnocracy' (2007: 19). Suthaharan Nadarajah and Luxshi Vimalarajah (2008: 16–17) also use the term 'ethnocracy' to refer to Sri Lanka. They make this characterisation on the basis that Sri Lanka's system of government provides uneven protection for political and civil rights 'across ethnic, class and territorial units', and because its last two constitutions are 'mono-ethnic' in character, enshrining 'Buddhism as a specially protected religion', and endorsing 'the unitary model of governance' that serves the interests of the island's Sinhala Buddhist community (Nadarajah and Vimalarajah, 2008: 16–17).

In this book, I refer to Sri Lanka as an ethnocracy not only for the above reasons, but also because it has exercised biopower (Foucault used 'biopower' and 'biopolitics' as synonymous terms) along ethnological lines, violating *en masse* the civil liberties and human rights of the Tamils. As we will see in Chapter 2 to Chapter 6, Sri Lanka transformed into an ethnocracy to improve the lives of its Sinhala Buddhist population; at the same time, it perpetrated mass atrocities on the Tamils because it saw them as a threat to this endeavour.

Sri Lanka's efforts to construct and secure a Sinhala Buddhist ethnocratic state order include attempts to rewrite the island's history by denying the precolonial existence of the Tamils and their kingdoms and principalities, and making the claims of the *Mahavamsa* (1912: 55), a Sinhala chronicle compiled by Buddhist monks in the sixth century C.E., that the island was given to the Sinhalese by Buddha for his religion (Buddhism) to be established, the 'truth'. In 'Society Must Be Defended', Foucault (2004: 68) argues that in Middle Ages Europe, history was used by rulers as the discourse of power to 'subjugate' people and to 'fascinate, terrorise, and immobilise' them. History, which 'spoke of the antiquity of kingdoms', sought to bring 'great ancestors back to life, and re-discovered the heroes who founded empires and dynasties' (Foucault, 2004: 66). The objective 'was to ensure that the greatness of the events or men of the past could guarantee the value of the present, and transform its pettiness and mundanity into something equally heroic and equally legitimate' (Foucault, 2004: 66). As we will see in Chapter 2 and Chapter 3, this is exactly what Sri Lanka has tried to do by invoking the *Mahavamsa*.

It is not only the history of the Tamils that Sri Lanka has sought to deny. It has also sought to deny that the island has long been the home of Muslims, though without any precolonial kingdoms or principalities of their own, but living within the Sinhala and Tamil kingdoms and principalities (see *Chapter 4*). In other words, Sri Lanka's biopolitics has been inextricably linked to the production of a narrative of 'truth' about the island's 'rightful' occupants.

For Foucault, a 'regime of truth' is often capable of making 'something that does not exist' become 'inscribed in reality' (2010: 20). In this sense, 'truth' is a manifestation of power:

> The important thing here, I believe, is that truth isn't outside power, or lacking in power: contrary to a myth whose history and functions would repay further study, truth isn't the reward of free spirits, the child of protracted solitude, nor the privilege of those who have succeeded in liberating themselves. Truth is a thing of this world: it is produced only by virtue

of multiple forms of constraint. And it induces regular effects of power. Each society has its regime of truth, its 'general politics' of truth: that is, the types of discourse which it accepts and makes function as true; the mechanisms and instances which enable one to distinguish true and false statements, the means by which each is sanctioned; the techniques and procedures accorded value in the acquisition of truth; the status of those who are charged with saying what counts are true.

(Foucault, 1980: 131)

In other words, 'truth' is 'linked in a circular relation with systems of power which produce and sustain it, and to effects of power which it induces and which extend it' (Foucault, 1980: 133).

As we will see in Chapter 3 and Chapter 6, it is not only the narrative of 'truth' on the island's 'rightful' occupants that Sri Lanka has sought to produce by exercising power in biopolitical mode. Following its transformation as an ethnocracy in 1972, and as part of its biopolitics of securing the ethnocratic state order, throughout the armed conflict and in its aftermath, Sri Lanka also sought to produce a 'truth' on the armed Tamil secessionist movement, in particular the LTTE. With the military defeat of the LTTE in May 2009, Sri Lanka sought to produce another narrative of 'truth' that there were 'zero' Tamil civilian casualties in its final military offensives. Torture (both physical and psychological), sexual abuse and rape have played key roles in these endeavours of the state.

In developing a biopolitical account of government and politics in Sri Lanka in this book, I do not seek to establish another form of 'truth'. Instead, I seek to make a contribution to what Foucault (2004: 7) called the 'insurrection of subjugated knowledges'. Foucault defined subjugated knowledges as either 'historical contents that have been buried or masked in functional coherences or formal systematizations', or 'a whole series of knowledges that have been disqualified as nonconceptual knowledges, as insufficiently elaborated knowledges' (Foucault, 2004: 7). Sri Lanka's policies and practices that have been subject to a biopolitical analysis in this book had largely remained masked in structural modes of analysis. In unmasking their biopolitical significance, this book makes a contribution to the literature on the insurrection of subjugated knowledges.

The book departs in two ways from mainstream Foucauldian scholarship.

Many Foucauldian scholars are reluctant to use Foucault's theoretical expositions to analyse the state on the basis that he posited a highly decentralised understanding of power. As David Chandler (2010: 141–142) puts it, they hold the view that there is 'the global disjunction between politics (confined to the nation-state) and power (alleged to be free-floating and unaccountable)'. This stems from the suggestion made by Foucault (1998: 88–89) in *The History of Sexuality: Volume 1* (first published in 1976), that the critique of power should go beyond the state; or to put it in Foucault's words, we need to 'cut off the head of the king' (the state) from 'political thought and analysis'.

However, in an interview in the year the work was published, Foucault clarified that in suggesting 'the king's head to be cut off' from political thought and analysis, he did 'not mean in any way to minimise the importance and effectiveness of state power'; instead, he merely wanted to highlight the dangers of taking power as the state's exclusive domain:

> I simply feel that excessive insistence on [the state] playing an exclusive role leads to the risk of overlooking all the mechanisms and effects of power which don't pass directly via the State apparatus, yet often sustain the State more effectively than its own institutions, enlarging and maximising its effectiveness.
>
> (1980: 72–73)

In an interview the following year, Foucault reiterated this point: 'I don't want to say that the State isn't important; what I want to say is that relations of power, and hence the analysis that must be made of them, necessarily extend beyond the limits of the State' (1980: 122). Later, in the lecture series *Security, Territory, Population*, delivered at the College de France in 1978, Foucault noted that the 'microscopic' analysis of power outside and beyond the state would, 'without paradox or contradiction', lead to understanding the 'general problems of the state' and government: 'an analysis in terms of micropowers comes back without any difficulty to the analysis of problems like those of government and the state' (2009: 358).

Though the focus of this book is the Sri Lankan state, its analysis is not confined to the power relations of the state. As we will see in Chapter 2 to Chapter 6, the book also analyses other power relations that exist outside/beyond the state, but have contributed, and to a large extent been used by the state. Thus, the analysis in this book is consistent with the way Foucault set out his exposition of power as both residing within and outside/beyond the state.

The second departure from mainstream Foucauldian scholarship in this book is its focus on law. In *The History of Sexuality: Volume 1*, Foucault suggested that 'we must construct an analytics of power that no longer takes law as a model and a code' (1998: 90). This, he argued, was necessary because modern power relations do not simply deal with 'deduction' and 'death' as law has historically done, but also operate on the basis of technique, normalisation and control (Foucault, 1998: 89). For Foucault, while 'law always refers to the sword', other forms of power relations that are not controlled by law, rather than displaying themselves in their 'murderous splendour', also 'qualify, measure, appraise, and hierarchize' life and thus distribute 'the living in the domain of value and utility' (1998: 144).

Consequently, many mainstream Foucauldian scholars have become accustomed to ignoring law (both in its domestic and international manifestations) in their studies on power relations. Although some scholars have examined the counter-terrorist practices of Western liberal states during the Global War on Terror (GWoT) using a Foucauldian framework, they have done so by placing counter-terrorism laws in a space without law (see, for example Neal, 2008; 2010). However, as the works of scholars such as Claudia Aradau (2007) and Mark Neocleous (2008) have demonstrated, it is possible to analyse law using Foucault's concepts.

Moreover, a close reading of Foucault's works and lectures reveals that he did not suggest that we should ignore law, especially if the focus of the analysis is the war-making functions of the state (whether internally or externally). As Foucault acknowledged also in *The History of Sexuality: Volume 1*, modern power relations do not make law fade into the background (1998: 144). This is a point that he reiterated in his later lecture series, *Security, Territory, Population* (Foucault, 2009: 10). For Foucault, it is law that, as well as setting out what is to be permitted and what is to be prohibited, also sets out the punishment for violations (2009: 5). In acknowledging the repressive powers of law in contemporary societies, Foucault (1998: 144) not only reiterated his earlier claim that law always means the sword, but also implied that it remains as forceful as it was before modernity, and is thus capable of producing the effects of battle, i.e., death, injury, submission, expulsion or the appropriation of persons or property. In other words, in equating law with the sword, Foucault acknowledged its war-making function in contemporary societies. Foucault suggested a study of power beyond law so that such a study would be able to grasp the productive dynamics of power, as opposed to only its repressive dynamics represented by law. Thus, one would not be going against Foucault's theoretical expositions of power by focusing on law if the concern of the study is the repressive actions of states that produce the effects of battle. As the discussions in this book will demonstrate, law, producing the effects of battle, has played a key role in Sri Lanka's biopolitics of constructing and securing a Sinhala Buddhist ethnocratic state order. For this reason, this book is justified in undertaking a Foucauldian analysis focusing on law.

This is not to say that only by undertaking an analysis of law one can understand the war-making functions of the state, apart from military action. As Foucault (1998: 144) noted in *The History of Sexuality: Volume 1*, all power relations, like law, are capable of producing the effects of battle, though they might not always be apparent. Chapter 4 to Chapter 6 will discuss these aspects.

One of the major criticisms that many Foucauldian scholars encounter is the relevance of Foucault's work beyond Western societies, and this is important to this study that takes Sri Lanka as a case for its analysis. Jan Selby (2007: 325 and 339), for example, claims that Foucault's work was primarily on the '"domestic" social arena' of Europe. In Selby's view, Foucault was preoccupied with biopower and governmentality in the 'domestic arenas of modern "governmentalised" societies', and as such his writings are suited only to 'analysing discrete techniques and practices of liberal governance' in European/Western societies (2007: 334).

This is a misreading of Foucault's works. Even though Foucault's analysis of power did not go beyond European/Western societies, it must be borne in mind that before the end of the Second World War, most states outside the Western hemisphere had either remained as colonies or protectorates of European powers where Western modes of governance were exercised, though this differed from country to country. Despite decolonisation, these states have not abandoned the Westphalian state system left behind by their European colonial masters and returned to their precolonial modes of rule. Moreover, as we will see in Chapters 2,

3 and 6, some of the techniques of government used in Europe before modernity and applied in Ceylon during British colonial rule have been incorporated in the biopolitical practices of the island-state in the postcolonial period. Notwithstanding this, in 'Society Must Be Defended', Foucault himself asserted the link between biopolitics and European colonialism (2004: 257). This suggests on the part of Foucault that his writings on Western societies can be used to explain the governmental practices of Europe's former colonies and protectorates. As Anna M. Agathangelou (2010: 703) notes, 'Foucault's recognition of colonialism opens up space for us to reconstruct a much longer genealogy of the international, not contained by European borders'. Moreover, many years before 'Society Must Be Defended' was published, Foucault's concepts were successfully used by scholars to analyse power relations outside the West (see, for example Said, 1977; Hyam, 1990; Escobar, 1995; Stoler, 1995).

Though this book undertakes a biopolitical analysis of government and politics in Sri Lanka, it would be misleading on my part to assert that the analysis here provides a comprehensive study of biopower on the island in the postcolonial period (in colonial Ceylon, biopower was exercised by the British Empire). Apart from the Sri Lankan state, biopower has also been exercised in the postcolonial period by at least three more power complexes: the *Janatha Vimukthi Peramuna* (JVP), which launched two failed Sinhala Marxist insurrections in 1971 and 1987, the LTTE, which spearheaded the armed Tamil secessionist movement from 1972 to 2009, and the Indian Peace Keeping Force (IPKF), which occupied the northern and eastern parts of the island from 1987 to 1990. A comprehensive understanding of biopower in postcolonial Sri Lanka would not be complete without subjecting these three power complexes to a biopolitical analysis. Such a task is beyond the scope of this book. This book is confined to a biopolitical analysis of one of the power complexes on the island, the state, and is thus confined to how biopower has been used by and in support of it.

Overview of chapters

Chapter 1 sets out the theoretical basis of the analysis undertaken in the book. It undertakes a discussion of the concept of biopolitics as introduced by Foucault, how it is being used by scholars today and how it can be understood to be a system of power inscribed with war.

In Chapter 2, the analysis sets out how postcolonial Ceylon went about transforming from a democracy to an ethnocracy. It examines the role of law, the violence of law and the violence of 'lawlessness' as Ceylon produced the effects of battle and transformed into an ethnocracy. The chapter also analyses the Ceylon state's use of emergency laws to crush the first Sinhala Marxist insurgency of the JVP in 1971, allowing its security forces to commit mass atrocities against Sinhala Buddhists suspected of involvement in the insurgency. In doing so, the chapter addresses the crucial question of how states are able to justify the use of violence against populations in whose interests they also claim to use violence against other populations existing within their borders.

8 *Introduction*

Chapter 3 concerns the period commencing in 1972 (when Sri Lanka became an ethnocracy) to 1990 (when the IPKF departed from Sri Lanka after occupying the predominantly Tamil-speaking Northern and Eastern Provinces for nearly 3 years). The focus of this chapter is on the Sri Lankan state's use of police brutalities and military violence to unleash terror on the Tamils. Next, it discusses the reforms made to the violence of 'lawlessness'. The consequence of these tactics by the state was to turn it into an unofficially organised form of terror. The chapter then moves to a discussion of the brief tactical alliances the state made, first with India in 1987 to counter the threat posed by the LTTE, and later in 1989 with the LTTE to oust the Indian troops from the island. Throughout this period, in the south of the island, the state faced another Sinhala Marxist insurgency from the JVP. The chapter concludes with an examination of Sri Lanka's use of tactics of terror during this tumultuous period of the island's history to crush the JVP insurgency, and solidify and unify the loyalty of the Sinhala Buddhists to the state.

Sri Lanka's efforts in the 1990s to regain state control over the territories it lost to the LTTE consequent to the Indian troop withdrawal from the North and East in March 1990 are examined in Chapter 4. The chapter provides an analysis of the tactical alliance that Sri Lanka made with the Jihadi extremists to drive the LTTE out of the populated areas of the Eastern Province. In doing so, it shows that even though biopower may be exercised along ethnological lines by states upholding ultranationalist ideologies, this does not mean tactical alliances cannot be made with power complexes that adopt competing extremist ideologies. The chapter also examines Sri Lanka's use of economic embargoes on the LTTE held areas of the Northern Province to weaken the LTTE's fighting capabilities and its ability to secure the territories that it controlled. This way, the chapter shows that it is not only law, but other power relations, in this case the economy, are also capable of producing the effects of battle.

Chapter 5 takes up the period, February 2002 (when a ceasefire agreement was signed between the LTTE and the Sri Lankan government) to the LTTE's military defeat in May 2009, for analysis. The chapter shows how Sri Lanka, exploiting the GWoT and advocating neoliberal economic policies, used diplomacy as a way of waging war on the LTTE, leading to the latter's eventual isolation at the international level; thus creating conditions for the state to commence the final military offensives to vanquish the armed Tamil secessionist movement. The chapter also deals with how Sri Lanka perpetrated mass atrocities, unprecedented in scale in the island's history, on the Tamils living in the LTTE held territories.

The final chapter is focused on the state's military defeat of the LTTE and its consequences for the Tamil people caught up in the zone of fighting. The state established mass internment camps to detain the hundreds of thousands of displaced and traumatised Tamils, and surrendered LTTE cadres in the immediate aftermath of the collapse of the LTTE's armed struggle. Using witness testimonies, the chapter expounds on how the use of rape, torture and mass scale 'disappearance' disciplined the displaced Tamil civilians and surrendered LTTE combatants into submission, and this became central to Sri Lanka's biopolitics of securing the ethnocratic state order. The chapter addresses how these methods produced the effect of battle and complemented the state's actions to produce a 'truth' about the LTTE, and to deny the mass atrocities perpetrated by its security forces in the final stages of the armed conflict.

As we saw earlier, the election of a pro-Western, pro-market government in Sri Lanka in January 2015, and the smooth transition from one regime to another, has led to Western leaders and diplomats hailing Sri Lanka as a resilient democracy. The Conclusion returns to the question of whether, following the biopolitical analysis set out in this book, the holding of regular elections, and the existence of state institutions based on those of Western liberal states, is sufficient to refer to Sri Lanka as a democracy.

References

Agathangelou, A.M. (2010) 'Bodies of Desire, Terror and the War in Eurasia: Impolite Disruptions of (Neo) Liberal Internationalism, Neoconservatism and the "New" Imperium', *Millennium – Journal of International Studies*, 38(3), pp. 693–722.

Aradau, C. (2007) 'Law Transformed: Guantanamo and the "Other" Exception', *Third World Quarterly*, 28(3), pp. 489–501.

Biswal, N.D. (2016) *Remarks Introducing Sri Lankan Foreign Minister Mangala Samaraweera*. Available at: http://www.state.gov/p/sca/rls/rmks/2016/253743.htm (Accessed: 26 February 2016).

Bush, G.W. (2005) *President Bush Says Sri Lanka Having Experienced Terrorism and Preserved, Understands the Threat that Terrorism Poses to Democracy and the World*. Available at: http://slembassyusa.org/embassy_press_releases/president-bush-says-sri-lanka-having-experienced-terrorism-and-persevered-understands-the-threat-that-terrorism-poses-to-democracy-and-the-world/ (Accessed: 8 January 2011).

Chandler, D. (2010) 'Globalising Foucault: Turning Critique into Apologia – a Response to Kiersey and Rosenow', *Global Society*, 24(2), pp. 135–142.

Chilcott, D.J. (2006) Interview for *Sunday Virakesari* reproduced by *Tamilnet*, 21 July. Available at: http://www.tamilnet.com/art.html?catid=13&artid=18870 (Accessed: 4 March 2011).

DeVotta, N. (2007) *Sinhalese Buddhist Nationalist Ideology: Implications for Politics and Conflict Resolution in Sri Lanka*. Washington: East West Center.

Doyle, M.W. (1986) 'Liberalism and World Politics', *The American Political Science Review*, 80(4), pp. 1151–1169.

Escobar, A. (1995) *Encountering Development: The Making and the Unmaking of the Third World*. Princeton: Princeton University Press.

Foucault, M. (1980) *Power/Knowledge*. Translated by Colin Gordon, Leo Marshall, John Mepham, and Kate Soper. Harlow: Pearson Education.

Foucault, M. (1998) *The History of Sexuality: Volume 1: The Will to Knowledge*. Translated by Robert Hurley. London: Penguin Books (Original work published 1976).

Foucault, M. (2004) *"Society Must Be Defended", Lectures at the College de France, 1975–76*. Translated by David Macey. London: Penguin Books.

Foucault, M. (2009) *Security, Territory, Population: Lectures at the College de France, 1977–1978*. Translated by Graham Burchell. Hampshire: Palgrave Macmillan.

Foucault, M. (2010) *The Birth of Biopolitics: Lectures at the College de France 1978–1979*. Translated by Graham Burchell. Hampshire: Palgrave Macmillan.

HC Deb 21 November 1947, vol 444, col 1478–1495. Available at: http://hansard.millbank systems.com/commons/1947/nov/21/ceylon-independence-bill#S5CV0444P0_ 19471121_HOC_94 (Accessed: 20 July 2013).

Hyam, R. (1990) *Empire and Sexuality: The British Experience*. Manchester: Manchester University Press.

Kemper, S. (1991) *The Presence of the Past: Chronicles, Politics, and Culture in Sinhala Life*. London: Cornell University Press.

Mahavamsa, Or the Great Chronicle of Ceylon. (1912) Translated by Wilhelm Geiger. London: Oxford University Press (Original work published in the sixth century C.E.).

Mandelbaum, M. (2002) *The Ideas that Conquered the World: Peace, Democracy, and Free Markets in the Twenty-first Century*. New York: Public Affairs.

Nadarajah, S. and Vimalarajah, L. (2008) *The Politics of Transformation: The LTTE and the 2002–2006 Peace Process in Sri Lanka*. Berlin: Berghof Research Centre for Constructive Conflict Management.

Neal, A.W. (2008) '"Goodbye War on Terror?" Foucault and Butler on Discourse of Law, War and Exceptionalism', in Dillon, M. and Neal, A.W. (eds.), *Foucault on Politics, Security and War*. Hampshire: Palgrave Macmillan, pp. 43–64.

Neal, A.W. (2010) *Exceptionalism and the Politics of Counter-Terrorism: Liberty, Security and the War on Terror*. Oxon: Routledge.

Neocleous, M. (2008) *Critique of Security*. Edinburgh: Edinburgh University Press.

Obama, B. (2015) *Statement by the President on the Election in Sri Lanka*. Available at: https://www.whitehouse.gov/the-press-office/2015/01/09/statement-president-election-sri-lanka (Accessed: 9 February 2016).

Paris, R. (2009) *At War's End, Building Peace after Civil Conflict*. New York: Cambridge University Press.

Reagan, R. (1984) *Remarks at the Welcoming Ceremony for President J.R. Jayewardene of Sri Lanka*. Available at: http://www.presidency.ucsb.edu/ws/?pid=40055 (Accessed: 10 November 2012).

Ribeiro, J. (1909) *History of Ceilao*. Colombo: The Colombo Apothecaries Co.

Said, E. (1977) *Orientalism*. London: Penguin.

Selby, J. (2007) 'Engaging Foucault: Discourse, Liberal Governance and the Limits of Foucauldian IR', *International Relations*, 21(3), pp. 324–345.

Stoler, A.L. (1995) *Race and the Education of Desire: Foucault's History of Sexuality and the Colonial Order of Things*. Durham: Duke University Press.

Thatcher, M. (1985) *Press Conference in Sri Lanka*. Available at: http://www.margaretthatcher.org/document/106022 (Accessed: 13 September 2012).

UN (2015) *Report of the OHCHR Investigation on Sri Lanka (OISL)*. Geneva: Office of the UN High Commissioner for Human Rights.

Yiftachel, O. (1999) '"Ethnocracy": The Politics of Judaizing Israel/Palestine', *Constellations*, 6, pp. 364–391.

1 Biopolitics as war

The term 'biopolitics' is used by scholars in various social science disciplines. It is even 'claimed by experts on biodefence, biosecurity, bioethics and biotechnology' (Aradau, 2012). This has led to the emergence of competing definitions of the term, thus making its usage both ambiguous and contentious. As Jorg Spieker notes, biopolitics today 'means different things to different thinkers' (2011: 94). So what is biopolitics? What did Foucault mean by it? How has it been reinterpreted by scholars after him? This chapter addresses these questions. In doing so, it also discusses ways of reconceptualising the term 'war'.

The chapter begins with a discussion of the concept of 'biopolitics', as used by Foucault, and examines how it is being used by scholars after him. It then moves on to discuss how biopolitics can be understood as a system of power inscribed with war, and capable of mobilising power relations, in addition to military action, to produce the effects of battle.

Grasping biopolitics

Although Foucault first coined the term 'biopolitics' in *The History of Sexuality: Volume 1*, and discussed it further in some of his subsequent lecture series, it was in the lecture series *Security, Territory, Population* that he provided the most clear cut definition of the term:

> By this I mean a number of phenomena that seem to me to be quite significant, namely, the set of mechanisms through which the basic biological features of the human species became the object of political strategy, of a general strategy of power, or, in other words, how, starting from the eighteenth century, modern Western societies took on board the fundamental biological fact that human beings are a species. This is roughly what I have called biopower.
>
> (2009: 1)

On the basis of this definition and a number of expositions Foucault made in his works and other lecture series, the concept of biopolitics can be understood in the following terms.

First, biopolitics deals with life at the level of populations (Foucault, 1998: 137). Unlike the ancient sovereign power of life and death that dealt with life at the level of the individual, biopolitics addresses the 'multiplicity of men' as a 'global mass'; it is a 'massifying' power directed at 'man-as-species' (Foucault, 2004: 242–243). This does not mean that in biopolitical rule, life at the level of the individual is completely ignored. Biopolitics also involves treating the body of the individual as a machine, using disciplinary mechanisms to optimise its capabilities, extort its forces, increase its usefulness and docility and integrate it into systems of efficient and economic controls (Foucault, 1998: 139; 2004: 242).

Second, biopolitics is not exterior to the exercise of political power: as a system of power concerned with 'the management of state forces', it deals with processes such as 'births and mortality, the level of health, life expectancy and longevity' and 'all the conditions that can cause these to vary' in populations. In other words, it is about improving the life chances of populations by carrying out interventions and imposing regulatory controls on processes that affect them in general (Foucault, 1998: 140; 2004: 243; 2009: 367; 2010: 317).

Third, remaining part and parcel of the exercise of political power, biopolitics is also the power to take human lives; as well as being a system of power that makes life live, it is also one that kills life. The ancient sovereign power over the life of the individual was largely exercised as the power of death (Foucault, 1998: 136). It was exercised 'as a means of deduction' that was 'levied on the subjects' to 'appropriate a portion of wealth, a tax of products, goods and services, labor and blood' (Foucault, 1998: 136). In seeking to make life live, biopolitics, however, has not put behind the ancient sovereign power of death/the right to kill: 'I wouldn't say exactly that sovereignty's old right – to take life or let live – was replaced, but it came to be complemented by a new right which does not erase the old right but which penetrates it, permeates it' (Foucault, 2004: 241). In biopolitics, the power of death/the right to kill is exercised as 'the right of the social body to ensure, maintain, or develop its life' (Foucault, 1998: 136). Thus, 'wars are no longer waged in the name of a sovereign who must be defended'; they are waged 'on behalf of the existence of everyone' (Foucault, 1998: 137). In Foucault's view, some power complexes resort to genocide not because they are obsessed with killings but because they largely exercise power biopolitically: if 'genocide is indeed the dream of modern powers, this is not because of a recent return to kill; it is because power is situated and exercised at the level of life, the species, the race, and the large-scale phenomena of population' (1998: 137).

As a system of power that deals with life at the level of populations and concerned with making life live, how is the power of death/the right to kill exercised? It is done by creating a binary division within the human species: the 'good' part of the human species that must be looked after and the 'bad' part of the human species that must be eliminated for the 'good' part of the human species to live (Foucault, 2004: 254–255). People of different races, political adversaries, the criminals, the mentally ill and people with various anomalies become defined as biological threats to the existence of the 'good' part of the human species (Foucault, 2004: 258–259 and 262). In other words, in the biopower system, killings are undertaken for the 'elimination of the biological threats to and the improvement of the species or race' (Foucault, 2004: 256). Thus, in biopolitical rule, massacres are seen to be vital for the human species to live: 'entire populations are mobilised for the purpose of wholesale slaughter in the name of life necessity' (Foucault, 1998: 137).

In *Homo Sacer*, claiming to correct and complete the Foucauldian thesis of biopolitics, and drawing on ancient Greek political thought, Giorgio Agamben (1998: 1 and 4) divides life as 'bare life' (meaning 'the simple fact of living common to all living beings') and 'qualified life' (meaning 'the form or way of living proper to an individual or group'). Claiming that Foucault had misconceived biopolitics as a development of modern power politics, and citing the ancient Roman law figure of the *Homo Sacer* (the criminal whose execution is 'classifiable neither as sacrifice nor as homicide') as an example, Agamben claims that the 'inclusion of man's natural life in the mechanisms and calculations of power' are not modern but 'absolutely ancient' (1998: 9 and 82). Modern politics is not so much characterised by the inclusion of bare life in politics or the use of life as 'a principal object of the projections and calculations of State power', but the entry of both bare life and qualified life into 'zone of irreducible indistinction' coupled with the 'processes by which the exception everywhere becomes the rule' (Agamben, 1998: 9). Though Agamben confines much of his study to the biopolitics of the Nazi state, he also touches on its thanatopolitical (the politics of death) character in 'democratically' constituted states: as both the 'bearer of rights' and 'sovereign subject', every individual is a *Homo Sacer*, who may be eliminated when he breaks the law (1998: 124 and 142). In essence, for Agamben, biopolitics is the thanatopolitics over the individual's life.

Contesting this claim of Agamben, in *Biopower Today*, Paul Rabinow and Nikolas Rose claim that biopolitics is not the power to take life but the power to foster life: it should be understood to 'embrace all the specific strategies and contestations over problematizations of collective human vitality, morbidity and mortality; over forms of knowledge, regimes of authority and practices of intervention that are desirable, legitimate and efficacious' (2006: 197). In their view, Foucault's concept of biopolitics 'operates according to logics of vitality, not mortality' (Rabinow and Rose, 2006: 211). While acknowledging that biopolitics includes 'circuits of exclusion', they argue that '*letting die* is not *making die*' [emphasis in original] (Rabinow and Rose, 2006: 211). Claiming the Nazi state to be 'one configuration that modern biopower can take', they criticise Agamben for characterising it as the 'hidden dark truth of biopower': biopower under the Nazi state, they argue, 'was dependent upon a host of historical, moral, political and technical conditions' that functioned alongside 'a complex mix of the politics of life and the politics of death' (Rabinow and Rose, 2006: 201).

In 'Society Must Be Defended', Foucault noted the Nazi state's appropriation of biopolitics to be 'a paroxysmal development' (2004: 259). Taking this characterisation at face value, Rabinow and Rose (2006: 199 and 201) claim that Foucault understood the Nazi state to be only an exceptional development in the history of biopolitics: they argue that Foucault understood biopolitics to be the techniques for 'maximising the capacities of both the population and the individual' within various domains of power – such as medicine, town planning and so on – and not the power to kill. This is an incorrect assertion. As we saw earlier, in introducing the concept of biopolitics to the study of power relations, Foucault presented both its productive and violent dynamics. Moreover, he did not refer to the appropriation of biopolitics by the Nazi state to be a paroxysmal development because it was the only state that exercised biopolitics as the power of death/the right to kill. Instead, Foucault made this characterisation on the basis that the Nazi state is an example of the state's use of the tight relationship between disciplinary power and biopower:

> After all, Nazism was in fact the paroxysmal development of the new power mechanisms that had been established since the eighteenth century. Of course, no State could have more disciplinary power than the Nazi regime. Nor was there any other State in which the biological was so tightly, so insistently, regulated. Disciplinary power and biopower: all this permeated, underpinned, Nazi society (control over the biological, of procreation and of heredity; control over illness and accidents too). No society could be more disciplinary or more concerned with providing insurance than that established, or at least planned, by the Nazis. Controlling the random element inherent in biological processes was one of the regime's immediate objectives.
>
> (2004: 259)

Rose further argues that the death pole of biopolitics should not be understood as the power to kill but as the power to allow death to occur through 'contraception, abortion, preimplantation, genetic diagnosis, debates about the right to die' and so on (2007: 64). Rose's argument, as Spieker (2011: 103) points out, was not actually derived from Foucault's works or lecture series. Thus, in developing a different conception of biopolitics based on reproduction and genomic medicine, Rabinow and Rose effectively depoliticise it.

This is not to suggest that Agamben's conceptualisation of biopolitics is not without its problems. Even though Agamben recognises the violent dynamics of biopower, the Roman metaphorical figure of *Homo Sacer* that he uses to develop his concept of 'bare life' ignores the massifying character of biopolitics. The metaphorical figure of *Homo Sacer* falls within the ambit of the ancient sovereign power of death that dealt with life at the level of the individual. Moreover, as Aradau (2012) notes, and as we saw earlier in this chapter, in contrast to the ancient sovereign power of death that was 'individualising', biopolitics is a 'massifying' technique: it 'captured the transformation of power from sovereign and disciplinary techniques to a technique which acts upon populations as collectives'. Agamben's work on biopolitics also ignores the fact that the power of death/ the right to kill in biopolitical rule is intimately linked to the power of making life live.

In *Empire*, Michael Hardt and Antonio Negri define biopolitics as the form of power that is concerned with administering the 'production and reproduction of life' in service of global capitalism: 'In the biopolitical sphere, life is made to work for production and production is made to work for life'; it is a power that 'extends throughout the depths of the consciousness and bodies of population' and 'across the entirety of social relations' (2001: 23–24 and 32). Though much of their work is concerned with the '*productive* dimensions of biopower', and how biopower is being used today in the service of global capitalism, Hardt and Negri (2001: 27 and 35) acknowledge its violent dynamics.

However, in *The Liberal Way of War*, while recognising the violent dynamics of biopolitics and its intimate relationship with capitalism, Michael Dillon and Julian Reid define it as 'an order of politics and power which, taking species existence' of humans 'as its referent object, circumscribes the discourse of what it is to be a living being to the policing, auditing and augmenting of species properties' (2009: 24 and 29). For Dillon and Reid (2009: 24–25), when Foucault coined the term biopolitics, economy (understood in terms of 'capitalist modes of production and exchange') was the key expression of species life in biopolitics. However, as a result of the 'confluence of the digital and molecular revolutions', economy has today become one, among many, of the primary expressions of 'species properties' of biopoliticised life (Dillon and Reid, 2009: 23–24 and 28–29). On this basis, Dillon and Reid argue that biopolitics today can only be understood by examining the life sciences (2009: 46).

Foucault (1998: 140–143; 2009: 1 and 367; 2010: 22 and 317) acknowledged biopolitics to be 'an indispensable element in the development of capitalism', though, as Aradau and Blanke (2010: 44–45) point out, his analysis dealt with capitalism's appropriation of biopolitics for disciplining individual bodies and governing circulation. Capitalism would not have been able to develop without 'the controlled insertion of bodies into the machinery of production and the adjustment of the phenomena of population to economic processes' (Foucault, 1998: 140–141). Biopolitics helped to adjust the 'accumulation of men to that of capital'; it went hand-in-hand with the 'growth of human groups', the 'expansion of productive forces' and the 'differential allocation of profit' (Foucault, 1998: 141). It also helped to prevent, contain and often eliminate, threats – such as epidemics and famines – to the human species and capitalism (Foucault, 1998: 142). With biopolitics working hand-in-hand with capitalism, the 'Western man' gradually learnt the meaning of existing as 'a living species in a living world, to have a body, conditions of existence, probabilities of life, and individual and collective welfare, forces that could be modified, and a space in which they could be distributed in an optimal manner' (Foucault, 1998: 142). Thus, Hardt and Negri cannot be faulted for asserting the relationship between biopolitics and capitalism. However, this does not mean that it is only about the production and reproduction of life in the service of capitalism.

For Foucault, it was not only capitalism that appropriated biopolitics; it was also used by European colonialism, the Nazi state and Soviet-type socialist states (2004: 257–263). It was European colonialism that first used biopolitics in a thanatopolitical mode (Foucault, 2004: 257). Despite being capitalist, European colonialism did not initially use biopolitics in a productive way, but used it in a destructive way, which Foucault calls 'colonizing genocide': biopolitics under

European colonialism was used to 'justify the need to kill people, to kill populations, and to kill civilizations' in colonies (2004: 275). This was also the case with the Nazi state, which was also capitalist. The Nazi state largely used biopolitics in its project of constituting the German race as the 'superior race' by seeking to eliminate and enslave other races (Foucault, 2004: 259–260). Soviet-type socialist states (in particular the Stalinist ones) also used biopolitics in a destructive manner to 'deal with the mentally ill, criminals, political adversaries, and so on' (Foucault, 2004: 261–262). Thus, biopolitics not only functions in the service of capitalism. Instead, it is a system of power that has been appropriated by various power complexes to manage populations in a calculated way. Each of them promote their own way of living for the human species and kill groups (the 'bad' part of the human species) that are seen to be a threat to the way of living they promote.

Foucault refers to this relationship of life and death – that is 'if you want to live, you must take lives, you must be able to kill' – as the 'relationship of war' (2004: 255). It is a relationship that has origins in the 'principle underlying the tactics of battle – that one has to be capable of killing in order to go on living' (Foucault, 1998: 137). Does this mean that when power is exercised in biopolitical mode, there is war? The next section will explore this.

Reconceptualising war

In his treatise, *On War*, Carl von Clausewitz defined war as 'a duel on an extensive scale' (1832/1997: 5). This definition has become the conventional wisdom that war is generally understood in terms of violence that involves military action. As a consequence, when wars are waged through other means, they are not seen as wars, except when the term is used metaphorically, i.e., 'war on drugs', 'war on gun crime' and so on. However, when Clausewitz wrote his treatise, there existed more than one definition of the term 'war'. This was acknowledged by Clausewitz himself, even though he did not elaborate what these different definitions were: 'We shall not enter into any of the abstruse definitions of war used by publicists. We shall keep to the element of the thing itself, to a duel' (1997: 5).

In the lecture series 'Society Must Be Defended', Foucault analysed politics and law through the matrix of war. For Foucault (2004: 16), politics 'sanctions and reproduces the disequilibrium of forces manifested in war'; it achieves this by perpetually reinscribing the 'relationship of force' in 'institutions, economic inequalities, language, and even the bodies of individuals'. As a form of power, law is, even in its most regular form, also inscribed with the mechanisms of war (Foucault, 2004: 50–51). This was also a point that Foucault made when he examined the violent dynamics of law in *The History of Sexuality: Volume 1*: 'Law cannot help but be armed, and its arm, *par excellence*, is death; to those who transgress it, it replies, at least as a last resort with that absolute menace. The law always refers to the sword' (1998: 144).

In 'Society Must Be Defended', Foucault (2004: 47–48) also inverted Clausewitz's (1997: 22) principle that war was the continuation of politics by other means. In this regard Foucault (2004: 48) claimed that he was not inverting Clausewitz's principle, but restating a thesis that had actually been in circulation in the seventeenth and eighteenth centuries before it was inverted by Clausewitz. Foucault did not unearth any scholarly work of those two centuries that specifically referred to politics as the continuation of war. However, to uphold his claim, he cited the works of a number of English and French thinkers of those centuries – of which the works of the English jurist Edward Coke and the French aristocrat and historian Henri de Boulainvilliers were the key ones – that formed the basis of political struggles to limit the powers of the absolute monarchy in England and France. Referring to those works collectively as a 'historico-political discourse', Foucault (2004: 49) argued that the latter understood war as 'a permanent social relationship, the ineradicable basis of all relations and institutions of power'. Citing the works of Coke in which Saxon laws were invoked to advance the claim that before the Norman invasion, the king 'exercised absolute and unchecked sovereignty over the social body' only in times of war, and those of Boulainvilliers in which it was argued that by possessing unlimited power the monarch was exercising the powers which were conferred to him in ancient French aristocratic societies only in times of war, Foucault (2004: 106 and 148) claimed that the works of both thinkers conceptualised the exercise of absolute power by the monarch in times of peace to be the continuation of war. For Foucault (2004: 165), it was this thesis that later inspired Clausewitz to conceptualise war as the continuation of politics (in his later lecture series *Security, Territory, Population*, Foucault (2009: 301–302) stated that Clausewitz's principle was also based on the fact that war also functioned as an instrument of diplomacy in the Balance of Europe system in the seventeenth century).

Although Foucault's arguments in this regard were actually his own interpretations of the works of Coke and Boulainvilliers (as well as some of their contemporaries and successors), most of them were credible interpretations. For example, in *The First Part of the Institutes of the Lawes of England* (first published in 1658), Coke defined peace to be the time 'when the Courts of Justice be open, and the Judges and Ministers of the same may by Law protect men from wrong and violence, and distribute Justice to all' (2003: 732). In contrast, 'when by invasion, Insurrection, Rebellions, or such like, the peaceable course of Justice is disturbed and stopped, so as the Courts of Justice bee as it were shut up, *Et silent leges inter arma* [amidst the clash of arms the laws are silent]', it becomes the time of war (Coke, 2003: 732). Coke elaborated further on his definitions of war and peace in following terms: 'So as hereby it also appeareth, that time of peace is the time of law and right, and time of warre is the time of violent oppression, which cannot be resisted by the equall course of Law' (2003: 733). When read together with *The Petition of Right 1627* (3 Cha. 1, c. 1), which was enacted in the English Parliament in 1628 under the guidance of Coke, these definitions reveal how the exercise of absolute powers by the monarch was understood at that time as war by other means. As well as seeking to curtail the English monarch's powers to raise forced loans to fund wars, section VIII of *The Petition of Right 1627* also sought to end the use of martial law, which allowed violence to be used in its naked form, in times of peace, and to ensure that ordinary laws prevailed when the country was not at war:

> And that the aforesaid Comissions for proceeding by Martiall Lawe may be revoked and annulled. And that hereafter no Comissions of like nature may issue forth to any person or persons whatsoever to be executed as aforesaid, lest by colour of them any of your Majesties Subjects be destroyed or put to death contrary to the Lawes and Franchise of the Land.
>
> (3 Cha. 1, c. 1)

In other words, in defining the 'time of violent oppression' as the time of war, which martial law under the reign of King Charles I produced in England, Coke (2003: 733) implied that when the monarch exercises absolute power in times of 'peace', politics becomes war.

This raises the question: can this historico-political discourse be used as the basis for conceptualising war beyond military action? In inverting Clausewitz's principle, and by establishing that he was restating a thesis that had actually been in existence before Clausewitz, Foucault challenged 'the idea that politics and war are in principle separate and different' (Spieker, 2011: 7). However, the historico-political discourse that he relied on to justify his arguments cannot be used as the basis for conceptualising war beyond military action in all contemporary societies. First, in contemporary Western societies that have constitutional monarchies (such as Britain), the monarch no longer exercises absolute power over the social body, either in times of 'peace' or in times of war. If this state of affairs is analysed within the context of the historico-political discourse that Foucault relied on to invert Clausewitz's principle, politics would signify peace, and not war. Second, as Foucault (1998: 144; 2004: 50–51) points out, law does not signify peace, even though Coke (2003: 733) argued in those terms. As Neocleous (2008: 50) established in *Critique of Security* (and as we will see in context of the use of emergency laws in postcolonial Ceylon/Sri Lanka), the very martial law that Coke and his contemporaries sought to confine to times of war through *The Petition of Right 1627* has today become part and parcel of 'ordinary' laws in 'the logic of emergency'. How then do we conceptualise war beyond military action? To do this, we need to turn to Foucault's other expositions on war.

In 'Society Must Be Defended', Foucault pointed out that before the 'state acquired monopoly on war', in the Middle Ages there existed a form of war known as 'day-to-day warfare', which was also called 'private warfare' (2004: 48). The state, 'endowed with military institutions', replaced 'the day-to-day and generalised warfare' as well as 'a society that was perpetually traversed by relations of war' (Foucault, 2004: 49). This was also a point that he made in *The History of Sexuality: Volume 1*, and reiterated later in the lecture series *Security, Territory, Population* (Foucault, 1998: 87; 2009: 300–301). For Foucault, before the monarchy established its supremacy over society, war had existed both as a private relationship (between individuals) and as a public relationship (between the princes):

> What, after all, was war in medieval conceptions? I was going to say that war was basically a judicial behaviour. Why did one go to war? One waged war when there was injustice, when there was a violation of right, or anyway when someone claimed a right that was challenged by someone else. In the medieval world there was no discontinuity between the world of right and the world of war. There was not even any discontinuity between the universe of private law, in which it was a matter of settling disputes, and the world of confrontations between princes, which was not, and could not be called international and public law. One was always in the realm of disputes, of the settlement of disputes – you have taken my inheritance, you have seized one of my lands, you have repudiated my sister – and one fought, wars developed, within this juridical framework of public war and private war. It was public war as private war, or private war that took on the public dimension. It was a war of right, and the war was settled moreover exactly like a juridical procedure, by a victory, which was like a judgement of God. You lost, therefore right was not on your side.
>
> (2009: 300–301)

Foucault also argued that the 'great institutions of power that developed in the Middle Ages' in the form of the 'monarchy' and 'the state with its apparatus' actually rose as 'agencies of regulation, arbitration, and demarcation' over other forms of war, i.e., 'feudal and private wars' as well as 'the private settling of lawsuits', that existed at that time (1998: 86–87). In its attempt to transcend all forms of war, the monarchy used law, through the 'mechanisms of interdiction and sanction', as 'a weapon' as well as the 'mode of manifestation and the form of its acceptability' (Foucault, 1998: 87). In this sense, law performed a war-making function for the monarchy, paving the way for the latter to establish its supremacy over medieval society.

Cross referencing these claims of Foucault with the works of two key social contract theorists of the Enlightenment brings to light that even in the early modern period, war as a relationship between individuals was not erased from society's memory. In *De Cive*, published in 1651, Thomas Hobbes claimed that 'the natural state of men, before they entered into society, was a mere war': it was 'a war of all men against all men' (1949: 29). Later, in the *Second Treatise of Government*, published in 1690, John Locke also argued that 'force, or a declared design of force, upon the person of another, where there is no common superior on earth to appeal for relief, is the state of war' (1980: 15). However, this state of war between individuals was understood to cease when they enter civil society. For Hobbes, on becoming part of civil society, individuals are understood to have 'conveyed their whole right of war and peace' to 'some one man or council' (1949: 73). Similarly, Locke argued that when individuals become part of political societies, they 'give up all the power' that they had in the state of nature

(1980: 53). Coke also advanced similar arguments, even though not within the framework of social contract theory. For Coke, individuals did not have the right to wage war and this right only belonged to the king: 'no subject can levie warre within the Realme without authority from the King, for to him it only belongeth' (2003: 969). In advancing these arguments, although Hobbes and Locke, as well as Coke, sought to denounce the right of the individual to wage war, in doing so they also revealed that war as a relationship between individuals had not been erased from the memories of society.

A close reading of the works of other political thinkers (see, for example Rousseau, 1999: 51) of the later years of the Enlightenment also reveals that even at the end of the eighteenth century, war as a relationship between individuals was not erased from society's memory. They not only saw the order established by the state through law as the substitute for the relationship of war between individuals, but also believed that when this order is challenged, it should trigger from the state the response to war (see Kant, 1887: 195–196; Rousseau, 1999: 71). They classified an individual who broke the law as the enemy of society, against whom the power mechanisms of the state had to be mobilised; he had to be treated as 'the common enemy', a 'traitor' and 'monster', against whom 'all the forces, all the power, all the rights' had to be used (Foucault, 1991: 90). This was in contrast to the arguments made earlier by Coke that only certain actions on the part of the individual can be construed as wars against the king. For Coke, when an individual rises to 'expulse strangers, to deliver men out of prisons, to remove Counsellors, or against any statute, or to any other end, pretending Reformation of their heads, without warrant', this becomes the 'levying of war against the King' (2003: 970). Similarly, if an individual rises to 'alter Religion established within the Realme, or Laws, or to go from Town to Town generally, and to cast downe enclosures', this also becomes 'a levying of war' (Coke, 2003: 970). However, in *The Social Contract*, published in 1762, Jean-Jacques Rousseau argued that when an individual breaks the law of his country, he makes 'war on it', and needs to be destroyed in order to preserve the state as well as the lives of his fellow countrymen (1999: 71). The offender 'becomes a rebel and a traitor to his country' and is put to death as 'an enemy rather than as a citizen': 'He who wills that his life may be preserved at the expense of others must also, when necessary, give his life for their sake' (Rousseau, 1999: 71).

In 1796, Immanuel Kant also made similar arguments. In Part I (*The Philosophy of Law*) of the *Metaphysics of Morals*, Kant argued that when an individual commits a crime, he endangers the 'Commonwealth' and can thus be destroyed: 'It is better that *one* man should die than that the whole people should perish' [emphasis in original] (1887: 195–196). For Kant, the right to punish a criminal was 'the Right of Retaliation (*jus talionis*)' (1887: 196). This was also the case with resistance against the state's laws. In Kant's view, when an individual rises against the state, 'he would expose himself as a Citizen, according to the law and with full right, to be punished, destroyed, or outlawed' (1887: 174). Resistance 'on the part of the people to the Supreme Legislative Power of the State', even when the monarch abuses power, 'is in no case legitimate' (Kant, 1887: 176). Any effort by the people to rise against the ruling order constitutes high treason:

> [W]hen the Supreme power is embodied in an individual Monarch, is there any justification under the pretext of his abuse of power, for seizing his person or taking away his life (*monarchomachismus sub specie tyrannicidi*)? The slightest attempt of this kind is *High Treason (proditio eminens)*; and a traitor of this sort who aims at the *overthrow* of his country may be punished, as a political parricide, even with Death. It is the duty of the People to bear any abuse of the Supreme Power, even though it should be considered to be unbearable [emphasis in original].
>
> (Kant, 1887: 176–177)

These arguments clearly indicate that in the early modern period, the concept of 'war' had at least three meanings. First, it was understood as a power relation between individuals. Second, it was understood as a power relation (primarily in terms of military action) between states. Third, it was understood as a power relation (in terms of military actions against internal rebellions, the prosecution of individuals who broke the law, and politics as the exercise of power that managed military actions and law) between a state and its citizens.

Foucault's key expositions on law's war-making function can be found in *Discipline and Punish*, published in 1975, in which he gave examples of how crimes from the Middle Ages to the early modern period triggered a response to war from the sovereign. For Foucault, in those years, the prince's 'right to punish' the criminal was understood to be 'an aspect of the sovereign's right to make war on his enemies'; in this respect, law, in the form of punishment that it meted on the criminal, preserved 'something of the battle' (1991: 48 and 51). In reference to the presence of the sovereign's troops, both armed and in large numbers, around the scaffold where the criminal was executed, Foucault claimed that, as well as having been intended to 'prevent any escape or show of force' by the criminal and 'to prevent any outburst of sympathy or anger on the part of the people', it was also intended to be 'a reminder' that every crime was 'a rebellion against the law', and 'that the criminal was an enemy of the prince' (1991: 50). Thus, in executing the criminal, the prince was performing his functions as the head of justice and as the head of war:

> As a ritual of armed law, in which the prince showed himself, indissociably, both as head of justice and head of war, the public execution had two aspects: one of victory, the other of struggle. It brought to a solemn end a war, the outcome of which was decided in advance, between the criminal and the sovereign; it had to manifest the disproportion of power of the sovereign over those whom he had reduced to impotence.
>
> (Foucault, 1991: 50).

Crime was thus understood to be 'an act of hostility'; it was the 'first sign of rebellion' (Foucault, 1991: 57). In witnessing the execution of the criminal and accepting the invitation to insult him, and often by attacking him, the people performed a 'scaffold service' to the sovereign: 'the people had to bring its assistance to the king when the king undertook "to be avenged on his enemies", especially when those enemies were to be found among the people' (Foucault, 1991: 59).

Although by the end of the eighteenth century public executions began to be looked upon with horror by the general public in Europe, and the 'scaffold service' that they were expected to offer to the sovereign often became that of 'confrontation between the violence of the king and the violence of the people', crime and the response of the state that it triggered nevertheless continued to be understood in terms of war (Foucault, 1991: 73 and 90). Foucault attributes this continuing state of affairs to the emergence of the social contract theory; having entered into the social pact, the 'citizen is presumed to have accepted once and for all, with the laws of society, the very law by which he may be punished' (Foucault, 1991: 89–90). As a result, when an individual breaks the law, he is understood to make war on society (Foucault, 1991: 90). In other words, the right to punish has now become the right of the society to defend itself (Foucault, 1991: 90). This brings us back to the life and death relationship of biopolitics – that is, killing life to make life live.

Scholars often criticise Foucault for equating 'law with pre-modern forms of power' (see Rose, 1984: 191–192; Hunt and Wickham, 1994: 59; Neocleous, 1996: 67). For Alan Hunt and Gary Wickham (1994: 59), Foucault's 'conception of law as the commands of a sovereign backed by sanctions imposed on bodies of the transgressors correspond to a somewhat simplistic, if albeit common, view of law which equates "law" with the punitive forms of criminal law'. This 'entirely ignores, eliminates, suppresses' the 'other faces of law' that 'make up its great bulk of provisions' and deal with 'the detail of economic and kinship relations and the distribution of social authority', as well as other social relations (Hunt and Wickham, 1994: 60). Law not only represses crime but also lays down 'detailed rules and procedures for a host of specialised areas of activity' such as 'detailed provisions concerning welfare entitlements, construction standards, product safety, credit transactions, and so on' (Hunt and Wickham, 1994: 67). In this regard, Gillian Rose also accuses Foucault of having simplified 'legal development by conflating sovereignty with monarchy and government with sovereignty' and thus making law seem 'monolithic and uniform' (1984: 191–192). In *Administering Civil Society*, Neocleous also takes Foucault to task for holding on to a 'command theory of law' (1996: 67). For Neocleous, law is not only 'concerned with saying "no"', but acts 'as a constitutive force across and throughout the whole of society' (1996: 67). Referring to the growth of tribunals in Britain 'during the early part of the twentieth century' to deal with issues such as 'health, social security' and 'professional discipline' outside the 'ordinary court system', Neocleous points out that as well as repressing crime, law also administers 'disputes between the individual and the state' (1996: 69). Thus for Neocleous, law not only performs the repressive function but also carries out 'constitutive, regulative, and policing functions' (1996: 67).

Foucault's expositions on law were confined largely to the Middles Ages and the early modern period. However, this is not a sufficient reason to dismiss them as being suitable for understanding only forms of law that function in repressive mode, i.e., criminal law. In contemporary societies, force remains central to all forms of law, whether they be civil or criminal. Force is the key to the enforceability of law. In this sense, Foucault's (1998: 144) assertion that law always signifies the sword is a valid one. However, the sword that law signifies is not a sword that is only concerned with repression. The sword that performs the repressive function is also the same sword that protects: it is the same law that prohibits theft that simultaneously protects the property of the individual; it is the same law that prohibits murder that protects the life of the individual; it is also the same law that empowers the individual to seek damages for negligence that takes away from the wrongdoer part of his wealth in the form of damages. Law therefore always performs a dual function: repression and protection. In this sense, even though Foucault was correct to equate law with the sword, he erred in asserting that it is only concerned with repression and does not have any other function.

A criticism that one encounters in using Foucault's expositions on war for an analysis of law and politics is the danger of stretching the term to render it as meaningless. In 'Society Must Be Defended', Foucault claimed that 'a battlefront runs through the whole of society', both 'continuously and permanently', placing everyone 'on one side or the other' (2004: 51). In making this statement, Foucault left every exercise of power to be conceptualised as war. In this regard, Neocleous (1996: 86) notes that this broad conceptualisation only 'encourages us to conflate all struggles into one universal struggle, rename it social warfare, and leave it at that'. Rose (1984: 193–194) also criticises Foucault for using the terminologies of war to explain power relations, in particular law and sexuality. However, it must also be borne in mind that before broadly conceptualising war, in 'Society Must Be Defended' Foucault also pointed out that in using war as the matrix for analysing power relations, he was 'simply taking an extreme [case] to the extent that war can be regarded as the point of maximum tension, or as force relations laid bare' (2004: 46). Clearly, Foucault also had reservations about conceptualising all forms of power relations as war.

All forms of power relations contain within them the potential for recourse to force, whether they be the power relations of the family, or that of the state. Similarly most institutions of power that function in a hierarchical way today are modelled on the military institution, as Foucault pointed out in *Discipline and Punish* (1991: 168). However, when force is exercised, it does not always produce the effects of battle, i.e., death, injury, destruction of property and so on.

How then can war be conceptualised as other than military action without at the same time rendering the term so broad as for it to become meaningless? Building on from Foucault's expositions on war, I treat power relations that produce the effects of battle to be ways of waging war. Those effects include death, injury and the expulsion of the enemy; destruction of the enemy's assets; appropriation of the enemy's land/property; and the submission or the disarming of the enemy/the enemy race. Therefore, biopolitics becomes war only when power is exercised to produce the effects of battle.

Within recent years, a body of scholarly work known as lawfare has emerged, affirming the relationship between law and war. Charles J. Dunlap (a US military judge), who first coined the term lawfare, defined it as 'the use of law as a weapon of war' and claimed that it has become 'the newest feature of 21st century combat': it is 'a method of warfare where law is used as a means of realizing a military objective' (2001: 1, 2 and 4). Later, expanding further on his earlier definition, Dunlap conceptualised lawfare as a 'strategy of using – or misusing – law as a substitute for traditional military means to achieve an operational objective' (2010: 122). Building on Dunlap's concept of lawfare, and the legal scholar David Kennedy's (2006: 33) characterisation of war as a 'legal institution', Eyal Weizman claims that 'the use of law as a weapon of war' (when war is understood in terms of military action) has two dimensions: on the one hand, law can be used by a weaker, non-state actor to 'constrain military action against it by claiming that war crimes have been committed'; on the other hand, states can also use law (in particular international humanitarian law) in wars as the 'ethical vocabulary for marking legitimate power and justifiable death' (2010: 13). Unlike Dunlap, Weizman (2010: 13) traces the original use of law in war to colonial times. Law was used in the seventeenth and eighteenth centuries by European powers to legitimise the 'tactics of Western warfare' in the colonies, and to 'delegitimize the subaltern violence of the colonised' (Weizman, 2010: 13).

Even though this new body of scholarly work acknowledges the relationship between law and war, three key limitations can be identified in its formulations. First, it fails to go beyond the conventional understanding of war in terms of military action. Second, it (with the exception of the work of Weizman) misconceives the use of law in wars to be the development of the twenty-first century. Third, it only assumes law to be a weapon in military conflict, and not a way of waging war. As discussed earlier in this section, Foucault traced the genealogy for the functions of law both as a weapon as well as a way of waging war to the Middle Ages (1998: 86–87). In doing so, he established the ground for conceptualising war beyond military action and for examining the actions of states since the Middle Ages through the matrix of war.

In this book, the term 'law' refers not only to ordinary laws but also emergency laws that allow violence to be exhibited in its naked form. In *State of Exception*, Agamben claims that although the state of exception – the basis of emergency laws – today appears in the form of laws, it is in fact 'the legal form of what cannot have legal form': it 'is not a special kind of law (like the law of war)', but 'a suspension of the juridical order itself' (2005: 4). The state of exception, Agamben argues, lies 'at the limit between politics and law' (2005: 1). Challenging this notion of Agamben, and scholars after him, Neocleous argues that emergency laws do not exist in a 'space without law', but being '*entirely constitutional*' they are themselves part of law: 'far from *suspending* the law, violent actions conducted in "emergency conditions" have been legitimated through law on the grounds of necessity and in the name of security' [emphasis in original] (2008: 41 and 71). In his study on British India, Nasser Hussain also argues that it is incorrect to assert that emergency exist in a lawless space (2003: 20). Similarly, in her study on the post-9/11 'exceptional' practices of Western governments, in particular the detention of terror suspects in Guantanamo Bay detention facility, Aradau points out that these practices are not undertaken in a space without law; having their own procedures, they signify the 'ongoing transformation of law' (2007: 490). As law 'governs the "realities" of society' it also adjusts to the 'imperatives of necessity' (2007: 499).

The next chapters will empirically establish the arguments advanced in this chapter.

References

Agamben, G. (1998) *Homo Sacer: Sovereign Power and Bare Life*. Stanford: Stanford University Press.

Agamben, G. (2005) *State of Exception*. Chicago: The University of Chicago Press.

Aradau, C. (2007) 'Law Transformed: Guantanamo and the "Other" Exception', *Third World Quarterly*, 28(3), pp. 489–501.

Aradau, C. (2012) 'What's Left of Biopolitics?', *Radical Philosophy*, 173(May/June). Available at: http://www.radicalphilosophy.com/reviews/individual-reviews/whats-left-of-biopolitics (Accessed: 1 December 2012).

Aradau, C. and Blanke, T. (2010) 'Governing Circulation: A Critique of the Biopolitics of Security', in de Larrinaga, M. and Doucet, M.G. (eds.), *Security and Global Governmentality: Globalisation, Power and the State*. Basingstoke: Palgrave Macmillan, pp. 44–58.

Clausewitz, C. (1997) *On War*. Hertfordshire: Wordsworth Editions (Original work published 1832).

Coke, E. (2003) *The Selected Writings and Speeches of Sir Edward Coke, Volume II*. Indiana: Liberty Fund.

Dillon, M. and Reid, J. (2009) *The Liberal Way of War: Killing to Make Life Live*. Oxon: Routledge.

Dunlap, C.J. (2001) 'Law and Military Interventions: Preserving Humanitarian Values in 21st Century Conflicts', *Humanitarian Challenges in Military Intervention*, Washington. 29 November. Available at: http://people.duke.edu/~pfeaver/dunlap.pdf (Accessed: 20 January 2013).

Dunlap, C.J. (2010) 'Does Lawfare Need an Apologia?' *Journal of International Law*, 43(1/2), pp. 121–143.

Foucault, M. (1991) *Discipline and Punish: The Birth of the Prison*. Translated by Alan Sheridan. London: Penguin Books (Original work published 1975).

Foucault, M. (1998) *The History of Sexuality: Volume 1: The Will to Knowledge*. Translated by Robert Hurley. London: Penguin Books (Original work published 1976).

Foucault, M. (2004) *"Society Must Be Defended": Lectures at the College de France, 1975–76*. Translated by David Macey. London: Penguin Books.

Foucault, M. (2009) *Security, Territory, Population: Lectures at the College de France, 1977–1978*. Translated by Graham Burchell. Hampshire: Palgrave Macmillan.

Foucault, M. (2010) *The Birth of Biopolitics: Lectures at the College de France 1978–1979*. Translated by Graham Burchell. Hampshire: Palgrave Macmillan.

Hardt, M. and Negri, A. (2001) *Empire*. Cambridge, MA: Harvard University Press.

Hobbes, T. (1949) *De Cive or the Citizen*. New York: Appleton Century Crofts.

Hunt, A. and Wickham, G. (1994) *Foucault and Law: Towards a Sociology of Law as Governance*. London: Pluto Press.

Hussain, N. (2003) *The Jurisprudence of Emergency, Colonialism and the Rule of Law*. Michigan: The University of Michigan Press.

Kant, I. (1887) *The Philosophy of Law: An Exposition of the Fundamental Principles of Jurisprudence as the Science of Right*. Edinburgh: T and T Clark (Original work published 1796).

Kennedy, D. (2006) *Of War and Law*. Princeton: Princeton University Press.

Locke, J. (1980) *Second Treatise of Government*. Indiana: Hacket Publishing Company.

Neocleous, M. (1996) *Administering Civil Society: Towards a Theory of State Power*. Hampshire and London: Palgrave Macmillan.

Neocleous, M. (2008) *Critique of Security*. Edinburgh: Edinburgh University Press.

The Petition of Right 1627 (3 Cha. 1, c. 1). London: HMSO. Available at: http://www.legislation.gov.uk/all?title=the%20petition%20of%20rights%201627 (Accessed: 10 June 2013).

Rabinow, P. and Rose, N. (2006) 'Biopower Today', *BioSocieties*, 1, pp. 195–217.

Rose, G. (1984) *Dialectic of Nihilism: Post-Structuralism and Law*. Oxford: Basil Blackwell Publisher.

Rose, N. (2007) *The Politics of Life Itself: Biomedicine, Power, and Subjectivity in the Twenty-First Century*. Princeton: Princeton University Press.

Rousseau, J. (1999) *The Social Contract*. Oxford: Oxford University Press.

Spieker, J.W.H. (2011) *Liberalism, Life and War: A Reflection on the Genealogy of Political Philosophy*. Unpublished PhD thesis. London: King's College.

Weizman, E. (2010) 'Legislative Attack', *Theory, Culture & Society*, 27(6), pp. 11–32.

2 Constructing an ethnocracy

On 4 February 1948, Ceylon attained independence from the British Empire. Unlike many of Britain's colonies, Ceylon's path towards independence was peaceful. With the exception of the rebellion of 1818 and the two riots of 1848 and 1915, for the best part of 152 years of British colonial rule, Ceylon had remained an obedient colony and accepted the liberal state-building undertaken by the British Empire. Thus, when Britain decided to grant independence, British officials were able to boast that they had completed their 'work and purpose' of turning Ceylon into a 'responsible democracy' (HC Deb 21 November 1947).

However, after independence, Ceylon did not emerge as a democratic success story. Despite holding onto electoral politics, it degenerated into an ethnocracy; a biopolitical transformation effected through law, the violence of law and the violence of 'lawlessness'.

War through law

One of the first tasks that Ceylon undertook after attaining independence was to secure the demographic composition of the Sinhala areas. When the Portuguese first set foot on the island in 1505, much of its Tamil population was confined to the northern and eastern parts, and some parts of the northwest (Kemper, 1991: 144). Though the Sinhala kingdom of Kandy in the central part had a Tamil monarch, Tamils were virtually non-existent in the area. After conquering Kandy, the British expelled the Tamil monarch's remaining relatives (Davy, 1821: 500).

In the 1840s, however, the demographic composition of the Kandyan area was transformed when the British brought in nearly a million Tamils from South India to work as labourers in the newly set up plantation (initially coffee, and later tea) sectors; sectors that the local Sinhalese had refused to work in. Although the newly inducted Indian Tamils were landless and lived in small plots allocated to them by British planters, their presence in the traditional Sinhalese area was seen as a threat by the local Sinhala population (Balasingham, 2004: 4–5).

The British colonial civil service on the island was also dominated by the indigenous Tamils of the North and East, though this can be largely attributed to the Buddhist clergy's preventing of Sinhalese from embracing Western education, and thus obtaining jobs in the colonial civil service (Snyder, 2000: 277). In the island's colonial capital city of Colombo, much of the trade and access to finance was dominated by Tamil investors from India (Bloom, 2003: 59). The island's import, export and retail sectors were also dominated by the Muslims of South India, many of whom used Tamil as their first language (see Chapter 4). The hostility of the Sinhalese towards the Indian Tamils (or those perceived to be of Indian Tamil origin) on the island was so high in colonial Ceylon that during a meeting with Mahatma Gandhi in 1940, J. R. Jayewardene, who later became the island's president, referred to the Indian Tamil settlers as 'exploiters' (cited in de Silva and Wriggins, 1988: 109).

In 1931, ethnic tensions escalated when the introduction of universal franchise gave the Indian Tamils voting rights (Wijemanne, 1996: 8). At that time the Indian Tamils formed 12 percent of the island's population (Wickramasinghe, 2006: 162). In the general election held in August – September 1947, 6 months before Ceylon attained independence, the Ceylon Indian Congress (CIC), the political party representing the Indian Tamils, won seven seats. This fuelled the fears of the Sinhalese that having already held sway over the island's economy and civil service, the Tamils were poised to become a powerful force in the island's polity, and hence a threat to Sinhalese control of the state legislature (Wilson, 1974: 29). At independence in 1948, in total, the Tamils of the North and East and the Indian Tamils constituted 33 percent of Ceylon's population. This meant that had the Tamil political parties forged a united front and contested elections, and coupled with the support of other ethnic and minority parties (especially the Muslims), they would have been in a position to act as a check on the potential of the Sinhalese to enact constitutional changes that required a two-thirds majority in the state's legislature.

Thus, within 6 months following independence, in August 1948, the democratically constituted Ceylon legislature introduced the *Ceylon Citizenship Act* No.18 of 1948, effectively disenfranchising large sections of plantation Tamils from South India. Under the Act, only the descendents of those who were born on the island before the legislation was enacted could claim Ceylonese citizenship. The majority of Indian Tamils in the plantation sectors were poor and uneducated, and travelled to the island without basic documents such as birth certificates, and they were not therefore in a position to stake a claim to citizenship (Wilson, 1974: 30–31). Only the 130,000 property owning and educated Indian Tamils were able to obtain citizenship; and the rest were made stateless, and thus left without voting rights (Balasingham, 2004: 7; Wickramasinghe, 2006: 162). Of those stateless Indian Tamils, around 600,000 were deported to India in the following years (Harris, 1990: 212). With the deportation of the Indian Tamils, the state had effectively cleansed the Kandyan areas of 600,000 Tamils: the demographic composition of those areas was reversed in favour of the Sinhalese. The state then proceeded to hand over the jobs of those deported Indian Tamils to the Sinhala peasantry (de Silva and Wriggins, 1988: 213).

In biopolitical rule, states wage wars 'as managers of life and survival, of bodies and race', and power is exercised for the 'improvement of the species or races'

(Foucault, 1998: 37; 2004: 256), and this can be achieved through measures other than military action. In the case of Ceylon, the state, using its elected legislature, implemented law, the *Ceylon Citizenship Act*, and produced an effect of battle – the expulsion of the Indian Tamils – and thereby improved the lives of sections of the Sinhala Buddhist race/species that it managed/fostered.

When the *Ceylon Citizenship Bill* was presented to parliament, Tamil leaders protested. S. Nadesan (1948), a prominent Tamil senator, drew parallels between Ceylon's action to Hitler's decision to decitizenise the Jews. Yet, the protests of Tamil leaders fell on deaf ears.

However, as the manager of the Sinhala Buddhist race/species, the state could not be satisfied that the expulsion of the Indian Tamils and the handing over of their jobs to the Sinhalese had made life better for the entire race/species that it managed/fostered. Eight years later, evoking its elected legislature again, Ceylon enacted further legislation, the *Official Language Act* No.33 of 1956. The legislation accorded to Sinhala the status of the only official language of Ceylon. Until then official transactions were conducted in Tamil, Sinhala and English, thereby opening up state employment to anyone versed in any one of these three languages. The new legislation, however, reversed this state of affairs. With the coming into force of the Act, Tamils not fluent in the Sinhala language were compelled to leave, or were expelled from state employment (Wilson, 1974: 21). Thus, the Act achieved its intended effect: following the implementation of the Act, the number of Tamils in the civil service fell from 30 percent to 6 percent (Harris, 1990: 213). Once again the state, with the use of law, produced an effect of battle: the dismissal of non-Sinhala speaking Tamils from the civil service – expulsion. In doing so, it also improved the lives of sections of the race/species that it managed/fostered: in the same way that the Sinhalese filled the jobs that became vacant in the plantation sectors after the expulsion of 600,000 Indian Tamils, the Sinhalese were now in a position to take up the jobs in the state's civil service left vacant by the thousands of Tamils excluded under the *Official Language Act*.

The *Official Language Act* also provided the opportunity for the island's Sinhala Buddhist leaders to assert the supremacy of their race on the island. A year earlier, when presenting the *Official Language Bill*, Ceylon's Prime Minister S.W.R.D. Bandaranaike (1955 cited in Wilson, 1974: 25) claimed that it was necessary to prevent the 'inexorable shrinking of the Sinhalese language'. Justifying the Bill, Jayewardene (1956 cited in McGowan, 1992: 161), the then Opposition Leader, went a step further. Jayewardene (1956 cited in McGowan, 1992: 161) argued that the bill signalled the beginning of the struggle of the Sinhala Buddhist people to give primacy to Sinhala language and the Buddhist religion on the island: 'The time has come for the whole Sinhalese race, which has existed for 2,500 years jealously safeguarding its language and religion, to fight without giving any quarter to save its birthright'. In other words, Jayewardene made it clear that the *Official Language Bill* was being enacted to institutionalise the *Mahavamsa's* idea that Ceylon belonged exclusively to the Sinhala Buddhists.

Law through 'lawlessness'

The enactment of the legislation that asserted the primacy to Sinhala Buddhist race on the island in 1956 presaged violence unleashed against the Tamils. Sinhala Buddhist extremists, led by Buddhist monks, attacked peaceful Tamil demonstrators protesting the enactment of the *Official Language Act*. This was followed by an all-out assault on the Tamils and the looting of Tamil businesses in Colombo. Ceylon's police refused to intervene against the assailants, allowing Tamils to be attacked (Vittachi, 1958; Ponnambalam, 1983: 100). According to Nadesan (1958 cited in Satyendra, 2007), no action was taken against the attackers 'because specific instructions had been given to the police that they should not shoot, should not arrest, should not deal with the lawlessness and disorder that was let loose'. Nadesan (1958 cited in Satyendra, 2007) went on to accuse some Sinhala parliamentarians of taking part in the violence being perpetrated against the Tamils. The state's complicity in the racist attacks, however, became apparent in Bandaranaike's address to the attackers who had gathered in front of Ceylon's parliament. Instead of condemning the violence and the attackers, and warning them that legal action would be taken against them if they persisted, he smiled and told them: 'Don't do that. Rain is coming down. They [the Tamil protestors] will be cooled in no time' (Bandaranaike, 1956 cited in Satyendra, 2007).

One of Foucault's central tenets in *The History of Sexuality: Volume 1* is that power is not always exercised in a hierarchical way, or only by the state (1998: 94). It is also exercised by those who are understood to be its targets; including the subjects/citizens of the state:

> It seems to me that power must be understood in the first instance as the multiplicity of force relations immanent in the sphere in which they operate and which constitute their own organisation; as the process which, through ceaseless struggles and confrontations, transforms, strengthens, or reverses them; as the support which these force relations find in one another, thus forming a chain or a system, or on the contrary, the disjunctions and contradictions which isolate them from one another; and lastly, as the strategies in which they take effect, whose general design or institutional crystallization is embodied in the state apparatus, in the formulations of the law, in the various social hegemonies.
>
> (Foucault, 1998: 92–93)

When analysed within this framework, it becomes apparent that the violence unleashed by Sinhala Buddhist extremists on Tamils during the enactment of the *Official Language Act* and its aftermath, and the inaction on the part of Ceylon's police, were in fact indirect actions of the state that manifested through certain sections of the race/species that it managed/fostered.

By challenging the *Official Language Act*, the Tamils had signalled that they would resist the ambitions of the Sinhala Buddhists to realise their supremacy over the entire island of Ceylon. In the words of Rousseau (1999: 57–58), in democratically constituted states, the sovereign, 'consisting solely of the individual persons which form it, has and can have no self-interest that is contrary to theirs'. For Rousseau, the will of the majority should always prevail (Rousseau, 1999: 58). Thus, in Rousseauian terms, in the 'democratically' constituted Ceylon, by rising against the *Official Language Act*, the Tamils had challenged the sovereign – the majority Sinhala Buddhist race/species. The state, which represented the sovereign, thus saw it fit to allow the violence of sections of the sovereign to be let loose on those who challenged its supremacy. Moreover, as Tarzie Vittachi (1958) notes, Bandaranaike's government, which came to power on a 'wave of popular acclaim', believed in letting the 'people have their way'.

The violence of the Sinhala Buddhist extremists on this occasion cannot also be equated with lawlessness and disorder, as Nadesan had suggested. Rather, it was the case of the law asserting itself through the people that it represented. By protesting against the *Official Language Act*, Tamils had not only challenged the supremacy of the Sinhala Buddhist race, but they had also dared to challenge the supremacy of the state's law: they had signalled that they would not be law abiding subjects. Thus, the violence of the Sinhala Buddhist extremists was an assertion of the state's law; the extremists were both subordinate to (being the state's subjects) and supreme to (being a part of the sovereign) the state's law. Thus, contrary to the way many commentators have argued, their violence cannot be construed or reduced to acts of lawlessness and disorder.

As Foucault says in *Security, Territory, Population*, the state does not always assert itself through law (2009: 262). There are occasions when it would also assert itself beyond law: 'Necessity, urgency, the need to save the state itself will exclude the game of these natural laws' (2009: 262). The state 'must be saved' regardless of 'whatever form may be employed to enable one to save it' (2009: 262). It is not only totalitarian states that have acted this way: some modern liberal states, as America did during the civil war, have also acted this way (Rositter, 1948: 11). Such actions are grounded in 'the theory of *Not kennt kein Gebot*, necessity knows no law' (Rositter, 1948: 12). Ceylon was therefore not an exception in asserting itself and its laws beyond law. However, it differed from liberal states in that it gave its 'people' (the Sinhala Buddhists) the power to assert their supremacy, and the state's law.

These can be compared to the scaffold service that the people were expected to perform to the prince in Middle Ages Europe by attacking a condemned man before he was executed: 'In calling on the crowd to manifest its power, the sovereign tolerated for a moment acts of violence, which he accepted as a sign of allegiance' (Foucault, 1991: 59). In Ceylon, the state allowed the Sinhala Buddhist extremists, as being both the subjects and part of the sovereign, to attack the protesting Tamils as a mode of affirming their allegiance to their race/species, and the state that represented them.

State connivance in the violence of the Sinhala Buddhist extremists was, however, manifest more explicitly in the massacres of Tamils in the border villages of the predominantly Tamil-speaking Eastern Province. Whilst the Tamils were attacked and their businesses looted in Colombo, in Paddipalai Aaru (renamed in Sinhala *Gal Oya*) area in the East, armed Sinhala Buddhist settlers went on a rampage, killing over 150 Tamils in 5 days (Ponnambalam, 1983: 100; Tambiah,

1996: 85–86). Cars, bulldozers and explosives belonging to state officials were used to execute these massacres (Tambiah, 1996: 85). When the Tamils demonstrated in the nearby Batticaloa town condemning the massacres, the state's police responded by firing at them, killing at least two of them (Tambiah, 1996: 85). The killings in Batticaloa were the case of law manifesting through officially sanctioned violence to complement the violence of the race/species that it managed/fostered. The message was clear. The 'lawlessness' of the species (people) that the state managed/fostered was acceptable because it was intended to assert the supremacy of law, the state and its species. However, the lawlessness of the species against whom the state was at war with could not be condoned even to the slightest extent.

The violence of the Sinhala Buddhist settlers against the Tamils operated at one level. On another level, while asserting the authority of law, the state and its species, it was intended to demonstrate through violence, the ideology that underpinned the emerging ethnocratic state order. In other words, Ceylon's Sinhala Buddhist leaders signalled to their people that they were entitled to use violence against the Tamils and take their lives to secure the land given to them by Buddha, as claimed in the *Mahavamsa* (1912: 55).

The *Mahavamsa* glorifies the killing of Tamils and any other races that do not adhere to Buddhism to be a historically acceptable phenomenon (Trawick, 2007: 24). It asserts that non-Buddhists are equivalent to beasts. When referring to the large scale killing of Tamils in a war between the Sinhala King Dutthagamani (also known in Sinhala as Dutugemunu) and the Tamil King Ellalan (referred to in Sinhala chronicles as Elara) that historians attribute to have taken place in the second century B.C. in which the former emerged victorious, the *Mahavamsa* recounts a statement purported to have been made by a group of Buddhist monks:

> The great king [Dutthagamani] greeted them [the Buddhist monks], and when he had invited them to be seated and had done them reverence in many ways he asked the reason of their coming.
>
> 'We are sent by the brotherhood at Piyafigudipa to comfort thee, O lord of men.'
>
> And thereon the king said again to them: 'How shall there be any comfort for me, O venerable sirs, since by me was caused the slaughter of a great host numbering millions?'
>
> 'From this deed arises no hindrance in thy way to heaven. Only one and a half human beings have been slain here by thee, O lord of men. The one had come unto the (three) refuges, the other had taken on himself the five precepts [of Buddhism]. Unbelievers and men of evil life were the rest, not more to be esteemed than beasts. But as for thee, thou wilt bring glory to the doctrine of the Buddha in manifold ways; therefore cast away care from thy heart, O ruler of men!'
>
> (1912: 178)

In other words, as Margaret Trawick (2007: 24) notes, the *Mahavamsa* not only imposes upon the Sinhala Buddhists the duty of unifying the island, but also advances the argument that such unification of the island under a single flag 'entails warfare and bloodshed'.

The massacre of over 150 Tamils in the border villages of the Eastern Province by gangs of Sinhala Buddhist settlers should therefore been seen as an act carried out by them in accordance with the so-called duty imposed on them by the *Mahavamsa*.

The law also played a role in facilitating these acts of the Sinhala Buddhist extremists. In the same year that the *Ceylon Citizenship Act* was enacted, Ceylon's Sinhala Buddhist rulers also enacted further legislation: *The Gal Oya Development Board Act* No.51 of 1949. When the Act was passed, the Tamils did not suspect that it had any motives other than creating a board to develop the areas south of Paddipalai Aaru in the Eastern Province. However, the real reasons behind the enactment of the legislation became apparent in 1952. The state, pursuant to subsection 6 (1) of the legislation, appropriated 163 square miles of Tamil lands in Paddipalai Aaru to create eight villages made up of Sinhala Buddhist settlers (Tharmalingam, 2007). In the guise of implementing the legislation, Tamil land was colonised by the state: Crown land in predominantly Tamil-speaking areas was handed over by the state to landless Sinhala peasants, whilst landless Tamil peasants were ignored. In this way, the state's insidious colonisation programme transformed the demographic composition of a predominantly Tamil-speaking region into a Sinhala area. If the *Ceylon Citizenship Act* was intended to keep Sinhala areas predominantly Sinhalese, *The Gal Oya Development Board Act* can be said to have been intended to diminish the Tamils' domination of the northern and eastern parts of the island where the precolonial Tamil kingdoms and principalities had existed.

Before Ceylon launched Sinhala colonisation programmes, the predominantly Tamil and Sinhala speaking areas were separated by 'vast forests and scrub wastes' (Vittachi, 1958). During the time of the composition of the *Mahavamsa*, however, this had not been the case, and race wars between the Tamils and Sinhalese were a feature of that period of history:

> When the Sinhalese Kingdom was centred in Anuradhapura, the proximity of the Sinhalese to the Tamils in the north provided the ideal setting for race warfare, and the agrarian wealth of the region provided the motivation for the economic competitiveness that inevitably led to open conflict. There was constant conflict between the two elements. But when the forest swept over this region and the centres of gravity of the population moved towards Kandy and the West Coast, separating the two major races, their internecine rivalry died down.
> (Vittachi, 1958)

In clearing these forest and scrub areas and creating new Sinhala Buddhist settlements in the postcolonial period, the state can be seen to be creating the context for a reawakening of ancient racial tensions (Vittachi, 1958). As Steven Kemper notes, from the Sinhalese perspective, the state's colonisation programmes were the reversal of the conquests by the Tamils in the medieval period of the parts 'given' to the Sinhalese by Buddha (1991: 161–163 and 144).

In the later years, the acceleration of the Sinhala colonisation programmes went hand in hand with the state arming the Sinhala Buddhist settlers (Fernando, 2008: 201), thus providing official legitimacy to this viewpoint. The Sinhalese settlers living in areas bordering the Tamil homeland evoked the epic term '*Sinhala Hamudawa*', meaning the Sinhala army, and they believed they constituted the fighting forces of the Sinhala Buddhist race (Vittachi, 1958). With the emergence of the armed Tamil secessionist movement in 1972, the state took measures to institutionalise this *de-facto* army. The *Mobilisation of Supplementary Force Act* No.40 of 1985 institutionalised an official paramilitary unit, the Home Guards, made up of Sinhala settlers.

1956 was, however, not the last occasion that Ceylon used 'lawlessness' to assert the supremacy of its law; and the Sinhala Buddhist race/species that it represented. In 1958, once again the state allowed the violence of the Sinhala Buddhist extremists to be let loose on the Tamils. The scale of death and destruction inflicted on the Tamils on this occasion was much greater in proportion than that 2 years earlier. As the Tamils also retaliated on this occasion, many historians refer to it as a Tamil–Sinhala ethnic riot; this is also how the mass violence of 1956 is referred to. However, in this book, I do not use the term 'riots' to describe the racial violence perpetrated against the Tamils because the violence that occurred was not the result of the state losing control over its populations. Rather, the violence was largely state orchestrated.

With the implementation of the *Official Language Act*, the state undertook to replace Tamil letters on the number plates of vehicles owned by Tamils with Sinhala letters. In the Tamil-speaking areas, the locals defied this and continued to use Tamil letters on their number plates. The use of those number plates became so common and popular that even vehicles plying between the Tamil-speaking areas and other parts of the island were inscribed with them. This, as Vittachi (1958) notes, 'brought the prestige of the Government and the police into abject disrepute. The impression among the Sinhalese in the south was that the Government had abdicated its authority in the northern and eastern provinces of Ceylon.' In other words, by using Tamil letters on their number plates, Tamils again challenged the state and its law.

The state initially responded to this civil disobedience of the Tamils by arresting and imprisoning those who used Tamil number plates on the grounds of contravening the *Motor Transport Act* No.48 of 1957. However, the use of law did not produce the intended effect. The Tamil politician S.J.V. Chelvanayagam travelled in a vehicle bearing the Tamil number plate and was subsequently jailed for 2 weeks (Ponnambalam, 1983: 106). Yet, his imprisonment failed to have an impact on the state's Sinhala only policy. The state therefore resorted to asserting law through 'lawlessness'.

In April 1958, Sinhala Buddhist extremists rampaged throughout the island for 3 days, painting tar on every Tamil letter found on vehicles and buildings, including shop bill boards. The Sri Lankan police refrained from intervening to halt the rampage; they had been 'given strict – but verbal – instructions not to interfere' in those actions (Vittachi, 1958). After tarring and erasing Tamil letters from public

Constructing an ethnocracy 35

places, the extremists vented their racism towards the Tamil people, tarring every Tamil person they encountered on the streets. It was only then the police intervened (Vittachi, 1958).

However, the tarring of Tamil letters (and Tamils) was only the first stage of the state using 'lawlessness' in 1958 to assert the authority of law and the supremacy of the Sinhala Buddhist race/species. The second stage of violence against the Tamils began the following month, when Chelvanayagam's political party, *Ilankai Thamil Arasu Katchi* (ITAK), decided to hold a major convention in the Tamil-speaking areas to assert the political and social rights of the Tamils. Citing the proposed convention, Sinhala Buddhist politicians spread rumours that the Tamils were preparing to launch a major invasion of the Sinhala areas (Vittachi, 1958). In response, and claiming to be the *Sinhala Hamudawa*, Sinhala Buddhist settlers and extremists from the villages bordering the Tamil-speaking Northern and Eastern Provinces launched attacks on the Tamils. As the violence against the Tamils spread throughout the island, including its capital Colombo, in the Tamil-speaking areas the Tamils retaliated. It was only then the state intervened and sent its armed forces to bring the situation under control. Though there have been no exact figures on the number of Tamils killed during the violence, hundreds of Tamils are said to have been massacred (Vittachi, 1958; Ponnambalam, 1983: 107).

Fearing further violence against them, the Tamils finally stopped using number plates bearing Tamil letters. Thus, in using 'lawlessness' to assert law and the supremacy of the race/species that it managed/fostered, Ceylon produced another effect of battle – submission. It made the Tamils submit to its law. Furthermore, the 1958 violence had the effect of partially cleansing the Sinhala areas of Tamils. In the violence of 1958, over 10,000 Tamils who lived in the Sinhala areas, including the capital Colombo, became refugees and had to return to the Tamil-speaking North and East in ships (Ponnambalam, 1983: 107). Thus, using 'lawlessness', the state produces two effects of battle – the submission and the expulsion of the 'enemy' race.

Ceylon's use of 'lawlessness' in 1958, however, posed a threat to the authority of the state. Elements amongst the Sinhala Buddhist extremists involved in perpetrating violence against the Tamils went to the extent of fighting the state's military when it intervened to bring the escalating situation under control. As a consequence, Sinhala soldiers killed some of the extremists from their own community (Vittachi, 1958; *The Sunday Times*, 2005). These killings were carried out under the powers vested by Ceylon's emergency law, the *Public Security Ordinance* No.25 of 1947 (the PSO), enacted by the British at the end of colonial rule.

The killing of its own people by the forces of the state would appear to contradict the argument that biopolitics is about making life better for the race/species that the state claims to represent. Foucault addresses this question in 'Society Must Be Defended' when he expands on the idea of 'good' and 'bad' amongst the human species. Though the idea of race is central to biopolitics, the binary division of the human species as 'good' and 'bad' is not always pinned to relations between biologically different racial groups: they go beyond the 'traditional form of mutual contempt or hatred between races' (Foucault, 2004: 258). In other words, the 'bad' part of the species that the state seeks to eliminate does not always have to belong to another group ethnically/biologically different to the 'good' race/species it seeks to foster. Anyone or any group with any anomalies within the 'good' species can be singled out and become targets for elimination. In Ceylon's case, the Sinhala Buddhist extremists who refused to submit to the state, when it sought to end 'lawlessness', fell into this category, and were killed.

The double-edged sword

Section 7 of the PSO allows the state to override ordinary laws when a state of emergency is in operation. The Act also deprives redress from the courts for those affected by the state of emergency. Whilst section 8 of the Act stipulates that any emergency regulation, order, rule or direction made or given under the statute cannot be questioned in any court, section 9 of the Act grants immunity to the government and anyone acting on its behalf from criminal and civil action for anything done whilst a state of emergency was in operation.

In the nineteenth century and the first quarter of the twentieth century, the proclamation of martial law in Ceylon provided the legal basis for the British colonial authorities to carry out mass detentions and summary executions, inflict injuries and cause damage to property (see HC Deb 20 February 1849; Torrington, 1851: 8 and 12; Finlason, 1872: 11; Ramanathan, 1916: 74). Though martial law had never existed in a codified form in English legal history and the last occasion that it was declared in England was in 1790 (Rossiter, 1948: 139–140; Neocleous, 2008: 42), in practice the British Empire used it in Ceylon and other colonies. In inscribing these draconian powers in the PSO before decolonisation, the British can be said to have codified martial law in Ceylon's legal system. This codification had already taken place in Britain through the enactment of the *Defence of Realm Act* 1914 and the *Emergency Powers Act* 1920 (Neocleous, 2008: 51). These legislations were seen to be necessary on the part of Britain for securing the liberal state order at home (Neocleous, 2008: 51). Likewise, the PSO may have been deemed by the British colonial authorities to be necessary for securing Ceylon's liberal democratic state order after independence.

However, for postcolonial Ceylon, from 1958 the PSO became an indispensible weapon in its efforts to transform from a democracy into an ethnocracy. As far as the state was concerned, the PSO was a double-edged sword. On the one hand, the legislation gave cover for the state to use draconian powers against sections of the Sinhala Buddhists who challenged its authority when it sought to bring an end to the state of 'lawlessness' that it had encouraged. On the other hand, it gave the state the legitimacy to use the same draconian powers to counter Tamil resistance to the discriminatory policies being implemented against them.

The PSO was first used against the Tamils in 1961. Dismayed by Ceylon's refusal to heed to their demand for equal rights and power over the affairs of the North and East, the Tamils launched a mass non-violent movement to set up a Tamil government (the *Thamil Arasu*) in the Tamil areas. Initially, the ITAK launched the *Thamil Arasu* postal service (Balasingham, 2004: 13). Measures were also taken to distribute Crown lands in the Tamil-speaking areas to landless peasants, and the creation of a Tamil police force for the region (Welhengama and Pillay, 2014: 202). These actions, though non-violent, were seen to be 'a direct challenge to the sovereignty and the territorial integrity of the island' (Welhengama and Pillay, 2014: 202).

In response to Tamil civil disobedience, the state declared a state of emergency under the PSO and despatched its armed forces to the North and East, unleashing violence on the Tamil population. Tamils who were engaged in mass demonstrations in their homeland in support of the formation of a regional Tamil government were brutally attacked by Ceylon's military. Leaders of the ITAK were also arrested. Moreover, a curfew was imposed in the Tamil-speaking areas to prevent any further mass uprising, resulting in the North and East remaining under military rule (Balasingham, 2004: 14).

Meanwhile, in Colombo and other Sinhala areas, gangs of Sinhala Buddhist extremists went on a rampage against the Tamils. But the violence of law perpetrated on the Tamils through the military was more aggressive than that of the 'lawlessness' let loose through gangs of Sinhala Buddhist extremists. Moreover, unlike in the previous years (1956 and 1958), in 1961, the violence of the Sinhala Buddhist extremists was quickly brought under control by the government. This could be attributed to the fact that Sinhala trade unions in the south had adopted a confrontationist course with the government; allowing gangs of Sinhala Buddhist extremists to go on a rampage without controls may have therefore been seen by the government to be favourable to trade unions, who would have used the state of 'lawlessness' to their advantage and create further chaos to destabilise the state.

But the violence of law in the biopolitical transformation of Ceylon became more aggressive in 1971. This time, it was not the Tamils who fell in the category of the 'bad' species: it was the Sinhala Marxist youth. As a consequence of economic hardships, in April 1971, the Sinhala youth, led by the JVP, rose against the state (Harris, 1990: 214). Under the cover of the PSO, the state mobilised the full power of its armed forces, and as a consequence 10,000 Sinhala youth suspected of taking part in the rebellion were killed (Harris, 1990: 214; McGowan, 1992: 32). The bodies of those massacred were thrown into rivers, lakes and canals as a way of deterring others. Thousands of Sinhala youth were also arrested under the PSO and detained for many months without trial (Tambiah, 1986: 14; Harris, 1990: 214).

The use of terror to suppress the insurrection of 1971 was not new to Ceylon; it was similar to that used by British colonial authorities on the island during the imposition of martial law in the nineteenth century and the first quarter of the twentieth century to crush rebellions and riots (see HC Deb 20 February 1849; Forbes, 1850: 27 and 30; Ramanathan, 1916: 74; Taylor, 2000: 165). For instance, during the riots of 1848 in Kandy, the British authorities shot dead a Sinhala Buddhist monk, who was accused of spearheading a rebellion against the British Crown, and hung his body on a tree for 4 days (HC Deb 20 February 1849;

Taylor, 2000: 165). This was done in accordance with the sentence passed by the court martial tribunal that tried the monk (HC Deb 20 February 1849; Forbes, 1850: 21).

In *Discipline and Punish*, Foucault argues that punishment is a political tactic of government, and public execution should be understood as a political ritual through which power is manifested (1991: 23 and 47). Thus, the logic behind the execution of the monk in 1848, and the displaying of his body in public for 4 days, was to deter others from rebelling in the future against the colonial state order. This reign of terror had already been tried successfully in European societies for centuries: 'sometimes the corpses of the executed persons were displayed for several days near the scenes of their crimes. Not only must people know, they must see with their own eyes. Because they must be made to be afraid' (Foucault, 1991: 58). Thus, justifying the reign of terror of 1848 in Ceylon, Sir Alexander Cockburn, then Britain's Attorney General, argued that individuals are punished under martial law not simply for the offences they committed but 'to deter others from following their example' (HC Deb 29 May 1851).

A similar argument was also advanced during an inquiry into the use of martial law in Jamaica during the Morant Bay Rebellion of 1866, wherein it was claimed that martial law was necessary to 'strike terror into the disaffected population' and protect the white population from the 'great danger of destruction' (Finlason, 1872: 17). Justifying the large scale killing of Jamaica's black population under the cover of martial law, Edward John Eyre, the British colonial governor claimed that when dealing with a rebellion guided by the 'evil passions of a race little removed in many respects from absolute savages', striking terror was the only choice (1866 cited in Finlason, 1868: xxvii). In the words of Serjeant Spankie, the British Advocate General of Bengal, the objective of martial law was 'self-preservation by terror' (cited in Finlason, 1872: 8).

In the same way the British Empire relied on martial law and naked violence to overcome threats to the colonial state order, postcolonial Ceylon in 1971 relied on the codified version of martial law and the naked violence it unleashed to overcome the threat to its ruling order. As a democracy degenerating into an ethnocracy, the use of naked violence through law under the logic of emergency was deemed to be justified. It sent out three message to the island's populations: the state would not tolerate the construction of any state order other than the specific one that it was constructing; it was capable of using the violence of law under the logic of emergency whenever it deemed it to be necessary; and it was prepared to kill, not only the Tamils, but also members of the race/species that it was fostering.

Completing ethnocratic state-building

Sri Lanka's ethnocratic state-building reached its conclusion in 1972 when it instituted its first republican constitution. Some scholars have argued that the constitution was enacted as 'a symbolic assertion of nationalism' (Coomaraswamy, 2012: 126). As the previous constitution, the *Ceylon (Constitution) Order in Council 1946*, was drafted by the British colonial rulers, Ceylon's Sinhala Buddhist nationalists 'had always felt disgruntled that their constitution was not a product of the nationalist struggles which had surrounded the drafting of the Indian constitution' (Coomaraswamy, 2012: 126). Others (see, for example de Silva, 1981: 542), however, have claimed that the Marxist insurrection of 1971, and the economic inequalities that fuelled it, hastened the government's efforts to write 'an autochthonous constitution for Sri Lanka'.

Although it had become an independent state in 1948, the functioning of a constitution drafted and enacted by its colonial master symbolised that Ceylon had not completely put its colonial legacy behind. Reflecting this, Ceylon's Prime Minister Srimavo Bandaranaike (1970 cited in Coomaraswamy, 2012: 126) asserted during a speech in parliament that by enacting a new constitution, the island's people would show that they had become 'a free, sovereign and independent people who have finally and forever shaken off the shackles of colonial subjugation'. Moreover, the *laissez faire* economic system institutionalised by the British Empire during colonial rule also did not help the state to overcome the economic hardships of the race/species that it managed/fostered. In the nineteenth century, the economic liberalisation programmes undertaken by the British Empire contributed to the transformation of Ceylon from a feudal economy to a commercial one (Mendis, 1946: 36–37). However, in postcolonial Ceylon, *laissez faire* liberalism failed to solve the economic inequalities faced by the Sinhala Buddhists (de Silva, 1981: 542). Neither the giving away of the jobs of the expelled 600,000 Indian Tamils and the thousands of Tamils forced out of the civil service, nor the Sinhala colonisation programmes of the Tamil areas, helped solve the economic difficulties of the Sinhala working class and peasantry. With 'the highest birth-rates in Asia', Sri Lanka could not cope with the economic hardships of the Sinhala Buddhist people, especially that of the 'poverty-stricken, unemployed and the frustrated elements ranging from articulate university graduates to the landless unemployed' (de Silva, 1981: 542).

However, these were not the only reasons to account for why Sri Lanka opted for a new constitution. The old constitution (*Ceylon (Constitution) Order in Council* 1946), though it failed to entrench fundamental rights of all ethnic groups (Soulbury, 1963: viii), remained an obstacle to the state's efforts to biopolitically transform the island into a Sinhala Buddhist ethnocracy. Article 29 (2) of the *Ceylon (Constitution) Order in Council* stipulated that no laws could be enacted to 'confer on persons of any community or religion any privilege or advantage which is not conferred on persons of other communities or religions'. Nevertheless, as discussed above, the island-state enacted the *Ceylon Citizenship Act*, contravening this constitutional provision. Yet, the legal challenge made by the Tamils to Ceylon's Supreme Court, and later the Judicial Committee of the Privy Council, was of no avail. The Privy Council held that 'the disqualification of a large number of Indians in Ceylon was not the necessary legal effect' of the legislation, and thus it did not violate Article 29 (2) of the *Ceylon (Constitution) Order in Council* (Wilson, 1974: 207). Furthermore, when a Tamil civil servant challenged the *Official Language Act* seeking damages from the state, Ceylon's Supreme Court refused to consider his case 'on the ground that a public servant had no right to sue the Crown' (Edrisinha and Selvakkumaran, 2000: 99). However, when the case went before the Privy Council, it overturned this decision and ordered Ceylon's Supreme Court to consider the case (*Kodeeswaran v Attorney General* 1969). The government responded by hastily enacting the *Court of Appeal Act* No.44 of 1971, thereby bringing an end to the Privy Council's oversight of the island's legal system (Marshall, 1973: 155). In other words, the act prevented the *Official Language Act* from being declared void by the state's judiciary.

To prevent the legislation from being nullified in any future judicial proceedings, and thus to uphold the supremacy of the Sinhala Buddhists on the island, Sri Lanka included a special provision in the new constitution of 1972, upholding the constitutional validity of the *Official Language Act*. Article 7 of the new constitution stated: 'The Official Language of Sri Lanka shall be Sinhala as provided by the *Official Language Act* No.33 of 1956' (*The Constitution of the Republic of Sri Lanka*, 22 May 1972).

In 1958, in an attempt to contain the rise of Tamil nationalism, Ceylon enacted the *Tamil Language (Special Provisions) Act No.28 of 1958*. Though the legislation did not accord to Tamil one of official status of the languages of the state, it allowed Tamil to be used as a medium of instruction in schools and higher education institutions, examination for public service for those with sufficient knowledge of the Sinhala language and its use in the Tamil-speaking areas for official correspondence and administrative purposes without prejudices to the Sinhala language. However, opposition from the Sinhala Buddhist clergy prevented the legislation from being enforced. Eight years later in 1966, the government enacted regulations for the use of the Tamil language in the manners prescribed by the Act, but mass demonstrations against the Act by Sinhala opposition parties forced it to refrain from giving force to them; and thus the legislation was never enforced (Ponnambalam, 1983: 135). Though the new constitution of 1972 upheld the validity of the *Tamil Language (Special Provisions) Act*, it did so by affirming the secondary status of the Tamil language given in the preceding years: Article 8 (2) of the new constitution stated that any regulations enacted earlier under the *Tamil Language (Special Provisions) Act* were to be deemed as subordinate legislation and 'shall not in any manner be interpreted as a provision of the Constitution' (*The Constitution of the Republic of Sri Lanka*, 22 May 1972). The new constitution also did not stipulate the implementation of the *Tamil Language (Special Provisions) Act*, effectively allowing the legislation to exist only on paper. In sum, the 1972 constitution affirmed the supremacy of the Sinhala language and the people (the Sinhala Buddhists) who spoke it. Thus, commenting on the new constitution, Chelvanayagam lamented at that time: 'The constitution has given everything to the Sinhalese and nothing to the Tamils' (1972 cited in Haniffa, 2012: 250).

The new constitution also affirmed the supremacy of Buddhism. Article 6 of the constitution stated: 'The Republic of Sri Lanka shall give to Buddhism the foremost place and accordingly it shall be the duty of the State to protect and foster Buddhism while assuring to all religions the rights granted by section [Article] 18 (1) (d)' (*The Constitution of the Republic of Sri Lanka*, 22 May 1972). Though

Article 18 (1) (d) affirmed that 'every citizen shall have the right to freedom of thought, conscience and religion' (*The Constitution of the Republic of Sri Lanka*, 22 May 1972), in giving the foremost place to Buddhism and imposing a duty on the state to protect and foster it, the new constitution affirmed the island as the land of the Sinhala Buddhists where those who practice other religions can exist only insofar as they do not pose a threat to Buddhism. In short, the 1972 constitution legalised the ethnocratic ideology originally enshrined in the *Mahavamsa*.

The *Mahavamsa's* (1912: 3) claim that the island was deemed by Buddha to exist as a single state unit was also legalised by Article 2 of the new constitution in that it affirmed the unitary character of the new state: 'The Republic of Sri Lanka is a Unitary State' (*The Constitution of the Republic of Sri Lanka*, 22 May 1972). The previous *Ceylon (Constitution) Order in Council* did not define Ceylon to be a unitary state. Therefore, in establishing a unitary state order, the new constitution also denied Tamils their claim of the North and East as their traditional homeland, where their precolonial kingdoms and principalities had existed.

The 1972 constitution further contributed to the island as an ethnocracy by renaming the state of Ceylon as Sri Lanka. Apart from invoking colonial memories, Ceylon, a Portuguese name, was devoid of any political meaning either for the Tamils or the Sinhalese. However, the name 'Lanka' is found only in ancient Sinhala chronicles, including the *Mahavamsa*, and Sanskrit/Pali language epics of North India. This name cannot be found in any ancient Tamil literary texts, and the Tamils refer to the island as 'Eelam'. Even the Tamil translation (made in twelfth century C.E.) of the Sanskrit epic *Ramayana* does not use the name 'Lanka' but 'Ilankai' to refer to the island. Thus, by renaming Ceylon using a Sinhala name, its rulers reinforced the *Mahavamsa's* claim that the island belongs to the Sinhala Buddhist race. Moreover, by adding the prefix 'Sri' – which means holy in Sanskrit, Pali and Sinhala – to 'Lanka', they gave a religious identity to the island, and thus the impression that it belonged to Buddha to be populated and ruled by the Sinhala Buddhists.

This ethnocratic identity was, however, partially entrenched 3 years after independence in Ceylon's national identity in the form of the national flag with a sword-wielding lion symbolising the *Mahavamsa's* alleged 'Aryan lion race' origins of the Sinhala Buddhists. The *Mahavamsa* (1912: 55 and 59) portrays the leader of the so-called founding father of the Sinhala people, Prince Wijaya, as the grandson of a lion and an Aryan princess from India. Anagarika Dharmapala, the founding father of Sinhala Buddhist nationalism, reformed and modernised this myth:

> Two thousand four hundred and forty-six years ago a colony of Aryans from the city of Sinhapura, in Bengal, leaving their Indian home, sailed in a vessel in search of fresh pastures, and they discovered the island which they named Tambapanni, on account of its copper coloured soil. The leader of the band was an Aryan prince by the name of Wijaya, and he fought with the aboriginal tribes and got possession of the land. The descendants of the Aryan colonists were called Sinhala after their city, Sinhapura, which was founded by

Sinhabahu, the lion-armed king. The lion-armed descendants are the present Sinhalese, whose ancestors had never been conquered, and in whose veins no savage blood is found.

(1902/1965: 479)

During British colonial rule, Sinhala Buddhist scholars frequently invoked this reformed and modernised Aryan lion race myth to portray the greatness of their people (Balasingham, 2004: 6). It was this idea that was symbolically represented and enshrined in postcolonial Ceylon's national flag embedded with a sword-wielding lion.

In many ways, it was the culmination of the efforts of the Sinhala Buddhist leaders during British colonial rule to romanticise the origins of the sword-wielding lion symbol. Despite depicting the Sinhalese as the descendents of an Aryan lion race, the *Mahavamsa* does not mention anywhere that any of the ancient Sinhala monarchs (or the Tamil monarchs who ruled the Sinhala kingdoms) ever had a sword-wielding lion embedded in their flags. Indeed, the Tamil monarch of the last Sinhala Kingdom of Kandy was not known to have had a sword-wielding lion embedded in his flag. Yet, in the closing years of British colonial rule, Ceylon's Sinhala Buddhist leaders made every effort to construct a history for the sword-wielding lion symbol.

In 1916, three Sinhala students studying in London made a claim that they had found three flags used by the last monarch of the Sinhala Kingdom of Kandy deposited at Chelsea Hospital. Though they did not bring back the so-called flags of the Kandyan king saying that they were hopelessly faded, they brought a sword-wielding lion flag created by a commercial artist in London claiming that it was a colour copy of one of the three faded flags of the Kandyan king (Pieris, 2016). This quickly became the conventional wisdom and in 1945, addressing the State Council, Jayewardene asserted: 'It is the flag that held sway over three portions of Lanka – Ruhuna, Rajarata and Mayarata [three ancient Sinhala kingdoms]. It is a yellow flag with a lion in the centre' (cited in *The Sunday Times*, 2007). Jayewardene even went to the extent of arguing that the same flag was carried by Prince Wijaya when he first set foot on the island (*The Sunday Times*, 2007).

Tamil leaders, including Nadesan and Chelvanayagam, objected to the idea of the sword-wielding lion being made the national flag of Ceylon. However, Sinhala Buddhist leaders went ahead with their plans and hoisted the sword-wielding lion flag on Independence Day. Many Tamil officials, including the deputy solicitor general, therefore responded by hoisting the bull flag of the last Tamil Kingdom of Jaffna on the same day (Pieris, 2016). Yet, 3 years later in March 1951, despite the opposition of many Tamil parliamentarians, using the political monopoly they held over the island's elected legislature, Ceylon's Sinhala Buddhist leaders officially made the sword-wielding lion the island's national flag.

In an attempt to show to the world that their national flag represented all of the major ethnic communities on the island, Sinhala Buddhist leaders added an orange stripe and a green stripe to the left hand side of the sword-wielding lion flag, claiming that these colours represented the Tamils and Muslims, respectively (see *The Sunday Times*, 2010). However, the adding of these coloured stripes had no value for those communities, in particular for the Tamils, as the orange colour was of no significance to them in terms of their language, culture or precolonial history on the island with their own kingdoms and principalities. Moreover, orange is a colour used to symbolise Buddha's teachings and is used in religious flags hoisted by the Sinhala Buddhists in their temples. Thus, the adding of the orange stripe to Sri Lanka's national flag can be said to have symbolised the Sinhala Buddhists and in no way the Tamils.

In 1972, Sri Lanka's Sinhala Buddhist leaders fully entrenched in the island's national identity the *Mahavamsa's* claim that the island was gifted to the Sinhalese by Buddha for Buddhism to be established by adding four Indian fig leaves to the corners of the sword-wielding lion flag. In Buddhist religious history, Buddha is said to have attained enlightenment under an Indian fig tree. Thus, having already made the lion to symbolise the Sinhala race and the sword to signify the sovereignty of the nation, Sinhala Buddhist leaders added four Indian fig leaves to the corners of the national flag to symbolise Buddhism (*The Sunday Times*, 2010).

In sum, the enactment of the new republican constitution in 1972 that gave the foremost place to Buddhism and the preeminent position to the Sinhala language and affirmed the island as a unitary state (thereby denying the precolonial existence of Tamil kingdoms and principalities on the island), coupled with the renaming of the island 'Sri Lanka' and the adding of Indian fig leaves to the sword-wielding lion flag to denote the *Mahavamsa's* idea that Buddhism would be protected by the armed Sinhala Aryan lion race, completed the ethnocratic state-building undertaken by the island's Sinhala Buddhist rulers.

The 1972 constitution can also be said to have affirmed the supremacy of the Sinhala Buddhist people. Although the *Ceylon Independence Act* 1947 passed by the UK government at the Westminster Parliament relinquished its right to legislate for the island after independence, in the postcolonial period, the British monarch continued to function as the head of state. In theory, the monarch's role was seen to be confined to ceremonial roles. However, in practice it enjoyed judicial prerogative over the island through the Judicial Committee of the Privy Council. In the 1960s, attempts were made by the island-state's judiciary to assert its supremacy, and in the case *R v. Hemapala* (1963), Ceylon's Court of Criminal Appeal ruled that the Privy Council did not have the authority to function as the island's highest court of appeal. However, the Privy Council overturned this decision in the case of *Ibralebbe v. R* (1964) and asserted its powers. In the *Ibralebbe v. R* (1964: 18) case, the Privy Council noted that although the British monarch only held nominal authority in the legislative and executive branches of Ceylon, it continued to have the prerogative to deal with judicial matters. The British monarch also continued to be the final authority on all legislation: no bill presented in Ceylon's parliament could become law until it received royal assent. This was because the *Ceylon (Constitution) Order in Council* made the British monarch a part of Ceylon's parliament.

Reversing these, Article 3 of the new constitution asserted that 'Sovereignty is in the People and is inalienable' (*The Constitution of the Republic of Sri Lanka*,

22 May 1972). Moreover, Article 13 of the constitution removed the British monarch from Sri Lanka's legislature, vesting the latter with all the powers of the former (*The Constitution of the Republic of Sri Lanka*, 22 May 1972). At the same time, Article 5 of the constitution made it a point to stress that Sri Lanka's new national assembly would remain the 'supreme instrument of State power of the Republic' and asserted that it would exercise the legislative, executive and judicial powers of the people (*The Constitution of the Republic of Sri Lanka*, 22 May 1972).

The fears that the Sinhala Buddhist leaders entertained over any legal rights the British monarch or the UK parliament may claim over the affairs of Sri Lanka in the future was evident from a request they made to the UK government when the new constitution was enacted. When the new republican constitution was to be enacted, Ceylon's government requested the UK government to also enact legislation in Westminster parliament reiterating the validity of the *Ceylon Independence Act*, and to note that it had changed its name to Sri Lanka (Wickremesinghe, 2014). The UK government conceded to this request and enacted the *Sri Lanka Republic Act* 1972.

Ceylon's biopolitical transformation to an ethnocracy is an issue that has largely been overlooked by the West. Any anxiety the West entertained regarding Sri Lanka's new republican constitution of 1972 stemmed essentially from Article 16 (2) of the constitution, which undermined the *laissez faire* economic policies that had been in force on the island since British colonial rule. The Article committed the state to 'carry forward the progressive advancement towards the establishment in Sri Lanka of a socialist democracy' (*The Constitution of the Republic of Sri Lanka*, 22 May 1972). This included 'the development of collective forms of property such as State property or co-operative property, in the means of production, distribution and exchange as a means of ending exploitation of man by man' (*The Constitution of the Republic of Sri Lanka*, 22 May 1972). It was the incorporation of these socialist principles that caused concern amongst many in the West (see Huntington, 1991: 19). Although these socialist principles were abandoned with the coming into force of the second republican constitution in 1978, the idea that Sri Lanka belonged only to the Sinhala Buddhist people was never abandoned. The next chapter sets out a biopolitical perspective on Sri Lanka's practices for securing the Sinhala Buddhist ethnocratic state order from 1972 onwards.

References

Balasingham, A. (2004) *War and Peace: Armed Struggle and Peace Efforts of Liberation Tigers*. London: Fairmax Publishing.
Bloom, M.M. (2003) 'Ethnic Conflict, State Terror and Suicide Bombing in Sri Lanka', *Civil Wars*, 6(1), pp. 54–84.
Ceylon Citizenship Act No.18 of 1948. Colombo: Government of Ceylon.
Ceylon (Constitution) Order in Council 1946. Colombo: Government of Ceylon.
Ceylon Independence Act 1947 (11 Geo. 6, c. 7). London: HMSO. Available at: http://www.legislation.gov.uk/ukpga/1947/7/pdfs/ukpga_19470007_en.pdf (Accessed: 10 March 2013).

The Constitution of the Republic of Sri Lanka, 22 May 1972. Colombo: Government of Sri Lanka.
Coomaraswamy, R. (2012) 'The 1972 Republican Constitution in the Postcolonial Constitutional Evolution of Sri Lanka', in Welikala, A. (ed.), *The Sri Lankan Republic at 40: Reflections on Constitutional History, Theory and Practice*. Colombo: Centre for Policy Alternatives, pp. 125–144.
Court of Appeal Act No.44 of 1971. Colombo: Government of Ceylon.
Davy, J. (1821) *An Account of the Interior of Ceylon and Its Inhabitants*. London: Longman, Hurst, Rees, Orme, and Brown.
de Silva, K.M. (1981) *A History of Sri Lanka*. London: Hurst & Company.
de Silva, K.M. and Wriggins, H. (1988) *J.R. Jayewardene of Sri Lanka: A Political Biography, Volume 1*. London: Anthony Blond.
Dharmapala, A. (1965) 'History of an Ancient Civilisation', in Guruge, A. (ed.), *Return to Righteousness: A Collection of Speeches, Essays, and Letters of Anagarika Dharmapala*. Colombo: Ceylon Government Press, 479–484 (Original work published 1902).
Edrisinha, R. and Selvakkumaran, N. (2000) 'The Constitutional Evolution of Ceylon/Sri Lanka 1948–98', in Lakshman, W.D. and Tisdell, C.A. (eds.), *Sri Lanka's Development Since Independence: Socio-Economic Perspectives and Analyses*. New York: Nova Science Publishers, pp. 95–112.
Fernando, J.L. (2008) *Religion, Conflict and Peace in Sri Lanka: The Politics of Interpretation of Nationhoods*. Zurich and Munster: Lit Verlag.
Finlason, W.F. (1868) *Justice to a Colonial Governor: Or Some Considerations on the Case of Mr. Eyre*. London: Finlason.
Finlason, W.F. (1872) *Martial Law*. London: Finlason.
Forbes, J. (1850) *Recent Disturbances and Military Executions in Ceylon*. Edinburgh and London: William Blackwood and Sons.
Foucault, M. (1991) *Discipline and Punish: The Birth of the Prison*. Translated by Alan Sheridan. London: Penguin Books (Original work published 1975).
Foucault, M. (1998) *The History of Sexuality: Volume 1: The Will to Knowledge*. Translated by Robert Hurley. London: Penguin Books (Original work published 1976).
Foucault, M. (2004) *"Society Must Be Defended": Lectures at the College de France, 1975–76*. Translated by David Macey. London: Penguin Books.
Foucault, M. (2009) *Security, Territory, Population: Lectures at the College de France, 1977–1978*. Translated by Graham Burchell. Hampshire: Palgrave Macmillan.
The Gal Oya Development Board Act No.51 of 1949. Colombo: Government of Ceylon.
Haniffa, F. (2012) 'Conflicted Solidarities? Muslims and the Constitution-Making Process of 1970–72', in Welikala, A. (ed.), *The Sri Lankan Republic at 40: Reflections on Constitutional History, Theory and Practice*. Colombo: Centre for Policy Alternatives, pp. 219–252.
Harris, N. (1990) *National Liberation*. London: I.B.Tauris.
HC Deb 20 February 1849, vol 102, col 1002–1003. Available at: http://hansard.millbanksystems.com/commons/1849/feb/20/colonial-system-ceylon-and-british-guiana#S3V0102P0_18490220_HOC_10 (Accessed: 20 July 2013).
HC Deb 29 May 1851, vol 117, col 220–243. Available at: http://hansard.millbanksystems.com/commons/1851/may/29/ceylon-adjourned-debate-second-night (Accessed: 20 July 2013).
HC Deb 21 November 1947, vol 444, col 1478–1495. Available at: http://hansard.millbanksystems.com/commons/1947/nov/21/ceylon-independence-bill#S5CV0444P0_19471121_HOC_94 (Accessed: 20 July 2013).

Huntington, S.P. (1991) *The Third Wave: Democratization in the Late Twentieth Century*. Norman: University of Oklahoma Press.

Ibralebbe v. R. [1964] A.C. 900.

Kemper, S. (1991) *The Presence of the Past: Chronicles, Politics, and Culture in Sinhala Life*. Itacha: Cornell University Press.

Kodeeswaran v. Attorney General [1969]. Available at: http://www.lawnet.lk/docs/case_law/nlr/common/html/NLR72V337.htm (Accessed: 5 December 2012).

Mahavamsa, Or the Great Chronicle of Ceylon (1912) Translated by Wilhelm Geiger. London: Oxford University Press (Original work published in the sixth century C.E.).

Marshall, H.H. (1973) 'Ceylon and the Judicial Committee of the Privy Council', *The International and Comparative Law Quarterly*, 22(1), pp. 155–157.

McGowan, W. (1992) *Only Man Is Vile: The Tragedy of Sri Lanka*. London: Pan Books.

Mendis, G.C. (1946) *Ceylon under the British*. Colombo: The Colombo Apothecaries' Co.

Mobilisation of Supplementary Force Act No.40 of 1985. Colombo: Government of Sri Lanka.

Motor Transport Act No.48 of 1957. Colombo: Government of Ceylon.

Nadesan, S. (1948) *Ceylon Citizenship Bill: Speech in the Ceylon Senate on 15 September 1948*. Available at: http://tamilnation.co/nadesan/ctizenship.htm (Accessed: 2 January 2015).

Neocleous, M. (2008) *Critique of Security*. Edinburgh: Edinburgh University Press.

Official Language Act No.33 of 1956. Colombo: Government of Ceylon.

Pieris, K. (2016) *National Flag of Sri Lanka*. Available at: http://www.island.lk/index.php?page_cat=article-details&page=article-details&code_title=140819 (Accessed: 23 February 2016).

Ponnambalam, S. (1983) *Sri Lanka: The National Question and the Tamil Liberation Struggle*. London: Zed Books and Tamil Information Centre. Available at: http://tamilnation.co/books/Eelam/satchi.htm (Accessed: 10 June 2015).

Public Security Ordinance No. 25 of 1947. Colombo: Government of Ceylon.

R v. Hemapala [1963]. Available at: http://www.lawnet.lk/docs/case_law/nlr/common/html/NLR65V313.htm (Accessed: 10 March 2013).

Ramanathan, P. (1916) *Riots and Martial Law in Ceylon, 1915*. London: St.Martin's Press.

Rossiter, C.L. (1948) *Constitutional Dictatorship: Crisis Government in Modern Democracies*. Princeton: Princeton University Press.

Rousseau, J. (1999) *The Social Contract*. Oxford: Oxford University Press.

Satyendra, N. (2007) *Indictment against Sri Lanka*. London: LTTE International Secretariat (Original work published in 1993). Available at: http://www.tamilnation.co/indictment/index.htm (Accessed: 5 January 2015).

Snyder, J. (2000) *From Voting to Violence: Democratization and Nationalist Conflict*. London: W.W.Norton and Company.

Soulbury, V. (1963) 'Forward', in Farmer, B.H. (ed.), *Ceylon: A Divided Nation*. London: Oxford University Press, pp. xvii–ix.

Sri Lanka Republic Act 1972 (19 Elizabeth 2, C. 55). London: HMSO. Available at: http://www.legislation.gov.uk/ukpga/1972/55/pdfs/ukpga_19720055_en.pdf (Accessed: 10 March 2016).

The Sunday Times (2005) *An Evolving Army and Its Role Through Time*. Available at: http://www.sundaytimes.lk/051016/plus/4.html (Accessed: 7 August 2010).

The Sunday Times (2007) *Odyssey of the Lion Flag*. Available at: http://www.sundaytimes.lk/070204/Independencesupp/59Independence9.html (Accessed: 7 May 2013).

The Sunday Times (2010) *The Sri Lankan National Flag*. Available at: http://www.sundaytimes.lk/100131/FunDay/fut_02.html (Accessed: 2 February 2010).

Tambiah, S.J. (1986) *Sri Lanka: Ethnic Fratricide and the Dismantling of Democracy*. London: I.B.Tauris & Co.

Tambiah, S.J. (1996) *Levelling Crowds: Ethnonationalist Conflicts and Collective Violence in South Asia*. Berkeley: University of California Press.

Tamil Language (Special Provisions) Act No.28 of 1958. Colombo: Government of Ceylon.

Taylor, M. (2000) 'The 1848 Revolution and the British Empire', *Past & Present*, 166(February), pp. 146–180.

Tharmalingam, K.N. (2007) *Development: Gal Oya Scheme – Early Example of State Discrimination against Tamils*. Available at: http://www.tamilcanadian.com/article/4821 (Accessed: 4 May 2015).

Torrington, V. (1851) *Speech of the Right Honourable Viscount Torrington on the Affairs of Ceylon*. London: George Woodfall and Son.

Trawick, M. (2007) *Enemy Lines: Warfare, Childhood, and Play in Batticaloa*. Berkeley: University of California Press.

Vittachi, T. (1958) *Emergency '58 – the Story of Ceylon Race Riots*. London: Andre Deutsch. Available at: http://tamilnation.co/books/Eelam/vitachi.htm (Accessed: 7 October 2011).

Welhengama, G. and Pillay, N. (2014) *The Rise of Tamil Separatism in Sri Lanka*. Oxon: Routledge.

Wickramasinghe, N. (2006) *Sri Lanka in the Modern Age: A History of Contested Identities*. London: Hurst and Company.

Wickremesinghe, R. (2014) *The New Republic*. Available at: http://www.sundaytimes.lk/141109/news/the-new-republic-126724.html (Accessed: 10 November 2014).

Wijemanne, A. (1996) *War and Peace in Post-Colonial Ceylon, 1948–1991*. Hyderabad: Orient Longman.

Wilson, J.A. (1974) *Politics in Sri Lanka, 1947–1973*. London: Palgrave Macmillan.

3 In defence of the race/species

In 'Society Must Be Defended', Foucault asserted that society, the law and the state are not 'armistices that put an end to war' (2004: 50). In Sri Lanka's case, this remained a valid assertion because the state's war (though having largely manifested through power relations apart from military action) against the Tamils did not end with the construction of a Sinhala Buddhist ethnocratic state order in 1972. The war continued with more intensity, this time incorporating military action.

In Middle Ages Europe, the sovereign power over life and death was exercised as the prince's right to 'either have people put to death or let them live' (Foucault, 2004: 240). In Sri Lanka, following its transformation as an ethnocracy, its biopolitics over the Tamil population was tilted in favour of this premodern sovereign power: the Tamils became a subject race who could either be put to death or allowed to live at the discretion of the state and the race/species that it managed/fostered.

The boomerang effect

In 1972, as a way of increasing higher education opportunities for the Sinhalese and thereby reducing unemployment within the Sinhala community, Sri Lanka introduced a system known as the standardisation of university entries (Harris, 1990: 215). Under this system, Sinhala students were placed at an advantaged position over their Tamil counterparts. For example, while the qualifying mark for admission to the medical faculties for the Sinhalese was set at 229, for the Tamils it was kept at 250 (Wilson, 2000: 102). Further measures were taken in 1974 to reduce the number of Tamils entering universities by introducing a system of district quota. In 1973, despite the system of standardisation, in the predominantly Tamil-speaking Jaffna district, 398 students qualified to enter university medical and biological science courses while 575 qualified to enter engineering and physical science courses (Horowitz, 2000: 663–664). This fell drastically with the introduction of the system of district quota. Under this system in 1974, only 34 places for medical and biological sciences and 37 places for engineering and physical sciences were made open for students from Jaffna (Horowitz, 2000: 663–664).

These actions of the state forced many Tamil students to seek higher education in Western countries, setting off the first wave of Tamil migration to the West (Harris, 1990: 215). As on previous occasions, using law, Sri Lanka was not only able to improve the race/species that it was fostering, but also indirectly expel a section of the 'enemy' race that it waged war against.

Sri Lanka's actions, however, also caused a boomerang effect. Angered by Sri Lanka's racist policies, the Tamil youth who either shunned foreign education, or did not have the means to go abroad, embarked on a militant path (Balasingham, 2004: 19). With the door to economic prosperity having been shut by the state, the Tamil youth deemed an armed struggle for creating an independent Tamil state, Tamil Eelam, encompassing the Northern and Eastern Provinces and the Puttalam district in the Northwestern Province, to be the only way forward (Balasingham, 2004: 20). As far back as 1961, when the state unleashed military violence on Tamils engaged in non-violent protests, many Tamils had come to the conclusion that non-violent campaigns against the state would not help realise their political rights, and 9 years later in 1970, a Tamil student organisation named Tamil Student Federation that 'articulated radical politics and encouraged student activists to take up the militant path' was formed (Balasingham, 2004: 22). Yet, the state, using its police and military, successfully vanquished this student movement by arresting and imprisoning its leaders (Balasingham, 2004: 22). However, following the introduction of the new constitution in 1972, closely followed by the system of standardisation and district quota to university entries, Tamil militancy gathered momentum. Angered by Sri Lanka's discriminatory policies, the youth (including school-going teenagers) formed underground guerrilla movements, of which the LTTE (initially known as the Tamil New Tigers), led by its 17-year-old leader Velupillai Pirapaharan, emerged as the most organised. In the early stages, the Tamil militancy manifested 'in the form of political assassinations, bombings, shootings, arson against government property and raids on state banks' (Balasingham, 2004: 23).

The militant path adopted by the Tamil youth also contributed to moderate Tamil politicians abandoning their demands for regional autonomy within a united Sri Lanka, and instead advocating for political independence. On 14 May 1972, 8 days before Ceylon enacted its first republican constitution, three Tamil political parties, including Chelvanayagam's ITAK, adopted a political programme that sought to achieve Tamil rights within a united Sri Lanka (Balasingham, 2004: 18–19). Five months later, with intensification of the violence of the Tamil youth, however, Tamil political leaders changed course and began to advocate secession. Chelvanayagam even resigned his parliamentary seat in October 1972 to protest against the new constitution, and announced that he would be contesting the bi-election on a platform of self-determination for the Tamil people:

> My policy will be that in view of the events that have taken place the Tamil people of Ceylon should have the right to determine their future whether they

are to be a subject race in Ceylon or they are to be a free people. I shall ask the people to vote for me on the second of these alternatives.

(1972 cited in Haniffa, 2012: 250)

This was followed by Tamil political leaders obtaining the popular mandate for secession in the general election of 1977. The Tamil United Liberation Front (TULF), made up of the ITAK and All Ceylon Tamil Congress (ACTC) that contested the general election on a manifesto of secession, won all the seats in the Tamil areas (Balasingham, 2004: 27–29).

Such was the influence of the Tamil militancy that Sri Lanka upgraded its war on the Tamils from one centred on improving the race/species that it fostered to that for defending it and securing the Sinhala Buddhist ethnocratic state order. In the 1950s and 1960s, the state's use of law and 'lawlessness' over the Tamils largely manifested as the biopolitics of state violence. From 1972 onwards, however, this assumed the character of biopolitics of state terror. The state's police, military and loosely organised gangs of Sinhala Buddhist extremists became the power complexes through which this reign of terror was unleashed.

The terror of law and the right to kill

Sri Lanka used two emergency legislations to unleash terror on the Tamil population: the *Prevention of Terrorism (Temporary Provisions) Act* (PTA) No. 48 of 1979, and the PSO.

Having used the PSO to crush the JVP insurrection in 1971, from 1972 onwards Sri Lanka turned its full force on the Tamils. This was the result of the legislation being given constitutional validity in the first republican constitution of 1972, and the second republican constitution of 1978 making it supreme, second only to the constitution. Article 155 (2) of the 1978 constitution stated:

> The power to make emergency regulations under the Public Security Ordinance or the law for the time being in force relating to public security shall include the power to make regulations having the legal effect of over-riding, amending or suspending the operation of the provisions of the Constitution.
>
> (*The Constitution of the Democratic Socialist Republic of Sri Lanka*, 7 September 1978)

The first occasion when Sri Lanka used the PSO to unleash terror on the Tamils after becoming a republic was in January 1974. Thousands of Tamils assembled at a Tamil conference of linguistic and cultural significance in Jaffna were attacked by armed Sri Lankan police officers. The government initially insisted that the Tamils hold the conference in Colombo because it feared that the Tamils might use it for political purposes if it was held in Jaffna (Balachandran, 2010), the capital of the last Tamil kingdom on the island. However, the organisers were adamant and the conference went ahead in Jaffna. The government allowed the conference to proceed for the first few days when there was no large public attendance. However, on the last day, when the Tamil public attended the conference in large numbers, the Sri Lankan police were quickly despatched to disperse the participants. The very fact that a state of emergency was already in force (citing the JVP insurgency and the Tamil militancy) provided the legal cover for the police to unleash terror. Firing tear gas and bullets, armed Sri Lankan police officers attacked the Tamils (Ponnambalam, 1983: 166). Some of the shots fired by the police brought down an overhead electric cable, killing nine Tamils (Wickramasinghe, 2006: 280). Many more Tamils were injured. The government's complicity in the attacks became apparent later when the senior police officer (an assistant superintendent of police) who led the attack was promoted for his 'patriotic act' (Tambiah, 1986: 17). By carrying out these attacks, the state conveyed the message to Tamils that any symbolic effort on their part to assert their language, culture and their history on the island would be met with the terror of law.

In July 1979, Sri Lanka complemented the PSO with the PTA. Though the preamble of the Act claimed that it was enacted as a 'special legislation to deal with acts of terrorism', in practice it became a special legislation to justify the perpetration of terror on the Tamils, and later the Sinhala Marxists led by the JVP who once again challenged the state order in 1987. Whilst the PSO allowed the state to use draconian powers only when a state of emergency was in force, the PTA allowed for the use of similar, and in some cases even more draconian, powers, even when there was no emergency. Whereas section 6 of the PTA gave the security forces the power to arrest individuals at their will and remand them 'until the conclusion of the trial', section 9 of the Act empowered ministers to order individuals to be detained. These orders, pursuant to section 10 of the Act, could not be challenged in the courts. Section 11 of the legislation also empowered ministers to issue orders restricting the movement of individuals. Moreover, section 16 of the legislation allowed confessions obtained through torture to be used as evidence in the courts.

Immediately after the PTA was enacted, the Sri Lankan President Jayewardene appointed one of his kinsman, Brigadier T. I. Weeratunge, as the military commander of the Northern Province with specific orders to eliminate the Tamil militancy within 6 months:

> It will be your duty to eliminate, in accordance with the laws of this land, the menace of terrorism in all its forms from the Island and more specifically from the [Northern] Jaffna District. I will place at your disposal all resources of the State. I earnestly request all law abiding citizens to give their co-operation to you. This task has to be performed by you and completed before 31 December 1979.
> (Jayewardene, 1979 cited in Dissanayaka, 2005: 37)

With the powers vested in him by the PTA, Weeratunge unleashed terror in the Tamil areas. Hundreds of Tamils suspected of involvement in the Tamil militancy were rounded up by the police and the military and detained without charges. Those who were arrested and detained earlier under the provisions of the PSO were also rearrested. Old Park, a compound in Jaffna used earlier by the chief civil administration officer for the district, was turned into a torture chamber by the military. Some of the detainees were killed (Hoole, 2001).

S. Saravanamuthu, an exiled Tamil journalist who was arrested at the age of 17 and detained at Old Park under the PTA in 1979, told the author during an interview in December 2015 that torture was used by the military and police as a key weapon for obtaining confessions and instilling fear among the Tamil youth who believed in an armed struggle for political independence. In each cell, between twenty to twenty-five detainees were held. During the day, a unit of police and military officers would arrive and routinely interrogate the detainees. However, at night another unit of police and military officers would arrive and enter each cell, dragging out the first detainee they encountered. The detainee would then be taken to another room and subjected to a continuous and ruthless beating. No questions would be asked. Sometimes the lights would be turned off, making it hard for the detainee to know who was attacking him and from which direction the blow would come. If the detainee fell on the floor whilst being attacked, he would be kicked and trampled upon. If he tried to resist being hit, the officials would then attack him with more vigour. At other instances, the detainee would be made to lie down and be beaten on the soles of his feet. Some of the detainees were stripped naked, and their genitals crushed. There were also instances when the detainee would be ordered to put his genital organ into an open cabinet drawer which would then be slammed shut. Sometimes the detainee would be hung upside down and beaten. An electric chair would be placed before the detainee and he would be threatened with electrocution if he did not confess. The torture would end at dawn, and the detainee would be taken back to his cell. A few hours later, another unit of police and military officials would arrive and treat the detainee kindly, telling him to confess and leave the country after release. Though Saravanamuthu survived the torture, not all inmates had been so fortunate; some became mentally ill and committed suicide after being released.

Similar testimonies have also been made by other Tamils who were held in Sri Lanka's prisons. In the words of S. A. David, who was held at Welikade Prison in Colombo in 1983:

> Almost every other day and whenever he was in the mood, Commander Udugampola would come drunk with a glass of arrack in his hand and open the cells, strip the detenus and assault and kick and curse them. I could hear cries of pain and groans throughout the nights and early morning and see naked colleagues hanging head down from high window bars. I saw naked detenus being chased around the courtyard and being assaulted and kicked by six to eight soldiers with PVC pipes and iron rods in their hands.
>
> One day, Commander Udugampola came drunk and opened my cell, ordered me to strip and lie face down on a concrete bench. He ordered three soldiers to trample my back and legs and hit me on my buttocks. They left me exhausted on the bench.

> On another day, he came drunk, entered my room with shoes in his hand and hit me on my head and face. My lips split and started bleeding. He allowed me to wash and ordered me to sleep naked throughout the night.
>
> (1983)

In his study of torture in Europe in the Middle Ages, Foucault argued that torture is 'not an extreme expression of lawless rage' but a technique in which 'a whole economy of power is invested' (1991: 33 and 35). This was exactly the case in Sri Lanka. Torture, as Foucault refers to it in relation to Middle Ages Europe, is 'an organised ritual for the marking of victims and the expression of the power that punishes' (1991: 34). In Middle Ages Europe, 'a policy of terror' through torture was used 'to make everyone aware, through the body of the criminal, of the unrestrained presence of the sovereign' (Foucault, 1991: 49) In Sri Lanka's case, the unrestrained presence of the Sinhala Buddhist race/species that had become the sovereign was manifested through the tortures carried out by Sri Lanka's military and police officials.

In Middle Ages Europe, torture remained 'the art of maintaining life in pain' (Foucault, 1991: 33). In Sri Lanka's case, torture was the manifestation of the sovereign's power over the life of the Tamil detainee. Like the sovereigns in Middle Ages Europe, the sovereign in Sri Lanka held the power to maintain the life of the Tamil detainee in pain, or put him to death. The fact that the Tamil detainee was made to strip naked and sometimes sleep in such a state in his cell, or run around the courtyard naked, should not simply be seen as an act of perversity on the part of Sri Lanka's military and police officials, but understood as an act that was intended to reduce the detainee to a state of nothingness. Nudity of the detainee was intended to remind him that not only his life, but his right to privacy no longer belonged to him: they all now belonged to the sovereign.

As well as reminding the Tamil detainee of the omniscient power of the Sinhala Buddhist race/species, torture was also used as an instrument for obtaining confessions. Saravanamuthu told the author that Sri Lankan military officials interrogating Tamil detainees showed more interest in extracting confessions from them, rather than verifying whether they were true:

> They would ask us questions as to what role we played in the Tamil militancy. If they ask whether I was part of a group that shot a pro-government Tamil politician, I had to say something that could be recorded as a confession. If I said, 'No,' they would torture me. But if I say, 'I didn't shoot him but threw a stone at him,' they would record that, and then I would not be tortured for that day. We then found out that if we say something, even if it was not true, we could escape torture for that day. Some of the detainees therefore made false accusations against random people to avoid torture. These people would then be arrested and tortured. When those new detainees learned the trick, they also started playing the same game.

Sometimes this game became dangerous. A prisoner, in an attempt to avoid torture, falsely confessed that he knew where the Tamil militants had hidden their explosives. He was immediately taken to the spot, and when he could not locate those 'hidden' explosives, he was buried neck-deep in sand, and threatened with decapitation. The prisoner was brought back to his cell only after soldiers realised that he had made a false confession to avoid torture.

In Middle Ages Europe, confessions through torture signified the victory of the sovereign in the ritualised production of 'truth' (Foucault, 1991: 41). In Sri Lanka, it was the case of military and police officials showing their loyalty to the race/species they served: by producing the 'truth' about the Tamil militancy, and taking into custody more of those from the 'enemy' race, they were protecting their race/species, and thus affirming their loyalty to it.

In June 1983, Sri Lanka vested, under the PSO, another sweeping power to the security forces by enacting *Emergency Regulation 15A*. The regulation allowed the security forces to dispose of bodies without an inquest (Amnesty International, 1984b: 10). A similar measure was introduced following the mass violence of 1958, paving the way for some officials to abuse power and get rid of their personal enemies (Vittachi, 1958). The new measure, this time, provided the cover for the security forces to shoot and kill any Tamil at their will, whilst at the same time avoid culpability for the crime of murder that may arise as a result of any subsequent inquest. The Sri Lankan government made this known explicitly even before the regulation was enacted:

> Certain regulations under the Public Security Act [Ordinance] will be enforced in the northern area to deal more effectively with terrorism. At present the armed forces are under restraint because in any incident that may result, there may be inquiries by coroners which may even lead later to trials before law courts. This puts the services at a great disadvantage in that terrorists can shoot and disappear at will and the Armed Services are unable to retaliate in self-defence. In order to free the services of these disabilities, security regulations will be published. They will remove the obligations to have coroners' inquests following any shooting incidents by Armed Services.
> (Sri Lanka Department of Information, 1983 cited in Amnesty International, 1984b: 10)

The regulation marked an important passage in the use of the power of death in Sri Lanka. Military and police officials no longer had to maintain the life of a Tamil detainee in pain. They could take his/her life if his/her existence was not deemed to be useful for producing the 'truth' on the Tamil militancy. At the same time, they could also take vengeance on the Tamils for any attacks carried out by Tamil militants on their colleagues.

After *Emergency Regulation 15A* was enacted, Amnesty International (1984b: 11) accused the Sri Lankan government of attempting to 'absolve members of the armed services from legal liability through prosecution in courts for extrajudicial killings' and thereby creating 'the impression that civilians can be killed by the security forces with impunity'. However, the Sri Lankan government hit back by claiming that the 'purpose of Emergency Regulation 15A was not to give additional powers to the services but to enable the authorities to bury or cremate a dead body in a manner that would not leave room for exciting communal tension' (Sri Lanka government, 1983 cited in Amnesty International, 1984b: 10). Yet, as Amnesty International and other international and local human rights groups later documented, the Sri Lanka security forces carried out mass killings after the enactment of the regulation. It is beyond the scope of this book to document all of the mass killings carried out by the Sri Lankan security forces on the Tamils. This chapter would therefore examine some of the infamous mass killings that reveal how the power of death was used by the Sri Lankan state as part of its biopolitics of defending the Sinhala Buddhist race/species and securing the ethnocratic state order.

On 24 July 1983, almost 1 month after *Emergency Regulation 15A* was enacted, the Sri Lankan security forces massacred scores of Tamils in Jaffna district in retaliation for the death of thirteen Sri Lanka soldiers in an ambush carried out by the LTTE the previous night. The exact number of Tamils killed in the aftermath of the ambush is not known because no inquests were held after the massacres, and the bodies of the victims were swiftly disposed of by the security forces. In the environs of the area where the ambush took place, sixty Tamil civilians were shot and killed by the Sri Lankan military (Balasingham, 2004: 39). Massacres were also carried out in other Tamil areas (Amnesty International, 1984a: 3–27). When these actions caused an international outcry, the Sri Lankan government absolved itself and the security forces of the massacres by claiming that these were isolated actions of some angry soldiers. Later, in a letter to Amnesty International, the Sri Lankan High Commissioner in London stated:

> When, however, on the night of 23 July, 13 Sinhalese soldiers were ambushed and killed by the terrorists in Jaffna, the pent up feelings of some of the soldiers got the better of their sense of discipline. A few soldiers acted on their own and 51 persons in Jaffna were killed. . ... The government does not condone the acts of these soldiers. I must stress that the commanding officer did all that was humanely possible to contain the situation.
> (1983 cited in Amnesty International, 1984b: 7)

However, as Amnesty International (1984a: 3–27) documented through sworn eyewitness testimonies, all of the massacres had a pattern in that soldiers would select and kill Tamil males. On one occasion, passengers travelling on a bus were stopped, the males and females made to line up on opposite sides, and any Sinhalese passengers told to come forward. When no Sinhalese passenger came forward, the security forces decided that all of passengers were Tamils, and shot the males in cold blood (Amnesty International, 1984a: 6–7). On another occasion, the Sri Lankan soldiers took control of a transport bus and, ordering the driver to keep driving, shot at every Tamil they encountered on the streets (Amnesty International, 1984a: 11). There were also instances in which Sri Lankan soldiers entered Tamil houses and 'shot at the inhabitants at point blank' (Amnesty International, 1984a: 11). The Sri Lankan state justified those mass killing 'by stating that civilians were killed during an "exchange of fire" with "terrorists"' (Amnesty International, 1984c: 3).

The mass scale killing of Tamil detainees by the security forces also became the norm. In December 1984, thirty-two Tamil detainees held at an army camp in the Northern Vavuniya district were shot dead by the military. When this caught the attention of the media, the Sri Lankan government simply stated that the detainees 'had died "trying to escape" while the camp was under attack' (Amnesty International, 1985: 245). When individual Tamil detainees died during torture, the Sri Lanka government would claim that they had committed suicide (Amnesty International, 1985: 245). On other occasions the soldiers carried out summary executions of individual Tamil detainees; the government would state they had been shot while trying to escape (Amnesty International, 1985: 245).

Following an international outcry, the Sri Lankan government repealed *Emergency Regulation 15A* in June 1984. Yet, the legal power it had vested on the security forces to kill Tamils and dispose of their bodies remained in place. The *Emergency Regulation 55 B-G*, enacted following the repeal of *Emergency Regulation 15A*, allowed the Sri Lankan security forces to conduct the initial investigations into the deaths of those killed by them, as opposed to a full enquiry by a magistrate (Amnesty International, 1985: 245). Moreover, the new regulation also gave the police the 'power to dispose of dead bodies without an inquest'; the regulation stipulated that this can be done 'in the interest of national security' (Amnesty International, 1985: 246). An inquest could only be held 'if the police applied for one and not at the discretion of the magistrate' (Amnesty International, 1985: 246).

The *Emergency Regulation 15A* and its successor *Emergency Regulation 55 B-G* not only instilled terror into the Tamil population, but they sent the message that it was the agents of the sovereign that held the power to determine the lives of the 'enemy' race/species. The life of every Tamil depended on the mercy of the individual Sinhala Buddhist soldier or policeman that he/she encountered: it was left to the soldier or the policeman to decide whether a Tamil should be allowed to live, his/her life managed in pain or taken away.

The author lived in the Jaffna peninsula in the Northern Province in 1984 and 1985 when some of those massacres were carried out by the Sri Lankan security forces. The author can recall moments when Tamil adult males in his village would run away from their homes and stay in hiding when the Sri Lankan troops carried out raids. Any Tamil who was not fortunate enough to avoid being arrested by the Sri Lankan security forces would return with scars all over his body due to torture. Some of the arrested never returned.

In the 1950s, 1960s and the early years of the 1970s, the state used law largely to produce one of the effects of battle – expulsion: the expulsion of sections of the Indian Tamils from the country; the expulsion of the indigenous Tamils from the civil service and universities; and ultimately created the conditions for the Tamils to favour migration as a possible avenue for survival and advancement. The violence of law through police brutalities and military violence was used when the Tamils tried to resist the 'lawless' violence of the Sinhala Buddhist extremists, or when they resorted to civil disobedience, as in 1961.

With the emergence of the armed Tamil secessionist movement in 1972, whatever constraints existed on the practices of the state and its armed forces in dealing with the Tamils were lifted. The sword of the law was turned on every Tamil who was not fortunate enough to avoid encountering it. In Sri Lanka's biopolitics of defending the race/species it fostered and securing the ethnocratic state order, law became the symbol of terror, and the manifestation of the power to kill the 'enemy' race/species.

In an attempt to avoid being accused by international human rights groups of militarising the Tamil areas, Sri Lanka set up a counter-insurgency unit – a part of its police force – in 1983. The Special Task Force (STF), as it came to be known, was initially made up of 3,000 police personnel. However, as the armed conflict intensified, this unit swelled to the size of a military division, encompassing up to 10,000 police commandos (Moorcraft, 2012: 73). The STF personnel were provided training to use infantry weapons and to conduct jungle warfare (Moorcraft, 2012: 73). Created as the 'third' force that existed between the military and the police, the STF was trained by around 100 ex-British Special Air Service (SAS) personnel (Moorcraft, 2012: 73). The STF was also said to have been trained by apartheid South Africa's notorious special police unit, the *Koevoet* (the 'crowbar') that was deployed against black guerrillas in South Africa and Namibia, and the Israeli internal security organisation, *Shinbeth*, also known for its notorious tactics against the Palestinians (Moorcraft, 2012: 73–74). As well as operating in small units to carry out commando raids against the Tamil guerrillas, the STF was infamous for making many hundreds of arrested Tamils 'disappear', and for mass killings (Amnesty International, 1994: 18). As Amnesty International later documented, Sri Lanka's tactic of making Tamils disappear in large numbers developed soon after the STF was created:

> [B]y late 1984 a new tactic of the security forces was evident: in an increasing number of cases where a person had been arrested by the security forces in front of witnesses, those forces denied holding the prisoner and their relatives were never able to establish their whereabouts. Whole groups of young men, who had been arrested together, simply "disappeared".
>
> This new tactic of "disappearance" developed in Sri Lanka soon after the creation of a new police commando unit, the Special Task Force (STF). Members of this unit, as well as members of the army, were frequently seen taking into custody young men who then "disappeared". Testimony after testimony by witnesses described how the "disappeared" had been rounded up in groups by the army or the STF and taken away. Less frequently police, air force and navy personnel were described as the arresting authority.
>
> Testimonies from released prisoners described the torture and killing of many prisoners in army or STF detention camps, and the secret disposal of

bodies, often by burning. "Disappearance" appeared to be used for two purposes: it facilitated torture without accountability, and it concealed the killing of prisoners.

(Amnesty International, 1994: 17–18)

The creation of the STF and the development of the tactic of 'disappearance' could be said to have allowed Sri Lanka to use the power of death in more innovative ways. It no longer had to manage the lives of members of the 'enemy' race in pain or kill them in public and risk being called a murderous state by the international community. It could simply arrest members of the 'enemy' race, but deny having made any arrests, and then manage the lives of the detainees in the pain of torture until the 'truth' on the Tamil militancy had been produced, and then eliminate them. In doing so, Sri Lanka created a new official status for many of the arrested Tamils – the 'disappeared'. Unofficially they were dead; but officially they were neither dead nor alive.

The reformed scaffold service

It was not only law that Sri Lanka used to unleash terror on the Tamils. The mass violence of 'lawlessness' was also used for this purpose.

In August 1977, a month after Tamils voted for secession, the mass violence of the Sinhala Buddhist extremists raised its head again. The violence spread after rumours circulated that Tamils were attacking the Sinhalese (Northern Provincial Council, 2015: 2). In reality no such attack by the Tamils had taken place. Instead, there was an altercation between a group of Sinhala police officers and the Tamil organisers of a carnival in Jaffna on the night before the mass violence (Hoole, 2001). Yet, rumours abounded that Tamil militants had killed two Sinhala policemen in Jaffna. This has become the established truth in literature published many years after the mass violence (see, for example Human Rights Watch, 1995: 86). However, further investigations carried out by local human rights groups have since revealed that no such killing of Sinhala policemen actually occurred (Hoole, 2001).

In 1956, 1958 and 1961, the role of the police in the racial violence was confined to non-interference, and allowing gangs of Sinhala Buddhist extremists to attack the Tamils. A notable aspect of the racial violence of August 1977, however, was that gangs of Sinhala Buddhist extremists who went on a rampage in the Tamil areas and other parts of the island were often led by armed police officers (Hoole, 2001). It was no longer the case of the state guarding the people, the Sinhala Buddhist extremists, while they meted out havoc on their enemies, the Tamils: it was the case of the state forces taking the lead in the violence of its people.

Statements made by Jayewardene, Sri Lanka's prime minister during the mass violence of 1977, exemplify this. Speaking in the parliament 2 days after the mass violence erupted, Jayewardene (1977a) blamed Tamil parliamentarians, claiming that their support for the Tamil militancy had inflamed the violence: 'If you want to fight, let there be a fight; if it is peace, let there be peace'. Jayewardene was quick to point out that these were not his words, but that he was articulating the voice of the people of the country: 'It is not what I am saying. The people of Sri Lanka will say that' (Jayewardene, 1977a). In claiming to speak on behalf of the people of the country, Jayewardene made it clear that the Tamils did not constitute a part of the people.

Jayewardene also warned Tamil leaders to expect even greater forms of violence if they continued to advocate secession: 'But I say, be careful of the words you use . . . And what has happened can happen in a greater degree if such words are used by responsible leaders' (Jayewardene, 1977a). Attacks on the Tamils intensified after Jayewardene's speech (Hoole, 2001). Though the exact casualty figures are not known, official estimates put it at 100 deaths (Human Rights Watch, 1995: 86). However, Tamil estimates have put the figure at 300 deaths (Northern Provincial Council, 2015: 2). Around 75,000 Tamils also became refugees (Samarakkody, 1977: 6). These included Indian Tamils who fled their homes and sought refuge in the North and East (Ponnambalam, 1983: 175; Human Rights Watch, 1995: 86).

Three months later, when confronted in the parliament by a Tamil parliamentarian on why the state had not taken action against police officers who led gangs of Sinhala Buddhist extremists, Jayewardene (1977b) claimed that he did not want to anger the Sinhala people:

> At that time we did not want to take any action against police officers because the situation would have aggravated. There was a Sinhala – Tamil dispute. It is all right for the Member now in the cool atmosphere of this air conditioned Chamber four months after the incident, to say that we should have interdicted that officer when there was rioting going on – the situation might have got worse.

Jayewardene's comments suggest that whenever the people meted their anger on their 'enemy' race, the state would do nothing to prevent its forces assisting and guiding them. This, in effect, signalled a reformed scaffold service. The scaffold service that manifested in the mass violence of 1956, 1958 and 1961 was one in which the people showed their vengeance on the 'enemy' race, while the state, symbolised by armed police and military officials, stood by their side, intervening only when the violence of 'lawlessness' went to the extent of threatening the state order. The mass violence of 1977 signalled a shift in this state of affairs in that the state would, as well as allowing its forces to stand by the people's side and protect them, allow them to guide the people in their mission to avenge their enemies. This was also beneficial to the state in that it held the reins of the violence of 'lawlessness' in its hands. The state could use the same police officers who led gangs of Sinhala Buddhist extremists to bring them under control.

The reformed scaffold service was once again used by the state in May 1981 to inflict terror on the Tamils. This time, it was more organised: two senior cabinet ministers, Cyril Mathew and Gamini Dissanayake, supervised the gangs of Sinhala Buddhist extremists being led by police officers and soldiers (Murray, 1984: 100). During this reign of terror, the Jaffna Public Library, home to irreplaceable literary and historical documents of the Tamils, was torched and razed to the ground (Tambiah, 1986: 19–20). A Tamil Hindu temple was burned, as were the offices and the printing press of a Tamil newspaper. Gangs of Sinhala Buddhist thugs also attacked and looted Tamil businesses in Jaffna (Murray, 1984: 100; Tambiah, 1986: 19–20; Balasingham, 2004: 33). The response of the Sinhala Buddhist thugs, with the collaboration of the military and the police, and egged on by Sinhala politicians, was a disproportionate response to shots being fired by Tamil militants at an election meeting (Murray, 1984: 100). Speaking in the parliament justifying the state-guided mass violence, W.J.M. Lokubandara, a ruling party parliamentarian warned:

> If the sleeping Sinhalese wake up to see the Tamils trying to establish a Tamil Eelam in Sri Lanka, then things may not be quite calm. It would be advisable for the Tamils not to disturb the sleeping Sinhala brother. Everybody knows that lions when disturbed are not peaceful.
>
> (1981: 6)

With the addition of the lion race terminology into the troika of politicians, the security forces and gangs of Sinhala Buddhist hardliners in the perpetration of anti-Tamil violence in 1981, it became apparent that 'lawlessness' was enjoying the status of an unofficial weapon to be used to defend the Sinhala Buddhist race/species and the ethnocratic state order. On previous occasions, in 1956, 1958 and 1961, the attacks on Tamils by Sinhala Buddhist extremists were largely confined to the Sinhala areas; and the violence against Tamils in their homeland was limited to newly erected Sinhala settlements. However, the racist violence of 1977 changed this, in that the violence had extended to the bastion of the last Tamil kingdom in the North. By burning the Jaffna public library and decimating Tamil businesses in Jaffna in May 1981, the state made it clear that it intended to take the war against the Tamils to their heartland, and attempt to assert the all-island sovereignty of the Sinhala Buddhist people. Reflecting this view, Wimala Kannangara (1981: 6), a cabinet minister in Jayewardene's government stated in a speech in the parliament a month later that: 'We are born as Sinhalese and as Buddhists in this country. Though we are in a majority, we have been surrendering to the minority community for years. Let us rule as a majority community'.

Almost as if on cue, later, in August 1981, the Tamils were subjected to another bout of state-guided racial violence. In this instance, a clash between Sinhala and Tamil students in Paddipalai Aaru in the Eastern Province escalated into mass scale violence. The violence quickly spread to other parts of the country (Tambiah, 1986: 20–21), and large numbers of Tamils were killed in the attacks (Balasingham, 2004: 32). Jayewardene (1981), who had now assumed the office of the president of the country, acknowledged the complicity of his ministers in those attacks: 'I regret that some members of my party have spoken in Parliament and outside, words that encourage violence and murders, rapes and arson that have been committed'.

However, compared to the state-orchestrated racial violence that occurred 2 years later in 1983, the scale of the violence of 1981 was much smaller. At midnight of 23 July 1983, the LTTE ambushed a military convoy in Jaffna, killing thirteen Sri Lankan soldiers (Balasingham, 2004: 38–39). The following day, gangs of Sinhala Buddhists extremists launched attacks on Tamils in Colombo and such attacks spread like wild fire to other parts of the country. Following a well-known pattern of racial violence, Tamil houses and businesses were targeted, the difference being that this time the attacks were carried out in a systematic way. The attackers carried in their possession 'lists of Tamil houses, buildings and businesses' (Kapferer, 1988: 29). According to Stanley Tambiah (1986: 21), the very fact that the attackers carried voter lists and addresses of Tamil owners and occupants of houses, shops and other property is evidence of prior intent and planning. Some government officials later admitted during private conversations that they had planned the attacks on the orders of their superiors (Wilson, 1988: 173). The author's residence in Colombo was also attacked by Sinhala Buddhist gangs. Whilst the author's residence on the first floor of an apartment was stoned by Sinhala Buddhist gangs, the residence of a Muslim trader below on the ground floor, was left intact (the author moved to Jaffna after the mass violence).

Such was the scale and the nature of the violence carried out in July 1983, unprecedented in Sri Lanka's history, that many Tamils have drawn parallels with the Nazi pogroms against the Jews (Kapferer, 1988: 29). As well as protecting and leading gangs of Sinhala Buddhist extremists, members of the Sri Lankan security forces also 'removed heaps of Tamils corpses for destruction, and supplied the gangs with refreshment' (*Tamil Guardian*, 2006: 2). The UK's Daily Telegraph had this to say in its report published 2 days after the mass attacks began:

> Motorists were dragged from their cars to be stoned and beaten with sticks during racial violence in Colombo, the Sri Lanka capital yesterday [24 July]. Others were cut down with knives and axes. Mobs of Sinhala youth rampaged through the streets, ransacking homes, shops and offices, looting them and setting them ablaze, as they sought out members of the Tamil ethnic minority . . . A Sri Lankan friend told me by telephone last night how he had watched horrified earlier in the day as a mob attacked a Tamil cyclist riding near Colombo's eye hospital, a few hundred yards from the home of Junius Jayewardene, the nation's 76 year old President. The cyclist was hauled from his bike, drenched with petrol and set alight. As he ran screaming down the street, the mob set on him again and hacked him down with jungle knifes.
> (*Daily Telegraph*, 1983 cited in *Tamil Guardian*, 2006: 2)

A Norwegian tourist who witnessed the massacre of Tamils told the UK's Daily Express:

> 'A mini bus full of Tamils were forced to stop in front of us in Colombo,' she said. A Sinhalese mob poured petrol over the bus and set it on fire. They

blocked the car door and prevented the Tamils from leaving the vehicle. 'Hundreds of spectators watched as about 20 Tamils were burnt to death.' Mrs. Skarstein added: 'We can't believe the official casualty figures. Hundreds, may be thousands, must have been killed already. The police force (which is 95% Sinhalese) did nothing to stop the mobs. There was no mercy. Women, children and old people were slaughtered. Police did nothing to stop the genocide'.

(Daily Express, 1983 cited in *Tamil Guardian*, 2006: 2)

These brutal killings were not confined to the streets of Sri Lanka. Tamil political prisoners held in high security prisons were also massacred by gangs of Sinhala Buddhist inmates. On 25 July at Welikade Prison in Colombo, while 'helicopters circled the prison roof, between 300 and 400 armed prisoners massacred thirty-seven [Tamil] political prisoners' (Murray, 1984: 105). Two days later, another 'eighteen [Tamil] political prisoners were butchered in the prison' (Murray, 1984: 105). A senior government minister later claimed that 'the Sinhalese were only "pacified" after the massacre at Welikade' (Murray, 1984: 105). A Tamil guerrilla leader, Kuttimani, held at Welikade, was ordered to kneel and pray to the Sinhalese; when he refused, his eyes were gauged out, and he was hacked to pieces, and his testicles cut out (*Tamil Guardian*, 2006: 2). Four months after the prison massacres, in a letter to Amnesty International, the Sri Lankan High Commission in London claimed that prison officials were powerless to stop the massacres because the attackers were a large crowd and 'feelings were high' (1983 cited in Amnesty International, 1984b: 13). No Sinhala inmate was charged for the massacres. The Sri Lankan High Commission also claimed that the 'judicial findings were of homicide due to a prison riot' (Amnesty International, 1984b: 13). However, in a sworn statement to Amnesty International, a survivor of the massacre implicated Sri Lanka's prison officials in the attacks:

> We asked those people as to why they came to kill us. To this they replied that they were given arrack [an alcohol] by the prison authorities and they were asked to kill all those at the youth offenders ward. When we asked them to reveal the name of the prison officer they refused to reply.
>
> (Amnesty International, 1984b: 14)

But the state's hand in the July massacres were evident from a statement made by Jayewardene in an interview with the Daily Telegraph 2 weeks earlier on 11 July 1983:

> I am not worried about the opinion of the Jaffna [Tamil] people now. . . Now, we cannot think of them. Not about their lives or of their opinion about us . . . The more you put pressure in the north, the happier the Sinhala people will be here . . . really, if I starve the Tamils out, the Sinhala people will be happy.
>
> (Jayewardene, 1983 cited in Janani, 2008: 9)

Two weeks after the massacres, speaking to BBC, Jayewardene claimed that his government took no action to stop the violence because the troops harboured anti-Tamil feelings: 'I think there was a big anti-Tamil feeling among the forces, and they felt that shooting the Sinhalese who were rioting would have been anti-Sinhalese' (1983 cited in Tambiah, 1986: 25).

The exact number of Tamils killed in the racial onslaught of July 1983 is unknown. The Sri Lankan government estimated that around 350 Tamils may have been killed (Tambiah, 1986: 22). However, other sources, including Tamil ones, cite a figure of between 2,000 to 3,000 Tamil deaths (see *The Times*, 1983a; Tambiah, 1986: 22; Balasingham, 2004: 40; Bose, 2007: 28). This was in addition to the destruction and the looting of billions of rupees worth of Tamil property. Thousands of Tamils were made refugees, with many of them fleeing to the Tamil-speaking North and East in ships organised by the Indian government (*The Economist*, 1983: 26). Some Indian Tamils even opted to permanently leave for India (Kalbag, 1983: 66).

The racial violence of July 1983 stands out not simply because of the scale of death and destruction it caused to the Tamils. Nor does it stand out because it was the last instance in which the state allowed the mass violence of the Sinhala Buddhist extremists to be let loose on the Tamils. Instead, it stands out as the height of Sri Lanka's use of the power of death as part of its biopolitics of defending the race/species it managed/fostered and securing the Sinhala Buddhist ethnocratic state order. The mass violence of July 1983 virtually left all Tamils at the mercy of the Sinhala Buddhists. Any Sinhala Buddhist who thought it fit to kill a fellow Tamil had the power to do so. During one instance, a group of Tamils who were travelling in a train were killed by fellow Sinhala passengers. The government justified the killings claiming that the killed Tamils were carrying hand bombs and guns that were discovered by fellow Sinhala passengers (Hamlyn, 1983), a claim never substantiated. The state, represented through its military, police, politicians and government officials, thus stood by the side of the Sinhalese man/woman who exercised the power of death. It was ready to help the Sinhala Buddhist people avenge their 'enemy' race: it was ready to provide them the list of Tamils to be eliminated, provide them armed security, issue refreshments, help in the disposal of the bodies of massacred Tamils and make justifications.

The Sinhala Buddhist man (or the woman) also had the power to decide whether a Tamil should be allowed to live. Not all Sinhalese participated in the mass violence; it is equally true that many of them opted to stand back and watch Tamils being massacred rather than join the attackers or prevent the massacres (Kapferer, 1988: 29). Some Sinhalese did shelter the Tamils out of compassion (Kapferer, 1988: 29). But that also sent a message to the beleaguered Tamils: only a Sinhalese man/woman had the power to allow the Tamil man/woman to live; only the compassion of the Sinhala Buddhists can save them. This power of death that the Sinhala Buddhist man/woman possessed over the Tamils was explicitly articulated by Jayewardene's senior cabinet minister Dissanayake (1983), who supervised the mass violence of 1981. A month after the racial conflagration of

July 1983 he said: 'Who attacked you? Sinhalese. Who protected you? Sinhalese. It is we who can attack you and protect you' (Dissanayake, 1983).

July 1983, which many Tamils refer to as 'Black July', also signalled the extent of violence the Sri Lankan state was prepared to use against the Tamils to ensure the all-island sovereignty of the Sinhala Buddhist people. The killing of fifty-four Tamil political prisoners (including militant leaders) in Welikade and the massacre of between 2,000 to 3,000 Tamils elsewhere, was intended to convey the message that for every Sinhalese soldier or policeman killed by the Tamil guerrillas, Tamils would face retaliation from the Sinhalese that would transcend any conception of proportionality. The key message to the Tamils was that the Sinhalese would not be satisfied with carrying out tit-for-tat killings: retaliation would go beyond that.

In allowing Sinhala Buddhist extremists, assisted by the security forces, to avenge the killing of thirteen Sinhala soldiers by the Tamil guerrillas, Jayewardene tacitly endorsed the scale of retaliation that was meted out by his people. In his televised address 5 days after the Black July mass violence began, instead of condemning the atrocities and expressing sympathy for the Tamils, Jayewardene (1983 cited in Hamlyn, 1983) warned that his government would no longer condone any form of Tamil secessionism: 'The government has now decided that the time has come to accede to the clamour and the request, the natural request, of the Sinhala people that we do not allow the movement for division to grow any more'. Jayewardene (1983 cited in Claiborne, 1983) was also quick to cite, albeit indirectly, *Mahavamsa's* claim that the island had all along belonged to the Sinhala people as a single state: 'The Sinhalese will never agree to the separation of a country that has been united a nation for 2,500 years'. The Jayewardene regime did not stop with words. Within weeks after the Black July mass violence, the Jayewardene regime enacted new legislation, the *Sixth Amendment to the Sri Lanka Constitution*, which amended Article 157 of the 1978 republican constitution, criminalising secessionist demands, even if it was advocated by political parties through non-violent means (see *The Constitution of the Democratic Socialist Republic of Sri Lanka (As Amended Up to 15th May 2015)*). The constitutional amendment, as well making secessionism an indictable offence, vested the state with the power to take away the civic rights of convicted secessionists for up to 7 years and confiscate their properties (The Constitution of the Democratic Socialist Republic of Sri Lanka (As Amended Up to 15th May 2015)).

In the aftermath of Black July, Jayewardene's government also made it clear that all property of the Tamils remained at the mercy of state. Immediately after the mass violence, the state took control of all properties destroyed or damaged during the attacks, claiming '[w]recked homes and factories would remain state property until it decides what to do with them under a rehabilitation programme' (*The Times*, 1983b).

To sum up, the use of the terror of 'lawlessness' in July 1983 paved the way for the state to not only assert the *Mahavamsa* based all-island sovereignty claim of the Sinhala Buddhist people and the power of death that they had over the Tamils, but also produced three effects of battle: the elimination of a section of the 'enemy' race; destruction and possession of parts of their properties; and the expulsion of a section of them from the Sinhala areas, and to an extent from the island's shores.

But the terror of 'lawlessness' also had negative implications for the state. If the state's standardisation and district quota policies of the 1970s pushed Tamil youth to take up arms and Tamil political parties to advocate secession, the massacres of Black July solidified the belief of many Tamils that an armed struggle for political independence was no longer the last choice, but inevitable. In the words of Anton Balasingham, the LTTE's theoretician:

> The July racial catastrophe opened the flood gates and Tamil nationalism swept across the continents fanning the flames of ethnic consciousness, identity and fraternity among Eelam Tamils. Fired by the passion of national patriotism, outraged by the unimaginable atrocities, thousands of Tamil youth flocked to join the armed resistance movement. The ranks of the LTTE suddenly swelled into the hundreds while thousands more yearned to join the freedom struggle. . ... For the other defunct Tamil groups hiding underground in Tamil Nadu, the new developments offered a golden opportunity for recruitment. With funds from the Tamil Diaspora and with new recruits, these groups were resurrected from oblivion.
>
> (2004: 42)

The implication of July 1983 massacres were not confined to the borders of Sri Lanka.

Shifting alliances and the 'enemy' within

As well as strengthening the armed Tamil secessionist movement, the mass violence of July 1983 also made India take a more active interest in the conflict and the politics of the island. India viewed the Tamil secessionist movement in the 1970s with anxiety. It was only in 1967 that through the devolution of power to the state of Tamil Nadu, India managed to contain the Tamil-led Dravidian secessionist movement that held sway in its southern flank (Krishna, 2000: 64 and 83). For Indian policy makers, the emergence of the Tamil secessionist movement in Sri Lanka was seen to have the potential to refuel secessionism back home (Dixit, 1990 cited in Krishna, 2000: 61).

Yet, in the initial years, India largely kept a distance from the conflict in Sri Lanka. This was because unlike during the JVP insurrection of 1971, the Sri Lankan government of Srimavo Bandaranaike did not seek India's support to crush the Tamil armed struggle and instead opted to deal with it in its own way. However, the politics of the island changed, particularly after Jayewardene assumed power in 1977. Like his predecessor, Jayewardene also did not seek India's support to crush the Tamil armed struggle. At the same time, he antagonised India by opting for counter-insurgency support from the West. Long opposed to Indian dominance in South Asia, Jayewardene took a distinctively anti-Indian stance upon assuming power. While reversing his predecessor's socialist policies enshrined in the 1972 constitution with a new constitution in 1978 (see *The Constitution of the Democratic Socialist Republic of Sri Lanka*, 7 September 1978), Jayewardene established close ties with the West – especially the US. As far back as 1954, when he was Sri Lanka's foreign minister, Jayewardene (1974: 46) made it clear that he expected India to keep its hands off the island: 'we do not expect India to play the role of trying to establish rights where they have no rights, or privileges where they have no privileges, or of trying to deprive other countries of their rights'. At that time, Jayewardene also made it clear that Sri Lanka would be closely aligned with the United States: 'We have been, and intend to be, on the terms of the greatest friendship with the USA' (Jayewardene, 1974: 46). Upon assuming power, Jayewardene kept his word and sought the support of the US and other Western countries, as well as their Cold War allies, to crush the armed Tamil secessionist movement (Dixit, 1998: 58; Balasingham, 2004: 50; Rajapaksa, 2013).

Sri Lanka's political and strategic alignment with the West and its allies was seen by New Delhi to be a threat to its national security. Following US support for Pakistan during the Indo-Pakistan War of 1971 and the close ties the US developed with China in the same year, India tilted towards the Soviet Union (Cohen, 2001: 275; Mohan, 2004: 121; Kapur, 2014: 259). India also became agitated when the US decided to set up a nuclear base on the island of Diego Garcia in the Indian Ocean (Jayapalan, 2001: 360). Tensions mounted further when the US decided to provide Pakistan, in the aftermath of the Soviet invasion of Afghanistan in 1979, with high-tech military equipment including F-16 jets (Jayapalan, 2001: 360). It was against this backdrop that Jayewardene sought Western counter-insurgency support. The situation was further complicated when Sri Lanka began receiving military equipment from the West through India's rivals, Pakistan and Israel (Dixit, 1998: 58; Balasingham, 2004: 50; Rajapaksa, 2013). India thus began to feel that its national security interests were being threatened by the Jayewardene regime (Dixit, 1998: 58; Jayapalan, 2001: 360).

With Prime Minister Indira Gandhi's return to power in 1980, tensions escalated further. Gandhi developed a foreign policy that was intolerant to 'external intervention in a conflict situation in any South Asian country if the intervention' was deemed to have 'implicit or explicit anti-Indian implication'; South Asian states were expected not to ask for external assistance if such assistance was intended to have 'an anti-Indian bias' (Gupta, 1983 cited in DeVotta, 1998: 457). Scholars have referred to this policy as the 'Indira Doctrine' (Rao, 1988: 422; DeVotta, 1998: 457; Chacko, 2012: 141). Warning Sri Lanka against seeking Western support, Gandhi spelled out this policy during a debate in the Indian Parliament on 5 August 1983 on the mass violence of July 1983: 'In this matter, India cannot be regarded just any country. Sri Lanka and India are the two countries who are directly concerned. Any extraneous involvement will complicate matters for both our countries' (1986: 409). Yet, Sri Lanka continued to obtain Western counter-insurgency support. It was under these circumstances that India decided to intervene in the conflict. In the words of J. N. Dixit, a former Indian high commissioner to Sri Lanka:

> India's involvement in Sri Lanka in my assessment, was unavoidable not only due to the ramification of Colombo's oppressive and discriminatory policies

against Tamil citizens, but also in terms of India's national security concerns due to Sri Lankan government's security connections with the US, Pakistan and Israel.

(1998: 58)

The Indian intervention in the conflict took two forms. On the one hand, using its mission in Colombo and its New Delhi based diplomats, India intensified political and diplomatic pressure on the Sri Lankan government to end the hostilities and seek a negotiated political settlement with the Tamils. On the other hand, India also conducted a 'clandestine military exercise to build-up and strengthen the Tamil armed resistance movement' (Balasingham, 2004: 52). Tamil fighters were taken to Indian military bases and provided with military training on 'all aspects of modern warfare', which included 'map reading, mine laying and the use of explosives and anti-tank and anti-aircraft systems' (Balasingham, 2004: 58–59). Although the quantity of arms that India supplied to the Tamil fighters was both 'small' and 'antiquated', thus remained 'unusable', New Delhi allowed them to bring in large quantities of arms from outside the Indian subcontinent and store them in their training bases in South India. In addition, the Tamil fighters also received direct financial assistance from the chief minister of Tamil Nadu (Balasingham, 2003: 14, 21–22, 25, 41 and 60; 2004: 62).

As Balasingham put it, India's support for the Tamil armed struggle was 'a moral, altruistic urgency and geo-strategic necessity' to 'contain a ruthless racist state bent on genocidal destruction of a minority Tamil nation in collusion with international forces with subversive intentions' (2004: 59). However, in turning the armed Tamil secessionist movement into 'a player' in its covert game against the West, New Delhi did not have any intentions to help establish a Tamil state on the island, even though some Tamil politicians entertained such hopes (Balasingham, 2004: 59–60). This policy of the Indian government was also officially conveyed to the LTTE in March 1985 by Girish Chandra Saxena, the head of India's external intelligence agency – the Research and Analysis Wing (RAW) – during a meeting with Pirapaharan and Balasingham (2004: 67–68), wherein he stated that 'India could not support the Tamil aspiration for a separate state since it would have far reaching implications' in its borders as it already had 'to deal with several secessionist movements'.

India believed that the Tamil–Sinhala conflict could be resolved and Tamils' secessionist demands contained by forcing Sri Lanka to accept a 'political settlement within a united Sri Lanka' that would meet the aspirations of the Tamils while at the same time ensuring Sri Lanka's 'sovereignty and territorial integrity' (Balasingham, 2004: 67–68). In the words of Balasingham, in providing military assistance to the armed Tamil secessionist movement, India expected the Tamil guerrillas to 'destabilise Jayewardene's regime and frustrate his militaristic approach' (2004: 60).

However, the tensions between India and Sri Lanka did not endure. After the assassination of Indira Gandhi by her bodyguards in October 1984, relations between India and Sri Lanka warmed, and Indian support for the Tamil armed struggle began to wane. Rajiv Gandhi, who assumed the office of the prime minister after his mother's death, avoided adopting a confrontationist approach with Sri Lanka. Rajiv Gandhi also renewed ties with the West.

It was against this backdrop that Jayewardene came to the conclusion that the Tamil armed struggle could be contained by appeasing both India and the West. This new approach culminated in an accord in July 1987 (the *Indo-Sri Lanka Accord)*, which guaranteed India a predominant role in dealing with Sri Lanka's security (Balasingham, 2004: 467–473). The signing of the *Indo-Sri Lanka Accord* was followed by the Jayewardene regime enacting the *Thirteenth Amendment to Sri Lanka Constitution*, making Tamil an official language and establishing provincial councils for all of the eight provinces on the island, including the Tamil-speaking North and East (see *The Constitution of the Democratic Socialist Republic of Sri Lanka (As Amended Up to 15th May 2015)*). Though the *Thirteenth Amendment* allowed Sri Lanka to claim at international forums that it had devolved power to the Tamils, in reality this was not the case. Whilst including a provision for making Tamil an official language, Article 18 (4) of the amended constitution stipulated that this specific provision could not be implemented until the parliament sets out measures for this purpose (The Constitution of the Democratic Socialist Republic of Sri Lanka (As Amended Up to 15th May 2015)); which has not happened within the past 3 decades. Even the provincial council system that allows for the Tamils to deal with local issues is constrained by Articles 154A to 155L of the amended constitution that vests the unelected governor appointed by the Sri Lankan president much of, if not all, the powers that should normally be exercised by elected provincial officials (The Constitution of the Democratic Socialist Republic of Sri Lanka (As Amended Up to 15th May 2015)).

Immediately after the Accord was signed, Indian troops landed on the shores of Sri Lanka, taking over Sri Lankan military bases in the Tamil-speaking North and East. The induction of Indian troops in those areas marked a turning point in Sri Lanka's biopolitics of defending the Sinhala Buddhist race/species and securing the ethnocratic state order. The state no longer had to shed Sinhala Buddhist blood to defend its race/species or secure the ethnocratic state order; or to confront the armed Tamil enemy. It had relinquished the job to the Indians. In essence, Sri Lanka's biopolitics had entered the stage of making a tactical military alliance with India that was expected to lead the island-state to victory, without shedding the blood of the Sinhala Buddhists.

However, Sri Lanka's calculations were proven to be wrong. In the Northern and Eastern Provinces, an all-out war broke out between the LTTE and the Indian troops, when the latter sought to disarm the former. The IPKF, assisted by anti-LTTE Tamil militant groups, committed wide scale atrocities, including the killing, enforced disappearance, rape and torture in custody of Tamil civilians suspected of supporting the LTTE (see Bobb, 1987: Amnesty International, 1990a: 2, 1990b: 13, 15 and 16–17). There were also cases of Tamil civilians being killed in indiscriminate airstrikes by the IPKF (Bobb, 1987). The LTTE also executed Tamils suspected of collaborating with the IPKF (Amnesty International, 1990b: 14). Amnesty International (1990a: 3) suggested in September 1990 that during the presence of the IPKF, as many as 10,000 Tamil civilians may have been killed in the North and East.

Meanwhile, in the Sinhala areas, taking advantage of the presence of the Indian troops to stir Sinhala nationalistic sentiments, the JVP launched another violent Marxist insurrection with the objective of overthrowing the capitalist state. Thus, the 'enemy' Sri Lanka confronted became one that existed within the race/species that it managed/fostered. However, its experience in dealing with the first JVP uprising of 1971 and the Tamil militancy meant that the state could unleash a reign of terror to deal with the 'enemy' within. Once again, under the cover of emergency, thousands of Sinhala youth suspected of involvement in the JVP insurgency were massacred by the state's security forces (de Mel, 2007: 70). Having at its disposal two draconian emergency laws, the PSO and the PTA, Sri Lanka unleashed the terror of law on the Sinhalese. As in the Tamil areas, the STF and the army played key roles in unleashing this terror (Amnesty International, 1994: 18). Extrajudicial killings and enforced disappearances also became the norm (Amnesty International, 1994: 18). The Sinhala youth, like their Tamil counterparts, were massacred (Trawick, 2007: 48). In the Sinhala areas, '[b]urnt bodies on roadsides, slumped corpses tied to lampposts and bodies floating down the rivers were a common sight' (de Mel, 2007: 70). Many of the bodies were either mutilated or burnt beyond recognition, and therefore impossible to identify (Amnesty International, 1994: 18). Severed limbs or heads of those killed were frequently displayed in public places (Amnesty International, 1994: 19).

The organised violence of 'lawlessness' also became a way of unleashing terror for the state. Various pro-government groups appeared under various names, issuing death threats to individuals, putting up posters in public places and sometimes placing posters beside dead bodies (Amnesty International, 1994: 18). Sri Lanka claimed that those atrocities were carried out by vigilantes who opposed the JVP, and over whom it had no control (Amnesty International, 1994: 18). However, evidence later emerged that 'the perpetrators were police or military personnel operating in civilian dress' (Amnesty International, 1994: 18).

In the same way that it had previously armed Sinhala settlers in the Tamil-speaking Eastern Province, the state armed civilian militias and the bodyguards of politicians in the Sinhala areas. These acted as the proxy forces of the state against the JVP with 'the same degree of immunity from prosecution as that enjoyed by the regular forces of the military and police with whom they collaborated' (Amnesty International, 1994: 18).

Consequently, an estimated 40,000 Sinhalese attained the official status of being neither alive nor being dead; they simply became the 'disappeared' people (see de Mel, 2007: 70; Jayasuriya, 2012: 5). The JVP matched the Sri Lankan state in its potential to perpetrate atrocities and to instill terror (Amnesty International, 1994: 18–19; de Mel, 2007: 70).

Both the JVP and Sri Lankan state did not differ on the *Mahavamsa's* idea of all-island sovereignty for the Sinhala Buddhists. Yet, they held competing views on improving the lives of their race/species. For the Sri Lankan state, the capitalist economic system provided the solution to the economic troubles of the Sinhalese. For the JVP, the solution lay in a communist system of government. It was this that kept both in a polarised position. In using the presence of the Indian troops as the justification for launching the second Marxist insurrection, the JVP was simply making an excuse to wage a war and overthrow the capitalist state. The JVP, despite its anti-Indian sentiments, did not throw even one stone at the Indian troops (Balasingham, 2001: 217). Instead it targeted the Sri Lankan state. Moreover, in June 1989, when Ranasinghe Premadasa, who succeeded Jayewardene, asked the Indian troops to end their 'peace-keeping' mission and leave the island, the JVP did not cease its violent campaign against the state. Instead, it continued the insurgency with the same vigour.

In November 1989, after unleashing terror for over 2 years in the Sinhala areas, Sri Lanka finally crushed the JVP insurgency. It was only 7 months earlier in April 1989, that the Premadasa regime formed an alliance with the LTTE to expel the Indian troops from the North and East. Fearing that 'Indian troops might stay on Sri Lankan soil indefinitely', President Premadasa provided the LTTE with arms and funds to fight the Indian troops (Balasingham, 2001: 211 and 244). After months of heavy fighting, and with a regime change in New Delhi in December 1989, the Indian troops finally withdrew in March 1990.

Sri Lanka's efforts to defend the race/species that it fostered and secure the ethnocratic state order thus ended with the making of an alliance with the very armed movement it had earlier sought to vanquish, and the unleashing of terror on its own race/species to weed out the 'enemy' within. In the Sinhala areas, the reign of terror unleashed by the state solidified the loyalty of the people. This was, however, not the case in the Tamil areas. Filling the vacuum left by the Indian troops in the Tamil-speaking areas, the LTTE emerged as a powerful force capable of confronting the state. The next chapter will explore Sri Lanka's use of biopower in the 1990s to retake the North and East from the LTTE.

References

Amnesty International (1984a) *Evidence of Extrajudicial Killings by the Security Forces in Sri Lanka, July – November 1983*. London: Amnesty International.

Amnesty International (1984b) *Review of Amnesty International's Current Human Rights Concerns in Sri Lanka, July – December 1983*. London: Amnesty International.

Amnesty International (1984c) *Sri Lanka: Current Human Rights Concerns and Evidence of Extrajudicial Killings by the Security Forces*. London: Amnesty International.

Amnesty International (1985) *Amnesty International Report – 1985*. London: Amnesty International.

Amnesty International (1990a) *Sri Lanka: The Indian Peace Keeping Force and "Disappearances"*. London: Amnesty International.

Amnesty International (1990b) *Sri Lanka, Briefing*. London: Amnesty International.

Amnesty International (1994) *"Disappearances" and Political Killings: Human Rights Crisis of the 1990s, a Manual for Action*. Amsterdam: Amnesty International.

Balachandran, P.K. (2010) *Sri Lankan Speakers Feel Ignored at Conference*. Available at: http://www.island.lk/index.php?page_cat=article-details&page=article-details&code_title=882 (Accessed: 28 June 2010).

Balasingham, A.A. (2001) *The Will to Freedom: An Inside View of Tamil Resistance*. London: Fairmax Publications.

Balasingham, A. (2003) *Liberation*. London: Fairmax Publications.

Balasingham, A. (2004) *War and Peace: Armed Struggle and Peace Efforts of Liberation Tigers*. London: Fairmax Publishing.
Bobb, D. (1987) *A Bloodied Accord*. Available at: http://indiatoday.intoday.in/story/after-16-days-of-bloody-battle-ipkf-finally-captures-ltte-stronghold-jaffna/1/337703.html (Accessed: 12 October 2014).
Bose, S. (2007) *Contested Lands: Israel-Palestine, Kashmir, Bosnia, Cyprus, and Sri Lanka*. Cambridge, MA: Havard University Press.
Chacko, P. (2012) *Indian Foreign Policy: The Politics of Postcolonial Identity from 1947 to 2004*. Oxon: Routledge.
Claiborne, W. (1983) 'Strife-torn Sri Lanka to Prohibit Separatist Groups', *The Washington Post*, 28 July. Available at: http://www.blackjuly83.com/Library_New.htm (Accessed: 10 December 2015).
Cohen, S.P. (2001) *India: Emerging Power*. Washington, DC: The Brookings Institution.
The Constitution of the Democratic Socialist Republic of Sri Lanka (7 September 1978). Colombo: Government of Sri Lanka.
The Constitution of the Democratic Socialist Republic of Sri Lanka (As Amended Up to 15 May 2015). Colombo: The Parliament of Sri Lanka.
David, S.A. (1983) *Detention, Torture and Murder*. Vavuniya: Gandhiam Society. Available at: http://sangam.org/2012/04/Eyewitness_Welikade_Massacre.php?uid=4690 (Accessed: 10 December 2015).
de Mel, N. (2007) *Militarizing Sri Lanka: Popular Culture, Memory and Narrative in the Armed Conflict*. London: Sage Publications.
DeVotta, N, (1998) 'Sri Lanka's Structural Adjustment Program and Its Impact on Indo-Lanka Relations', *Asian Survey*, 38(5), pp. 457–473.
Dissanayaka, T.D.S.A. (2005) *War or Peace in Sri Lanka*. Mumbai: Popular Prakashan.
Dissanayake, G. (1983) 'Speech', *Executive Committee Meeting*. Lanka Jathika Estate Workers' Union, Colombo, 5 September.
Dixit, J.N. (1998) *Assignment Colombo*. New Delhi: Konark Publishers.
The Economist (1983) 'Sri Lanka Puts a Torch to Its Future', 6 August, pp. 25–26.
Foucault, M. (1991) *Discipline and Punish: The Birth of the Prison*. Translated by Alan Sheridan. London: Penguin Books (Original work published 1975).
Foucault, M. (2004) *"Society Must Be Defended": Lectures at the College de France, 1975–76*. Translated by David Macey. London: Penguin Books.
Gandhi, I. (1986) *Selected Speeches and Writings 1982–84*. New Delhi: Government of India.
Hamlyn, M. (1983) 'Colombo Acts to Appease Mobs', *The Times*, 28 July. Available at: http://www.blackjuly83.com/Library_New.htm (Accessed: 10 December 2015).
Haniffa, F. (2012) 'Conflicted Solidarities? Muslims and the Constitution-Making Process of 1970–72', in Welikala, A. (ed.), *The Sri Lankan Republic at 40: Reflections on Constitutional History, Theory and Practice*. Colombo: Centre for Policy Alternatives, pp. 219–252.
Harris, N. (1990) *National Liberation*. London: I.B.Tauris.
Hoole, R. (2001) *Sri Lanka: The Arrogance of Power; Myths, Decadence and Murder*. Colombo: UTHR-J. Available at: http://www.uthr.org/Book/Content.htm (Accessed: 2 February 2016).
Horowitz, D.L. (2000) *Ethnic Groups in Conflict*. London: University of California Press.
Human Rights Watch (1995) *Playing the "Communal Card"*. New York: Human Rights Watch.

Janani, J.T. (2008) 'The Blind Spot in Genocide Theory', *Tamil Guardian*, 4 June, pp. 9 and 19.

Jayapalan, N. (2001) *History of India: From National Movement to Present Day – Volume IV*. New Delhi: Atlantic Publishers and Distributors.

Jayasuriya, M. (2012) *Terror and Reconciliation: Sri Lankan Anglophone Literature, 1983–2000*. Lanham: Lexington Books.

Jayewardene, J.R. (1974) *Selected Speeches*. Colombo: H.W.Cave & Company.

Jayewardene, J.R. (1977a) *Hansard*. 18 August, vol 23(2), col 246. Colombo: Parliament of Sri Lanka.

Jayewardene, J.R. (1977b) *Hansard*. 28 November, vol 24(7), col 1459–1483. Colombo: Parliament of Sri Lanka.

Jayewardene, J.R. (1981) Interviewed by Michael T.Kaufman for *New York Times*, 11 September. Available at: http://www.nytimes.com/1981/09/11/world/harassed-sri-lanka-minority-hears-call-to-arms.html (Accessed: 10 December 2015).

Kalbag, C. (1983) 'The Aftermath', *India Today*, 15 September, pp. 66–76.

Kannangara, W. (1981) 'Let Us Rule', *Tamil Times*, November, p. 6.

Kapferer, B. (1988) *Legends of People: Myths of State, Violence, Intolerance, and Political Culture in Sri Lanka and Australia*. Washington: Smithsonian Institution Press.

Kapur, S.P. (2014) 'India and the United States from World War II to the Present: A Relationship Transformed', in Ganguly, S. (ed.), *India's Foreign Policy, Retrospect and Prospect*. New Delhi: Oxford University Press, pp. 219–252.

Krishna, S. (2000) *Postcolonial Insecurities: India, Sri Lanka and the Question of Nationhood*. New Delhi: Oxford University Press.

Lokubandara, W.J.M. (1981) 'Do Not Disturb the Sleeping Lion', *Tamil Times*, November, p. 6.

Mohan, R.C. (2004) *Crossing the Rubicon: The Shaping of India's New Foreign Policy*. New York: Palgrave Macmillan.

Moorcraft, P. (2012) *Total Destruction of the Tamil Tigers: The Rare Victory of Sri Lanka's Long War*. South Yorkshire: Pen and Sword Books.

Murray, N. (1984) 'The State against the Tamils', *Race and Class*, July, 26(1), pp. 97–109.

Northern Provincial Council (2015) *Resolution: Sri Lanka's Genocide against Tamils*. Jaffna: Northern Provincial Council.

Ponnambalam, S. (1983) *Sri Lanka: The National Question and the Tamil Liberation Struggle*. London: Zed Books and Tamil Information Centre. Available at: http://tamilnation.co/books/Eelam/satchi.htm (Accessed: 10 June 2015).

Prevention of Terrorism (Temporary Provisions) Act No. 48 of 1979. Colombo: Government of Sri Lanka.

Rajapaksa, G. (2013) Interviewed by Shamindra Ferdinando for *The Island*, 20 June. Available at: http://www.island.lk/index.php?page_cat=article-details&page=article-details&code_title=81746 (Accessed: 20 June 2013).

Rao, V.P. (1988) 'Ethnic Conflict in Sri Lanka: India's Role and Perception', *Asian Survey*, XXVIII, 4(April), pp. 419–436.

Samarakkody, E. (1977) 'Behind the Anti-Tamil Terror: The National Question in Sri Lanka', *Workers Vanguard*, 7 October, pp. 6–7 and 10.

Tambiah, S.J. (1986) *Sri Lanka: Ethnic Fratricide and the Dismantling of Democracy*. London: I.B.Tauris & Co.

Tamil Guardian (2006) 'July 1983: Anatomy of a Pogrom', 26 July, pp. 2–3 and 8.

The Times (1983a) 'Sri Lanka Focus in Delhi, Tamil Leader Says 2,000 May Have Died in Unrest', 11 August. Available at: http://www.blackjuly83.com/Library_New.htm (Accessed: 3 January 2016).

The Times (1983b) 'Sri Lanka Troops Went on a Rampage', 7 August. Available at: http://www.blackjuly83.com/Library_New.htm (Accessed: 10 December 2015).

Trawick, M. (2007) *Enemy Lines: Warfare, Childhood, and Play in Batticaloa*. Los Angeles: University of California Press.

Vittachi, T. (1958) *Emergency '58 – the Story of Ceylon Race Riots*. London: Andre Deutsch. Available at: http://tamilnation.co/books/Eelam/vitachi.htm (Accessed: 7 October 2011).

Wickramasinghe, N. (2006) *Sri Lanka in the Modern Age: A History of Contested Identities*. London: Hurst and Company.

Wilson, J.A. (1988) *The Break-Up of Sri Lanka: The Sinhalese-Tamil Conflict*. London: C.Hurst & Co.

Wilson, J.A. (2000) *Sri Lankan Tamil Nationalism: Its Origins and Development in the 19th and 20th Centuries*. London: Hurst Publishers.

4 Unleashing Jihadism and starving the 'enemy'

When the last contingent of Indian troops left the shores of Sri Lanka in March 1990, the LTTE had under its control almost all of the eight districts of the North and East (see Amnesty International, 1990: 14; UTHR-J, 1990a: 5; Balasingham, 2001: 256). Though the Sri Lankan military had bases at strategic points of those districts and a number police stations existed in the populous areas, with the state's security forces confined to their barracks and police stations, almost all of the districts and their populations remained under the control of the LTTE: its military cadres were able to move freely through those areas. However, by the time the Norwegian-sponsored ceasefire agreement was signed with the Sri Lankan government in February 2002, the LTTE had lost most of the populous areas of the North and East to the Sri Lankan state.

This is not to say that the LTTE was militarily weakened by 2002. Despite losing the populous areas by changing its tactics, the LTTE was able to develop its conventional fighting capabilities in the late 1990s, and by 2002 achieve strategic parity with the Sri Lankan military (Balasingham, 2004: 382; Stokke, 2006: 1022). By then, the LTTE had also developed a *de-facto* state apparatus (Stokke, 2006: 1022). Yet, it had under its full control only two districts in the North: Killinochi and Mullaithivu. Though the LTTE controlled a sizeable portion of the rural areas in the Mannar and Vavuniya districts of the North, some of the Tamil-dominated rural areas of the Batticaloa district in the East, and pockets of territories in the Eastern districts of Trincomalee and Amparai, it did not control as many territories and populations as it had under its control when the Indian troops departed in March 1990 (for a discussion on the territories and the populations that remained under the control of the LTTE in February 2002, see Stokke, 2006: 1022–1023; Sarvananthan, 2007a: 1186–1188). In the North, the Jaffna peninsula, considered the cultural capital of Tamils and the most populous Tamil area, remained, with the exception of a land strip in the southeastern coast, under the full control of the Sri Lankan military. This was also the case with the Eastern district of Trincomalee, long held to be the capital of the future state of Tamil Eelam. In the Eastern district of Amparai, where the Muslims remain the majority, the LTTE only controlled pockets of the Tamil-dominated rural areas adjoining the jungles of the district. How did this state of affairs come about? What had the Sri

Lankan state done to regain the territories that it lost to the LTTE following the departure of the Indian troops?

Throughout the 1990s, in an attempt to regain the North and East, the Sri Lankan state launched a series of military offensives, some of which were successful, especially those launched in the East and the Jaffna peninsula, while others were humiliating failures, such as *Operation Victory Assured* launched in 1997 to retake the Vanni region. Sri Lanka's success in retaking large parts of the East and the Jaffna peninsula can be attributed to its calculated use of biopower in those areas prior to and, in the case of the East, parallel to, its military offensives. In the East, Sri Lanka's biopolitics manifested in the form of making a tactical alliance with Jihadi extremists, extending the power of death over the Tamils to the Islamists. In the North, its biopolitics manifested in the form of a tough regime of economic embargo that sought to drive a wedge between the 'bad' species (the LTTE) and the 'enemy' race/species (the Tamils). As Sri Lanka calculated, the economic embargo brought the Jaffna Tamils to their knees. The LTTE's policies to counter the embargo and minimise its effects on the armed struggle exacerbated the situation, forcing Jaffna's upper and middle classes to reconsider support for a Tamil state, thereby placing constraints on the LTTE's ability to increase its manpower and firepower. This subsequently made it easier for Sri Lanka to retake the populous Jaffna city in December 1995 and the rest of the peninsula in April 1996. This chapter explores these biopolitical aspects.

Background to Tamil–Muslim relations

As a form of biopolitics that divides the populations of Sri Lanka as 'good' and 'bad' on the basis of their affiliation to the Sinhala language and the Buddhist religion, Sinhala Buddhist extremism has never had reasons to consider the Muslims a part of the 'good' species. The animosity of the Sinhala Buddhist extremists towards the Muslims developed during British colonial rule. This was due to the commercial monopoly the Muslims enjoyed under British rule. As we saw in Chapter 2, in the early years of the twentieth century, Ceylon's import and export sectors were dominated by Muslims (Nuhuman, 1998: 4). This was also the case with retail trade. In the urban and rural areas, the retail trade was monopolised by the Muslims (Nuhuman, 1998: 4). This angered the Sinhala entrepreneurs, who found it difficult to compete with the economically powerful Muslims. Dharmapala (1915 cited in Nuhuman, 1998: 4), the patriarch of Sinhala Buddhist nationalism, denounced the Muslims as 'an alien people' whom he claimed had 'by Shylockian method' become 'prosperous like the Jews'. For Dharmapala and other Sinhala Buddhist extremists, deporting the Muslims to Arabia (the home of Islam) was the only way to curtail their commercial monopoly on the island (see Ali, 1997: 259).

Muslims were also the first ethnic group in colonial Ceylon to face the violence of the Sinhala Buddhist extremists. In 1915, what started off as a dispute between local Muslims and Sinhalese on a Buddhist religious procession passing a mosque in the central hill town of Kandy escalated into an island-wide riot against the entire Muslim community. Gangs of Sinhala Buddhist extremists attacked Muslims and their businesses, looting their properties, forcing many Muslims to flee the island (Ramanathan, 1916: 38–39). This is not to say that violence was meted out only by the Sinhala Buddhist extremists. Muslim extremists also carried out provocative attacks against the Sinhalese, resulting in a number of deaths (Ramanathan, 1916: 7–9). However, the casualties sustained by the Muslims, both in terms of life and property, were much greater than those sustained by the Sinhalese. The riots were brought to an end only after the British colonial authorities imposed martial law and adopted heavy-handed tactics, including the summary execution of suspected Sinhala rioters (Ramanathan, 1916: 80–87). In an attempt to facilitate the return of Muslim traders to the island, British colonial authorities also ordered the Sinhalese, including those who had no role in the riots, to pay damages to all of the affected Muslims (Perera, 1915: 27). Sinhala community leaders in the affected areas were coerced to sign debt bonds to guarantee those payments (Perera, 1915: 27).

As a minority community facing the wrath of the Sinhala Buddhist extremists in colonial Ceylon, it would seem that the most prudent strategy for Muslims would have been to align with the Tamils in a struggle to secure their rights in postcolonial Ceylon, particularly in view of the fact that for the majority of Ceylon's Muslims, Tamil was their first language. Furthermore, the combined population of Tamils and Muslims had the potential to emerge as a major force in the predominantly Tamil-speaking Northern and Eastern Provinces, and the Northwestern district of Puttalam. However, in postcolonial Ceylon, many Muslims sought to distance themselves from the Tamils and their politics. A number of reasons can be advanced to account for the estrangement of Muslims from the Tamils during this period.

First, the origin of the Muslims on the island is diverse and distinct from the history of the Tamils on the island. Whilst there are some Muslims who are descendents of Tamil Hindu converts, the majority are of Middle Eastern, Afghan, Indo-Pakistani and Javanese (Malay) descent. The first migration of Muslims to the island began 1,000 years ago with the arrival of Arab traders (Ali, 1997: 254; Nuhuman, 1998: 4–5; Balasingham, 2004: 1 and 3). They were followed by Muslims of Javanese (Malay) descent, brought to the island in the seventeenth century by the Dutch as part of an army of mercenaries (Wilson, 1974: 55–56). The third bout of Muslims' settlement on the island was during British rule in the nineteenth century. These Muslims, known as the Hambayas, are mainly of Indian origin, with roots in both Tamil Nadu and the non-Tamil-speaking states of South India (Ramanathan, 1916: 1 and 7; Ali, 1997: 254).

Second, the British introduced a series of reforms of the island's legislature in the nineteenth century that allowed for representation of all ethnic groups, and this fostered a sense of distinct ethnic identity amongst the Muslims. The claim by Sir Ponnambalam Ramanathan, the Tamil representative at Ceylon's Legislative Council, at the Council and later at the Ceylon Branch of Royal Asiatic Society, that the Muslims 'were ethnologically Tamils though they follow a different religion', drew a sharp response from the Muslim community (Nuhuman, 1998: 4). It angered the community and many of them viewed Ramanathan's assertions as a 'plot to prevent their separate representation in an expanded Legislative Council' (see Ali, 1997: 257; Nuhuman, 1998: 4).

The rift widened between the Muslims and Tamils following the Sinhala–Muslim riots of 1915. Ramanathan, rather than sympathising with Muslims as victims of racial violence, campaigned against Muslims in support of Sinhala Buddhist leaders imprisoned by the British colonial authorities on suspicion of instigating the riots (Ali, 1997: 257; Nuhuman, 1998: 4). In a book published as part of his campaign to secure their release, Ramanathan (1916: 1) suggested that the 'intolerance and aggressiveness' of the Hambaya Muslims were the root causes of the riots. He accused the Hambayas of not having understood the 'necessity of living in peace with their Sinhalese fellow-subjects and being tolerant to their religious observances' (Ramanathan, 1916: 2). Making representations at Ceylon's Supreme Court, and leading a Sinhala delegation to Britain, Ramanathan was able to secure the release of imprisoned Sinhala Buddhist leaders (Ali, 1997: 257). With their release, 'members of the Sinhala elite celebrated the event and pulled the cart on which Ramanathan was seated through the Colombo streets' (Nuhuman, 1998: 4). Thanking Ramanathan, Dharmapala (1915 cited in Weerasekara, 2014), who was held under house arrest in British India on charges of instigating the riots, said: 'The day you are taken away from Ceylon, from that day there will be no one to defend the poor, neglected Sinhalese. They are a doomed people with no one to guide them and protect them'.

Muslims too watched carefully the political developments unfolding in their large neighbour, India. The breakup of British India as postcolonial India and Pakistan in 1947, with the latter being established as an Islamic country, contributed to the estrangement of Muslims from Tamils in Ceylon. The formation of Pakistan as an Islamic country encouraged the Muslims of Ceylon to maintain a distinct identity for themselves and to remain aloof from the politics of the mainly Hindu Tamils on the island (Ali, 1997: 257). The Tamils as mainly Hindus (though there are also Christian Tamils) was reason enough for Muslims to view them with suspicion as sympathisers of the predominantly Hindu India (though officially a secular country), and thus the enemies of Islamic Pakistan (Ali, 1997: 257).

This is not to imply that Muslims found life in postcolonial Ceylon any better for themselves than the island's Tamils. Muslims were not affected by the *Official Language Act* of 1956, as many of them were not employed in the civil service, but instead were engaged in trade. The statist and semi-statist economic policies implemented by Ceylon's socialist governments in the 1960s (Ali, 1997: 256), however, had severe ramifications for the Muslim community. The nationalisation of Ceylon's banking, transport, real estate, import and export sectors, coupled with state-led reforms in the agricultural sector in favour of Sinhala landowners and peasants, had a deep impact on Muslim entrepreneurs, the urban middle class and the farmers (Ali, 1997: 256). Postcolonial Ceylon's statist and semi-statist policies led to Muslims losing the commercial monopoly they held during British colonial rule. Additionally, in the 1970s, Muslims living in Sinhala areas and in Puttalam, a Northwestern district with a large Muslim population, were subjected to periodic episodes of racial violence perpetrated by Sinhala Buddhist extremists. Muslim businesses were either burned down or looted (Ali, 1997: 256). The hand of the state forces was also visible during some of those atrocities (Ponnambalam, 1983: 167). In 1976, seven Muslims praying inside a mosque in Puttalam were shot dead, and two Muslims were burnt alive by the Sri Lankan police (Ponnambalam, 1983: 167).

However, neither the violence of the Sinhala Buddhist extremists, nor the participation of the state police in murderous acts against members of their community were sufficient to drive Muslims to forge a unity, and to identify and politically align with Tamils in a struggle for their rights and against injustice and oppression. Similarly, the injustices to which they were subjected and the consequences of the state's economic policies on the lives of the Muslim community failed to create Muslim resistance against the state. On the contrary, for the Muslims, the advantages of supporting the state outweighed the advantages of aligning with the Tamils, or rebelling against the state. While the 1972 standardisation policy and the quota system in 1974 reduced the number of Tamils in higher education and hence constrained their future prospects, Muslims, like the Sinhalese, benefitted from these policies: the policies paved the way for more opportunities in higher education for Muslims living outside the Tamil-dominated Northern Province, thereby creating 'a new professional class and an educated elite' within the community (Nuhuman, 1998: 6). Muslims also greatly benefited from the economic liberalisation policies implemented by Sri Lanka's pro-Western, pro-market governments starting with the Jayewardene regime from 1977 onwards (Ali, 1997: 257). For Muslims, the Tamil demand for the creation of a separate state in the North and East was thus seen as unfavourable to furthering their commercial interests: as entrepreneurs, many of the Muslims saw greater economic opportunities in a wider market in a united Sri Lanka, rather than a divided island (Ali, 1997: 256). State violence against Muslims was also sporadic and of lesser intensity than that inflicted on Tamils, though this may be attributed to Sinhala Buddhist extremists viewing Tamils as a greater threat to Sinhala Buddhist dominance over the island, especially following the emergence of the armed Tamil secessionist movement in 1972 (Ali, 1997: 260).

In the 1970s and 1980s, the Tamils United Liberation Front (TULF), the largest Tamil political party, and the LTTE, the largest armed Tamil secessionist organisation, made an attempt to appease Muslims by accommodating the latter's interests in their political manifestos. Claiming Muslims, along with Tamils and other communities that had adopted the Tamil language as their mother tongue, to be part of the Tamil nation, the TULF made a pledge that within the future state of Tamil Eelam, an autonomous province for the Muslims would be established, with Muslims being accorded 'the right to secede' from Tamil Eelam 'on the basis of the right to self-determination' (TULF, 1977). However, while the LTTE did not recognise in its manifesto the right of Muslims to secede from a Tamil state, it accepted that they 'constitute themselves as a unique ethnic group with distinct religio-cultural identity' and made the commitment to guarantee 'the safety, well-being and economic prosperity of the Muslim people' (LTTE, 1985: 13). It also pledged 'to safeguard and promote their religio-cultural identity' (LTTE, 1985: 13). An analysis of the LTTE's publications in the 1980s indicate that it saw Muslims as integral to the struggle for a separate state, and encouraged Muslim youth, whom it frequently referred to as 'Islamic Tamils', to join the armed struggle; and many Muslims joined the LTTE in the 1980s (see LTTE, 1985: 13; *Liberation Tigers*, 1986: 5).

However, the political commitment to Muslims from the Tamils failed to convince the entire Muslim community to accept a Tamil national identity, and embrace the Tamil secessionist movement. The heavy-handed tactics adopted against the Muslims by anti-LTTE Tamil militant groups in the mid-1980s led to a number of small scale riots between the Tamils and Muslims in the East, and the killings and counter-killings by Sri Lanka's Muslim paramilitary unit, the Jihad Group, and anti-LTTE Tamil militant groups (see UTHR-J, 1990b: 48–49). Often, the violence of the anti-LTTE Tamil militants spilled over to the North, and in 1985, three Muslim worshipers were gunned down in a mosque in the Northern town of Mannar (Ali, 1997: 258).

However, the LTTE continued to enjoy goodwill among Muslims. When Tamil–Muslim communal tensions developed in some parts of the East in 1985, the LTTE supported Muslims and punished Tamils who looted Muslim businesses (Sivaram, 1992). In most of the operations that it carried out against the Jihad Group in the East, as well as using its Tamil fighters, the LTTE also deployed its Muslim cadres (UTHR-J, 1990b: 49).

The goodwill enjoyed by the LTTE among Muslims in the East in the 1980s became more apparent when the Indian troops took control of the North and East in July 1987. During the presence of the Indian troops, the LTTE was not only able to gain new Muslim recruits but 'its survival in the East' depended on the support of the Eastern Muslims (Sivaram, 1992; Hoole, 2001). The collaboration between anti-LTTE Tamil militant groups and the Indian troops also pushed Muslims closer to the LTTE (Sivaram, 1992).

This state of affairs, however, did not last long. With the departure of the Indian troops from the North and East in March 1990, the relations between the LTTE and the Eastern Muslims began to sour. Frictions developed after Muslims began to demand greater autonomy in their religious and cultural affairs in the Northern and Eastern Provinces, as promised in the LTTE's political manifesto (Hoole, 2001). These frictions were exacerbated by the LTTE's efforts to promote the Muslim United Liberation Front (MULF), an organisation that first aligned with the TULF and later the LTTE, among the Eastern Muslims (Sivaram, 1992). Many Eastern Muslims supported the Sri Lanka Muslim Congress (SLMC), the MULF's rival, and were therefore not happy with the LTTE's closeness to the latter (Sivaram, 1992). Tensions mounted further after leaders of the LTTE's political party, the People's Front of Liberation Tigers (PFLT), led by the LTTE's deputy leader K. Mahendirarajah alias Mathaya, exerted pressure on the Eastern Muslim leaders to join their political party (UTHR-J, 1990a: 31).

Jihadism vs. the LTTE

The state took advantage of these tensions when armed hostilities resumed in June 1990. The state reintroduced the Jihad Group, by now made up of radicalised Muslim youth, into the conflict (Tissainayagam, 2014). Islamic fundamentalism had already been on the rise from the 1950s in Sri Lanka following the formation of three Muslim fundamentalist organisations, the *Jamaat e Islami*, the *Tableq Jamaat*, and *Jam Iyyathu Ansaris Sunnathul Muhammatiyya* (Nuhuman, 1998: 7). Leaders of those organisations sought to reform Islam on the island by eliminating what they regarded 'as un-Islamic practices' of the Muslims (Nuhuman, 1998: 7). These ranged from rejecting 'all the customary folk religious practices from shrine worship to religious feasts' (practiced by the Hindu Tamils and adopted by local Muslims); expanding mosques to all Muslim villages and towns to make it easier for all Muslims to attend prayers; replacing Tamil or Tamil blended Arabic names of Muslims with purely Arabic names; the naming of Islamic institutions in Arabic; trying to curtail Muslim women from seeking employment; compelling Muslim women to accept female segregation and subordination to men; preventing Muslims from enjoying 'performing arts like music, dance, drama and the film'; and forcing Muslim women to wear the *fardah* to cover their whole body (Nuhuman, 1998: 7–12). Through these efforts to 'Islamise' Muslims, Islamic fundamentalists sought to rout *Sufism*, the South Indian version of Islam that was 'culturally integrated with the local Tamil environment' and replace it with *Wahabism*, a version of Islam 'sanctioned and practiced in ultra-conservative Saudi Arabia' (Balachandran, 2007). Arguably, *Wahabist* resurgence in Sri Lanka can be said to have had, to an extent, sediments of anti-Tamil feelings, especially given the fact that *Sufism* was culturally integrated with the Hindu Tamils of India and Ceylon.

It was against this backdrop that the Sri Lankan state inducted radicalised Jihadi gunmen into the East in June 1990. The presence of those gunmen, assuming the role of civilians when unarmed and playing the role of security forces when armed, was sufficient to create Tamil–Muslim communal tensions. For those Tamils in the East who had experience of the Sri Lanka military and police brutalities in the 1980s, the collaboration of Muslims as civilians *cum* paramilitary operatives with the state's military forces, created a situation where Tamils viewed Muslims as instruments of state oppression. Indeed, some Jihadi gunmen had previously been members of the Sri Lankan paramilitary forces in the 1980s, and this was known to the local Tamils (UTHR-J, 1990a: 40).

This sense of mistrust was further compounded by the atrocities committed by those Jihadi operatives, who, dressed in military uniforms, roamed Tamil villages assisting Sri Lankan troops, with 'widespread anger against the Muslims' amongst the Tamils being a legacy (see UTHR-J, 1990a: 40–41; Amnesty International, 1992: 1–2; Tissainayagam, 2014). Tamils suspected of supporting the LTTE were rounded in large numbers and summarily executed by Jihadi gunmen (UTHR-J, 1990a: 40–41; Amnesty International, 1992: 1–2; Tissainayagam, 2014). In some parts of the East, entire Tamil hamlets and villages were destroyed by the Jihadists (Jeyaraj, 2005). Tamil policemen working for the Sri Lankan state were also killed (Amnesty International, 1991: 3). These included Tamil policemen arrested and released by the LTTE, but rearrested by the STF, and later handed over to the Jihad Group (Amnesty International, 1991: 3). A large number of Tamil women were also abducted, raped and killed, or made to disappear (UTHR-J, 1990a: 41). Tamil Hindu temples were destroyed (Ariyanetthiran, 2015). In some instances, Tamil babies as young as 2 years old were hacked to death (Amnesty International, 1992: 4). There were also cases of armed Sinhala home guards killings Tamil civilians and the LTTE retaliating by killing Sinhala settlers (Amnesty International, 1992: 2 and 4)

There is a high possibility that Sri Lanka developed its strategy of exploiting LTTE–Muslim tensions at least 2 months before the resumption of armed hostilities in June 1990. In April 1990, heeding the longstanding call of the island's Muslim population, the Sri Lankan government demanded the US embassy in Colombo shut down its Israeli Interest Section, ironically used in the 1980s by the state to acquire weapons directly from Israel and other Western countries to fight the LTTE (see Balasingham, 2004: 49). The demand to shut down this Section helped Sri Lanka to claim, both to the local Muslim population and the Islamic world, that it would not allow 'anti-Muslim' elements to function on its soil. But it was not just the demand to shut down the Israeli Interest Section that signalled Sri Lanka's biopolitical shift in accepting Muslims as a 'friendly' species. After demanding the closure of the Israeli Interest Section, Sri Lanka announced that ties with Israel 'would be restored only after Israel recognised the PLO [the Palestinian Liberation Organisation], withdrew from all occupied [Palestinian] territories and agreed to participate in an international conference to solve the Arab–Israeli conflict' (Abadi, 2004: 302). In putting forward this demand, Sri Lanka emerged, in the eyes of many Muslims on the island, as the champion of the Islamic world in South Asia. In light of the LTTE–Muslim tensions in the East, this public relation exercise also allowed the state to project its security forces, assisted by its Jihadi paramilitary operatives, as the defenders of the Eastern Muslim community.

The handling of LTTE–Muslim relations by the LTTE's Eastern command under Vinayagamoorthy Muraleetharan, alias Karuna, played into the hands of the state. Whilst the LTTE released a number of surrendered Muslim policemen in the Northern areas it controlled, in the Eastern Batticaloa and Amparai districts under the command of Karuna, a large number of Muslim policemen who surrendered, along with their Sinhalese colleagues, simply vanished, presumed to have been executed (UTHR-J, 1990a: 12; Hoole, 2001). There was also the disappearance of 242 Muslims in July 1990 in the Batticaloa district, allegedly taken into custody by Karuna's cadres. The Federation of Kattankudi Mosques and Muslim Institutions (1990 cited in Sheriffdeen, 2014) accused the LTTE of massacring them. However, the LTTE denied these accusations and suggested that they may have been made to disappear by the Sri Lankan military (UTHR-J, 1990b: 16–17).

Tamil–Muslim tensions reached their height on 3 August 1990, when two mosques in the predominantly Muslim town of Kattankudi in Batticaloa district were attacked by gunmen disguised as Muslim worshipers. One hundred and six Muslims praying in the two mosques were killed in the attack, and many sustained injuries (with some of them later succumbing to their injuries). Initially there was confusion among the survivors as to who was responsible for the massacre (Shaheeb, 2012). Though the state media was quick to pin the blame on the LTTE, survivors expressed disbelief, given the cordial relations the Muslim community in Kattankudi had earlier maintained with the LTTE (Shaheeb, 2012).

The Sri Lankan military was also slow in responding to the massacre. When some local Muslims ran to the nearby army camp to seek help, the Sri Lankan military was initially reluctant, claiming that it would not be able to get to the scene of the attack because the roads may have been mined by the LTTE (UTHR-J, 1990a: 43). By the time the Sri Lankan military arrived, the attackers had escaped, and rumour abounded of state collusion in the attack (UTHR-J, 1990a: 43). In an interview with the BBC Tamil Service the following day, Karuna's deputy S. Karikalan denied the LTTE's involvement in the atrocity (UTHR-J, 1990b: 16). However, in a statement strongly rebuking the LTTE's denial, the Federation of Kattankudi Mosques and Muslim Institutions (1990 cited in Sheriffdeen, 2014) claimed that the massacres were carried out by a group of LTTE cadres led by one of its fund collectors, Nagarajah, alias Ranjith Appa. It also accused Ranjith Appa of playing a key role in the disappearance of 242 Muslims a month earlier (Sheriffdeen, 2014).

In its analysis of the Kattankudi atrocity, University Teachers for Human Rights – Jaffna (UTHR-J) (1990a: 44), a local human rights group, suggested that the massacre represented 'a leadership crisis' within the LTTE. Given that the LTTE released arrested Muslim policemen from its custody in the North and some parts of the East not under the command of Karuna, the UTHR-J (1990a: 43) noted that the LTTE's hand in the Kattankudi massacre seemed to be 'puzzling'. In a statement made to the Sri Lankan Parliament a few days later, Ranjan Wijeratne (1990, cited in UTHR-J, 1990a: 43), the country's defence minister, claimed, citing intelligence reports, that Karuna 'had radioed the Jaffna High Command [of the LTTE] mid-night 4 August, that his boys [cadres] had fired at Sri Lankan army trained Muslim youth at Kattankudi'. UTHR-J suggested that Wijeratne's statement implied that the Kattankudi massacre was carried out by the LTTE's Eastern Command, without the prior knowledge of its top leadership based in the Northern Jaffna peninsula (UTHR-J, 1990a: 44). For its part, the LTTE's Jaffna-based leadership pinned the blame for the massacre on the Sri Lankan government, claiming they were 'organised by the Government to drive a wedge between Tamils and Muslims, and to get help from Arab countries' (Menon, 1990). To support this claim, the LTTE's leadership cited Wijeratne's visits, coinciding with the Kattankudi massacre, to Iran, Egypt and Libya to procure arms (Menon, 1990; UTHR-J, 1990b: 17).

Initially, as the killing of Muslims spread to other parts of the East, M.H.M. Ashraf, the leader of the SLMC, suggested that the Sri Lankan government may be collaborating with the LTTE in those killings (UTHR-J, 1990b: 9). In response to the killing of Muslims attributed to the LTTE in the Eastern town of Eravur a week after the Kattankudi massacre, Ashraf (1990, cited in UTHR-J, 1990b: 9) stated: 'The massacre of defenceless Eravur Muslims is raising doubts whether the LTTE is going ahead with its barbaric attacks on the Muslims with the connivance of the government'. Ashraf's accusation was based on the behaviour of the Sri Lankan armed forces during the Eravur massacre, and the way the attackers behaved. If during the Kattankudi massacre the Sri Lankan armed forces arrived at the scene only after the attackers had escaped, during the Eravur massacre, the military refused to send its troops to the scene of the attack until the next day, claiming that it was not safe to do so (UTHR-J, 1990b: 18). Some of the Muslim survivors claimed that the perpetrators of the Eravur massacre spoke in Sinhala, calling out the Muslims to come out of their houses and either hacked them to death or fired at them (UTHR-J, 1990b: 18–19). Some of the victims' heads were severed (UTHR-J, 1990b: 18–19). The Jihadists retaliated by massacring Tamils in the adjoining villages (UTHR-J, 1990b: 19).

Whatever the truth behind these massacres, they were not the last episode in the killing of Eastern Muslims attributed to the LTTE, nor did these massacres put a check on the massacre of Tamil civilians attributed to the Jihad Group. The anti-Muslim stance of Karuna towards the Muslims only served to alienate the Eastern Muslims and reinforced suspicions that the LTTE was involved in those massacres. Unlike the LTTE's Eastern command in the 1980s that was staffed by its Northern leaders who were sympathetic to the Muslims and maintained a cordial relationship with them, its Eastern command in the 1990s led by Karuna was intolerant of Muslims (Sivaram, 1992). Despite the LTTE's persistent denials of involvement, the frequent massacre of Muslims in the East only served to challenge the credibility of its denials. At that time, neither the LTTE's Eastern command nor its Northern leadership did anything substantial to reconcile with Muslims, or allay their fears that the LTTE was taking an anti-Muslim stance. Though no Muslims were killed in the LTTE-controlled North, the fact that Muslims in the East were frequently massacred reinforced suspicions that the LTTE's handling of the Muslim question was wanting. It also reinforced suspicions that the LTTE's Jaffna-based leadership had only nominal control over its Eastern command, which could formulate its own policy and behaviour towards Muslims. This seems plausible given the fact that in the North, the LTTE was largely dependent on the recruits that Karuna regularly sent from the East. Even after the 2002 ceasefire, Karuna's men continued to harass Eastern Muslims, hampering the prospects for improved Tamil–Muslim relations in the East (see Jeyaraj, 2002). Karuna's then deputy Karikalan also toed an anti-Muslim line (Jeyaraj, 2002). At one point, when the LTTE's top leadership tried to reconcile with Muslims in April 2002, Karikalan claimed in a media interview that whatever deals Muslims make with the LTTE's top leadership, it cannot be enforced without the support of the Eastern command (Jeyaraj, 2002). The frictions between the LTTE and Eastern Muslims eased partially after Karikalan was removed from the post of political leader for Batticaloa and Amparai districts in August 2002, and to a greater extent after Karuna and his loyalists split from the LTTE in March 2004.

The killing and counter-killing of Tamils and Muslims in the East in the early 1990s also brought divisions within the rank and file of the LTTE, leading to a large number of its Muslim cadres deserting the movement, and surrendering to the Sri Lankan military (Hoole, 2001). Some of those deserters who opted to go into hiding instead of surrendering were caught by the Sri Lanka military and killed (Hoole, 2001). However, many who surrendered became part of the state's intelligence apparatus, helping to identify LTTE camps, cadres and supporters (see *Liberation Tigers*, 1990: 11; UTHR-J, 1991: 23 and 34).

With the mutual killing of Tamils and Muslims escalating in the East, in October 1990, the LTTE expelled Muslims living in its Northern territories, an act which was later admitted to be a grave 'political blunder' by LTTE theoretician Balasingham in 2002 (cited in *Tamilnet*, 2002). The LTTE never gave a clear explanation for the expulsion of the Muslims, but critics claim that it was triggered by the discovery of seventy-five swords concealed in a shop in the North owned by a Muslim trader. The trader's vehicles regularly made trips to government-controlled areas, and the LTTE's intelligence wing suspected that the Northern Muslims were planning to stage violence on a scale similar to that in the East (Jeyaraj, 2005). A month after the expulsion, the LTTE's official organ, *Liberation Tigers* claimed that the LTTE had lost 'faith' in Muslims following the mass killing of Tamils by the 'Muslim people' (*Liberation Tigers*, 1990: 11). The LTTE's official organ also claimed that 'by refusing to align with the Tamils and the LTTE whilst the [Tamil armed] struggle was taking place', and by 'seeking to destroy the LTTE and the Tamil people', the 'Muslim people' had committed 'a historical blunder and a historical treachery' (*Liberation Tigers*, 1990: 11). In *The Tamils' Quest for Statehood: In the Context of the Birth of New States in the Former Soviet Union and Yugoslavia*, published 2 years after the expulsion, Viswanathan Rudrakumaran (1992: 18), the LTTE's US-based legal advisor justified the expulsion, claiming that the entire Muslim community in Sri Lanka was working to sabotage the Tamil secessionist movement: 'In Sri Lanka the Sinhalese-controlled *government uses the Muslim population as a pawn* in their war game against the Tamils, in an effort to crush their quest for statehood' [emphasis added]. In response to this vilification of the entire Muslim community, Dharmeratnam Sivaram (1992), a leading Tamil military analyst who criticised the expulsion, suggested that Rudrakumaran was vilifying Muslims as a 'subnationality' who were being used by the state 'like the South Ossetians in the former Soviet Union to destabilise the creation of a separate [Tamil] state when international conditions are ideal'. Warning that Rudrakumaran's vilifications signified a 'dangerous trend', Sivaram (1992) argued that 'genocide' and 'ethnic cleansing' were on the agenda of the LTTE. However, in his annual policy address, published in the same issue of the LTTE's official organ that justified the expulsion, LTTE leader Pirapaharan was silent on the Muslim issue. Yet, 4 years later, in an interview with BBC Tamil Service, Pirapaharan (1994) expressed regret over the expulsion of Muslims: 'Those people [the Muslims] belong to the Jaffna soil. Because of some unfortunate developments at a certain point of time, they were forced to become refugees. We express our regret over this'. A year later, in an interview with the Indian journal *Outlook*, Balasingham went a step further and apologised for the expulsion:

> It was an unfortunate affair and we apologise. But there was communal tension and we asked them to leave the place without doing any harm to them. It was a mistake. We have told them that they have an inalienable right to live in peace in the North-east.
>
> (Balasingham, 1995)

In April 2002, 7 years later, Balasingham (cited in *Tamilnet*, 2002) said the expulsion 'could not be justified' and added: 'Let us forget and forgive the mistakes made in the past. Tamil Eelam is also the homeland of the Muslims and we have to live in harmony and amity to promote peace and prosperity in the region'. This was followed by Pirapaharan signing an agreement with Rauf Hakeem, the leader of the SLMC, which had emerged as the largest Muslim party, for the return and resettlement of Northern Muslims. Pirapaharan also agreed to grant tax concessions to Muslim traders (Imtiyaz and Iqbal, 2011: 383). This, despite the strain that the actions of Karikalan and Karuna caused in LTTE–Muslim relations in the East, helped to develop some goodwill between the LTTE and Muslims in the North.

What is interesting about these attempts of Pirapaharan and Balasingham to reconcile with Muslims from 1994 onwards is that it exposes the unofficial split and, to an extent, the crisis of leadership that existed on the Muslim question in 1990 within the LTTE, as claimed by UTHR-J (1990a: 44). Though it is often claimed in the Sinhala media (see, for example Jeyaraj, 2005) that LTTE's decision to expel Muslims from the North was the result of Karuna's then-deputy Karikalan's success in convincing Pirapaharan, a close analysis of the justifications made in the LTTE's official organ in November 1990 for the expulsion shows the role of Mathaya, under whose control, as the leader of the PFLT and the deputy leader of the LTTE, the movement's *de-facto* civil administration for the North functioned. The LTTE's official organ also functioned under Mathaya's purview. This is not to say that neither Karuna nor Karikalan may have had no role in the expulsion. Given their anti-Muslim stance, it is highly likely that they would have also influenced the decision to expel Muslims from the North.

An important fact that that has also been overlooked by many critics is that the Muslims were expelled from the North 6 days after Mathaya returned from the East (see Mahendirarajah, 1990: 5). Before the expulsion, Mathaya had stayed in the East for 41 days (Mahendirarajah, 1990: 5). In a statement printed in the LTTE's official organ alongside Pirapaharan's policy statement that was silent on the expulsion, Mathaya appealed to Northern Tamils to provide aid to Eastern Tamils displaced by the war and even went to the extent of suggesting that Tamils do not have to care about the Muslim community: 'The Sinhala people have the Sri Lankan government to help them. The Muslim people have the Sri Lankan government and the Arab countries to help them. But it is us [the Tamils] who should help the Tamil people' (Mahendirarajah, 1990: 5).

Close scrutiny of the LTTE's publications during that particular period also reveals Mathaya's role in the expulsion, and the existence of an unofficial split within the LTTE's leadership. The LTTE's overseas journal *Erimalai* published a series of articles in 1991 on Mathaya's tour of the East before the expulsion. In one of the articles, Karuna was quoted as having told Mathaya: 'They [the Muslims] have made a decision. Now, the question is how we are going to respond. Now, we have to make a firm decision' (*Erimalai*, 1991a: 9). In another article, Karuna was quoted as having said to Mathaya: 'They [the Muslim leadership] believe that whatever they do to the Tamils, we [the LTTE] would not take action beyond a certain limit. I think the time has come for us to prove that this belief is wrong' (*Erimalai*, 1991b: 8). Around the same period of time that these statements were made, Sathasivam Krishnakumar alias Kittu, a loyalist of Pirapaharan and the LTTE's then international leader, wrote in *Erimalai*: 'The full rights of the Muslims will be ensured in Tamil Eelam. Their aspirations will be met' (1991 cited in *Erimalai*, 1991c: 25). Kittu, who signed an agreement with Muslim leaders in India in August 1987 guaranteeing their rights in an Indian-backed Northern and Eastern regional government (before armed hostilities between the IPKF and the LTTE broke out), made this statement 3 months after Muslims were expelled from the North; and 3 months before Karuna's statements to Mathaya were printed in *Erimalai*. In the same journal, Kittu also said: 'When some Tamil groups fight alongside the Sri Lankan state against our people, we do not consider it to be a major issue that *some Muslims* are opposing us' [emphasis added] (*Erimalai*, 1991c: 25). This was in contrast to the vilification of the entire Muslim community in the LTTE's official organ in November 1990 and its legal advisor Rudrakumaran's booklet in 1992.

An analysis of some of Karuna's statements in *Erimalai* during this period also reveals the notorious manner in which he handled Tamil–Muslim tensions within the LTTE's rank and file. In one of the articles on Mathaya's tour of the East, Karuna was quoted as accusing all of the LTTE's Eastern Muslim cadres of betraying the Tamil armed struggle (*Erimalai*, 1991a: 9). Whilst accusing some of the LTTE's ex-Muslim cadres to be Jihad Group infiltrators, Karuna claimed that others who deserted their ranks, despite being loyal to the movement earlier, did so after being convinced by the local Islamic clerics: 'One day, the mosques functioning in all of the villages called all of the Muslim youth in the movement [the LTTE] for a meeting and spoke with them. Immediately after that all of them left the movement' (*Erimalai*, 1991a: 9). It has been claimed by critics that following the tensions in the East, a large number of LTTE's Muslim cadres were executed by their Tamil colleagues (see UTHR-J, 1991: 17; Jeyaraj, 2005). Karuna's claim that all of LTTE's Muslim cadres left the movement on a single day suggests that some of them may have been executed. As Karuna's forces in the East functioned under a hierarchised military command structure, it is highly unlikely that all of LTTE's Muslim cadres would have had the opportunity to meet mosque leaders simultaneously and then desert their ranks. Karuna's story suggests a meticulously planned rebellion by the LTTE's Muslim cadres, which is highly improbable. Given Karuna's human rights record during the years he was in command of the LTTE in the East (see Human Rights Watch, 2013), and the way he executed some of his Tamil colleagues for being Pirapaharan's loyalists immediately after he split from the LTTE in 2004, it is probable that he may have also executed a number of Muslim cadres, if not a large number of them.

The new 'friendly' species

Whatever the truth, and whatever efforts Pirapaharan and Balasingham took from 1994 to reconcile with Muslims, the expulsion of Muslims in October 1990 from the North only pushed the entire Muslim community towards the state. As the killings in the East escalated, and to avoid further accusations that it had a hand in the killing of Muslims, Sri Lanka stationed its STF commandos outside mosques, providing security to Muslim worshipers (Menon, 1990). This helped to enhance the developing goodwill between the state and the Muslim people.

As well as providing security to mosques, the state also provided arms training and weapons to hundreds of Muslim youth, thereby strengthening its paramilitary unit, the Jihad Group. The Federation of Kattankudi Mosques and Muslim Institutions (1990 cited in Sheriffdeen, 2014) aggravated the situation by urging Muslims to prepare to confront death in order to defend Islam. In a statement released after the Kattankudi massacre, the Federation asked the Muslims: 'Would any Muslim worry about dying for holy Islam?' (Sheriffdeen, 2014). This, and similar statements made by Islamic clerics that elevated the communal tensions to a life and death question for the religion of Islam in Sri Lanka, only served to whip up Islamist sentiments, thereby radicalising Muslim youth and strengthening *Wahabist* ideas. Muslim youth were issued with assault rifles by the state to keep at their homes (*Asian Tribune*, 2007). Sri Lanka's Defence Minister Wijeratne justified these actions claiming that Muslim youth had 'come forward to help government forces' (1990 cited in UTHR-J, 1990a: 43).

Muslims, not just from the East but also those from the North, were also inducted into Sri Lanka's regular military units, and its military intelligence apparatus. Whilst claiming that 'the actions of the LTTE had precluded the recruitment of Tamils into the armed forces', Wijeratne announced that Muslims would be recruited into the armed forces until their numbers reached 'their ethnic proportion of 7%' (UTHR-J, 1990b: 8). These actions provided a dual advantage to the state: on the one hand, the Muslim recruits provided the state with a Tamil-speaking intelligence base; on the other hand, it was able to function without apprehensions of LTTE infiltrations in its security forces, as anti-LTTE sentiments amongst Muslims ran high. Anti-LTTE Tamil groups (though small), were also at the disposal of the military. They had switched allegiance to Sri Lanka after the departure of the IPKF and functioned as paramilitary forces of the state, engaging in operations against the LTTE and often carrying out summary executions of LTTE suspects/supporters (Amnesty International, 1991: 4).

As well as using Jihadi gunmen to absolve its security forces of any responsibility for the atrocities perpetrated against Tamils, Sri Lanka also used them as proxies in its efforts to retake LTTE-held territories in the East. The armed Islamists in predominantly Muslim areas of the East contributed to the withdrawal of the LTTE from those areas, effectively turning them into government-controlled territories. Furthermore, with the assistance of Muslims in its intelligence apparatus, the state had control over the populous areas of the East where both Tamils and Muslims resided. The effective intelligence network created difficulties for the LTTE to establish control over, or to move through Tamil areas sandwiched between Muslim areas and those with mixed populations. In strategic terms, the existence of Tamil–Muslim tensions and the large scale presence of armed Jihadists in the East pushed the LTTE from the towns and rural areas of the East and into the jungles. Thus, Islamist paramilitary operatives functioning as an effective and reliable force, freed up the manpower of the Sri Lankan military in the East: whilst the Islamists cleared and secured Muslim areas and those with mixed populations of LTTE activity, and the military, with the assistance of anti-LTTE Tamil groups, deployed its troops in military operations in the predominantly Tamil areas of the East and in the North. The presence of armed Sinhala settlers in colonies previously established by the state in the East also made it difficult for the LTTE to take control of, or move through these areas and their adjoining Tamil villages.

In mid-1995, the LTTE managed to regain some of the strategically insignificant Tamil-dominated rural areas (the Paduvankarai region) of the Batticaloa district, but this was attributable to the Sri Lankan troops withdrawing from those areas for major military operations in the North. Nevertheless, the predominantly Muslim areas and those with a mixed population (as well as Sinhala colonies) continued to remain under the government's control. In Amparai district, where Muslims are a majority, the LTTE's control was limited to pockets of Tamil-dominated villages adjoining the jungles. Even in those areas, frequent incursions by the Sri Lankan armed forces made it difficult for the LTTE command to maintain a civil administration in the area. This was also the case in Trincomalee district where many Tamil and Muslim villages are sandwiched between each other. With the withdrawal of troops in mid-1995 for deployment to the north, the LTTE was only able to take control of a Tamil-dominated small land strip, Muthur East, in the south of Trincomalee district (adjoining another small land strip, Vaharai, in Batticaloa district), a geographical location suitable only for launching artillery and mortar attacks on the Sri Lanka military.

The biopolitical alliance the state made with the Jihadists by treating Muslims as a 'friendly' species and its efforts to project itself as the defender of the Muslim people also had political, economic and diplomatic benefits. At the political level, the state's control over vast tracts of Muslim territory made it possible for Sri Lanka to reject the Tamil claim of the Northern and Eastern Provinces as the Tamil homeland. Though the Tamils are the majority in the East, the combined population of Muslims and Sinhalese (as a result of the state's Sinhala colonisation programmes since the 1950s) make them a minority community there, thus allowing the state to challenge their homeland claim.

On the economic front, Sri Lanka was able to receive aid from Islamic countries to support reconstruction and resettlement programmes in the Muslim areas, meaning that it could claim that it was developing the Muslim areas, whilst not expending its own resources.

On the diplomatic front, playing the Muslim card, as the Muslims were largely sympathetic to Pakistan, Sri Lanka was able to keep India in check (Tissainayagam, 2014). With the Muslims pitched against the Tamils, and closely aligned with the state, Sri Lanka was able deny India the legitimacy to carry out another intervention in the North and East on behalf of the Tamil-speaking people, which included the Muslims. As a consequence of the Tamil–Muslim tensions, Muslim political parties chose to align with the state to further the interests of their community, and for obtaining political authority with the allocation of ministerial positions for their leaders. The MULF too distanced itself from Tamil politics and later merged with the SLMC (Johansson, 2012: 1). This allowed Sri Lanka to claim at the international level that it was not only representing the interests of the Sinhala Buddhists, but the inclusion of Muslims in the government was further evidence of its commitment to pluralism.

Although Sri Lanka gained strategic, political, economic and diplomatic benefits by arming the Jihadists in the East, and the division of Tamil and Muslim communities as a result, it also created conditions for Islamic extremism to emerge as a potentially dangerous force on the island. At the time of the Tamil–Muslim crisis in June 1990, only the Jihad Group existed in the East. Even then, it existed as a paramilitary unit of the state, functioning under the purview of local Sri Lankan military commanders. However, during the ceasefire between the LTTE and the Sri Lanka government in 2004, this had increased to eight Islamist groups: the Jihad Group, the Al Fatah Group, the Sadam Group (named after Sadam Hussein) the Osama Group (named after Osama bin-Laden), the Jetty Group, the Knox Group, the Mujahadeen Group and the Islamic Unity Foundation (IUF) (see Lunstead, 2004; also see *Asian Tribune*, 2007). Some of these groups were identified by the US Embassy in Colombo (Lunstead, 2004). Members of these groups, according to the US ambassador, received arms training not only from the Sri Lankan state: some were trained in the Kashmir region of India; others received arms training after joining to fight for Jihadists in other Islamic countries (Lunstead, 2004). The weapons these groups had in their possession were not only those issued by the state: some were also bought from Karuna after he split from the LTTE in March 2004 and led a Tamil paramilitary unit for the state; others were either smuggled in from India or bought from Sri Lanka's criminal gangs (Lunstead, 2004).

The biopolitical nurturing of violent Islamic fundamentalism in the East in the 1990s seems to have had top level support from the Sri Lankan government. Six months after the Kattankudi massacre in August 1990, the Sri Lankan President Premadasa visited the area, showing solidarity with the Muslim community (UTHR-J, 1991: 8–9). However, he refrained from visiting the adjoining Valaichenai area, where a large number of Tamils had been massacred by Jihadists (UTHR-J, 1991: 9). During his visit to Batticaloa Town, a group of Tamil mothers asked him to look into the disappearance of 125 Tamils taken away by the Sri Lankan military from a makeshift refugee camp at Eastern University (UTHR-J,

1991: 8–9). Premadasa was, however, adamant, and refused to look into the matter. His comments to the distressed mothers were: 'The mothers of those killed by the JVP are crying. The mothers of dead security forces are crying' (1991 cited in UTHR-J, 1991: 9). In other words, Premadasa implied that since he was preoccupied with consoling the Sinhala relatives of the dead soldiers (presumably killed by the LTTE) and the victims of atrocities committed by the JVP, it was not possible for him to look into the disappearance of Tamils. Inquiring into the disappearance of Tamils would open up the Sri Lanka military forces to investigation, a politically untenable position for Premadasa as the commander-in-chief of the island-state's armed forces. Premadasa's statement, as the UTHR-J noted, was, for the Eastern Tamils, 'a piece of sarcasm completely evading the fact that the President has an obligation to be accountable' (UTHR-J, 1991: 9).

Another ploy used by Sri Lanka to gain the sympathy and political and diplomatic support from the Islamic world and to project itself further as the defender of Islam and the Muslim people on the island was to accuse the LTTE of working hand-in-hand with Israel (UTHR-J, 1990a: 11). A few days after the resumption of armed hostilities in June 1990, M. H. Mohamed, a Sri Lankan Muslim cabinet minister who played an influential role in the Sri Lanka–Arab Friendship Society, made the spurious and unsubstantiated claim that 'Israeli experts had joined the LTTE to create trouble and turmoil' (UTHR-J, 1990a: 11).

However, while Muslims have enjoyed relatively friendly relations as contributors to the security of the state in the 1990s, a biopolitical analysis of the history of racist violence perpetrated against them suggests that their security rests on political contexts. The mass violence unleashed against the Muslims in southern Sri Lanka by government-backed Sinhala Buddhist extremists in June 2014 after the demise of the LTTE exemplifies the fragility of the security of the Muslims on the island. With the military defeat and the obliteration of the politics of the LTTE in May 2009, the Muslims reverted from being a 'friendly' race/species for the state, to the category of an 'enemy' race/species (see Chapter 6). The hostility Sri Lanka demonstrated towards Muslims in the post-LTTE period also strengthened the Islamic fundamentalism that it earlier nurtured in the 1990s. Reports in recent years indicate that Islamists in Sri Lankan have joined the terror group Islamic State. Sri Lankan Islamists, supported by Pakistan's intelligence service, also plotted to launch attacks on US and Israeli consulates in India in 2014 (Tissainayagam, 2014; Nanjappa, 2016). Regardless, one cannot deny that it was Sri Lanka's biopolitical nurturing of Jihadism and treating Muslims as a 'friendly' species that allowed the state to bring under its control the populous areas of the East in the 1990s.

The power of economic embargoes

Like the biopolitical nurturing and unleashing of Jihadism in the East, Sri Lanka used the economic embargo in the North to produce the effects of battle in the prelude to the implementation of its military strategy to retake control of the LTTE stronghold, Jaffna. An economic embargo was put in place with a view of 'softening' up Jaffna's Tamil population, and the LTTE, and thus driving a wedge between the two in preparation for launching a decisive military offensive to dislodge the LTTE and bring the area under state control. In 'Society Must Be Defended', Foucault (2004: 16) asserted that economic inequalities are capable of reproducing 'the disequilibrium of forces manifested in war'. In Sri Lanka's case, the economic inequalities its economic embargo produced for the Tamils weakened the LTTE's support base in Jaffna, making it increasingly difficult for the LTTE to compensate for manpower and firepower shortages.

The economic embargo was imposed in June 1990 immediately after the resumption of armed hostilities. Though the embargo was partially relaxed in September 1994 after a new government led by President Chandrika Kumaratunga assumed office, it was reimposed in April 1995 after the collapse of peace negotiations between the Kumaratunga regime and the LTTE, and continued until the February 2002 ceasefire.

Sri Lanka imposed the embargo in two ways: officially through Gazette notifications issued by its Defence Ministry prohibiting items that it deemed the LTTE could use for military purposes; unofficially, military officials on border sentry points curtailed goods to the North. There were cases of the government sending supplies of food and medicine to the North through civilian run co-operative societies (Ranawana, 2000; Sarvananthan, 2007b: 44). However, military officials manning border crossings determined when to send them and the quantities in which they should be sent (*The Sunday Times*, 2001). Quantitative restrictions were even imposed on painkillers and surgical supplies (Sarvananthan, 2007b: 44). These restrictions were, again, not imposed through law but beyond law.

Sri Lanka's economic embargo had two effects on the Northern Tamil population. On the one hand, it pushed the poor sections of the Northern Tamils, many of whom supported the LTTE, to the brink of starvation. The high cost of living brought about by the economic embargo compelled all able-bodied members of the family to search for employment opportunities. Families either had to induct more than one member of their household as labourers to improve the income of the family, and in other cases, sell their land to pay human smugglers to send them abroad. Consequently the recruitment base of the LTTE in the North shrunk. On the other hand, the high cost of living also made life difficult for the Northern upper and middle classes, who saw a better life in economic terms existing outside LTTE held territories and abroad.

The LTTE's efforts to tap into the incomes and savings of the upper and middle classes of Jaffna through enforced loan contributions, and the taxation of traders to fund its relentless demand for military hardware, and to cover the costs of sustaining a large politico-military organisation and its cadres, exacerbated the situation, causing deep resentment and hostility towards the organisation from those sections of the population. Consequently, sympathy for an LTTE-administered state began to wane among those classes in Jaffna.

In the meantime, apart from the economic embargo, Sri Lanka put pressure on the Northern Tamil population and the LTTE with constant airstrikes on populated areas of the North (McGirk, 1994; Ranawana, 2000). This also made life unsafe for all sections of Northern Tamil society, making many Tamils, especially those in the Jaffna peninsula, want to leave LTTE-held areas at the first opportunity.

Despite Sri Lanka's persistent denials, a handful of foreign journalists who managed to visit the LTTE-held Northern territories were able to witness and document the extent of the economic embargo and the hardships it caused for the Tamils. The ban on diesel and petrol imposed by the state forced auto rickshaws and lorries to run on coconut oil, 'after firing the engine with a few drops of petrol that every driver kept zealously in a dropper in his shirt pocket' (see Jayaram, 2013; also see McGirk, 1994). Electricity to the North was also cut off, forcing people to use for lighting 'specially made earthen-lamps, a few drops of kerosene [also heavily restricted] and paper wicks' (Jayaram, 2013). The ban on iron rods and cement prevented people from reconstructing their homes destroyed in airstrikes, and forced them to live in huts built from mud with grass roofs (*World Socialist Web Site*, 2002). Fertilisers were also banned, hitting farmers and bringing the agricultural sector to a grinding halt (Ranawana, 2000). But it was not only these items that were banned; an endless list of items ranging from candles to notepads were also banned (McGirk, 1994).

Marie Colvin (2001), the late American journalist who made a clandestine visit to the LTTE-held Vanni region in April 2001 and was injured in a rocket attack by the Sri Lanka military on her way back to Colombo wrote about the hardships caused by Sri Lanka's economic embargo: 'I had travelled though villages in the Vanni and found an unreported humanitarian crisis – people starving, international aid agencies banned from distributing food, no mains electricity, no telephone service, few medicines, no fuel for cars, water pumps or lighting'.

The author lived in the Jaffna peninsula until 1992 and can recall the hardships the economic embargo caused to the people. Sugar became a sought after commodity after its flow to the North was severely restricted by the state. People would rush to co-operative shops and wait in long queues whenever the news spread that 100 grams of sugar was being rationed out. Many got used to drinking black tea without sugar. Some even opted to have cold black tea so that it could be consumed quickly, without feeling the bitter taste. Potatoes became expensive (a fact also documented by a visiting British journalist (see McGirk, 1994)). Soaps and detergents were scarce, forcing people to wash clothes using the acidic pulp of palmyra fruit and sometimes ashes. The restrictions placed on the flow of papers resulted in newspapers sometimes being printed on thin cardboards. Travelling by automobile became expensive following the ban on petrol and diesel, forcing people to use bicycles. Though people sought to use earthen lamps for light at night, the scarcity of kerosene and coconut oil, which were largely used in vehicles, meant earthen lamps also became expensive to use. As a result, children were forced to study before dusk fell, meaning they could not play in the evening after returning from school, thereby being deprived of exercise. Playing at night also became dangerous due to the presence of venomous snakes in the dark. Airstrikes and artillery shelling by the Sri Lankan military on civilian settlements became a frequent occurrence, forcing people to build underground shelters in the vicinity of their houses. The absence of light at night made it dangerous for people to seek refuge during artillery shelling in shelters often infested with venomous snakes and scorpions. The presence of fortified underground shelters in the vicinity of each house made them resemble a mini camp, making it easy for the state to claim that these were LTTE shelters and bombard them. A ban on batteries meant people could not listen to radios. People therefore opted to listen to BBC Tamil Service and other radio broadcasts by spinning the wheel on their bicycles fitted with dynamos, which produced the electricity needed to make radios work, also documented by a CNN journalist who visited Jaffna after the military retook control of the peninsula (see Ranawana, 2000).

In October 2001, the BBC (cited in Kumaratunga, 2001), citing international aid agencies, claimed that the economic embargo had resulted in 40 percent of children living in the LTTE-held Vanni region being 'undernourished or malnourished'. Kumaratunga (2001) dismissed these allegations and argued: 'There is no economic blockade, that is nonsense'.

However, Kumaratunga (2001) acceded that the previous governments (those of Premadasa and his successor D. B. Wijetunga, who held power between 1990 to 1994), had imposed 'a very big economic blockade' and it was '*an official one*' [emphasis added]. Note Kumaratunga's use of the word 'official' to denote the economic embargo imposed by her predecessors. A letter sent to the army commander by Sri Lanka's defence secretary on 22 March 2001, which was also made available to the defence attachés of foreign missions in Colombo, announcing the relaxation of the free flow of twenty-four items showed the existence of an unofficial economic embargo also under the Kumaratunga regime (see *The Sunday Times*, 2001). The letter was worded: 'Ban on the following items has been lifted with immediate effect. Please instruct the officers concerned immediately' (*The Sunday Times*, 2001). The relaxed items included fruit juice packets, coconut oil, aspirin based tablets (pain killers), vitamins, anti-malaria pills, rice, eggs, non-instant noodles, papers, soap and sleeping mats (*The Sunday Times*, 2001). The Gazette notification issued by the Kumaratunga regime on 20 April 1995 had not listed these items as prohibited. The April 1995 Gazette notification had, among a number of other items considered to have potential military use for the LTTE, had prohibited the flow of petrol, diesel, batteries, iron, cement and spare parts for motor vehicles (*The Sunday Times*, 2001). Though the government later claimed that the March 2001 letter of the defence secretary had been erroneously worded, the issuing of orders to military officials to relax the free flow of twenty-four items not listed in the Gazette notification of April 1995 implied that the government of Kumaratunga had enforced an unofficial ban on them and other unknown items. When a foreign defence attaché inquired about the ban on instant noodles to the Vanni region, a Sri Lankan army officer claimed: 'the people there (in the Vanni) did not know how to prepare them' (*The Sunday Times*, 2001). Even if this was true, or that all of the people of the Vanni region were illiterate (which was not the case), and could not read the instructions on the instant noodles packets, the army officer's response indicates that it was the state that could determine what the people of Vanni should consume; and this depended on the state being able to confirm that they were not illiterate. In other words, for Sri Lanka, those who did not belong to the biopolitical category of the 'good' species, or belonged to an 'enemy' race/species, did not even have the right to choose what they should consume.

The use of economic embargo as part of its biopolitics of retaking the Northern territories was not the innovation of the Sri Lankan state in the 1990s. It had already been tested and tried during the presidency of Jayewardene in early 1987, a few months before the Indian troops took control of the Northern and Eastern Provinces. An Indian journalist who visited the Jaffna peninsula in February 1987 observed: 'The Sri Lankan government deliberately imposed the economic blockade on Jaffna in the hope that the suffering northern Tamils would pressure the Tigers [LTTE] to come to a settlement with Colombo' (Venkatramani, 1987). The Indian journalist cited the statement made by Sri Lanka's then National Security Minister Lalith Athulathmudali (1987 cited in Venkatramani, 1987) who justified the economic embargo in following terms: 'what we want is the dismantling of the LTTE's civil administration and that the Tigers should come to negotiate with us'. This statement of Athulathmudali is not surprising given the fact that 2 weeks before the Black July mass violence of 1983, Jayewardene (1983 cited in Janani, 2008: 9) had said in an interview with the UK daily, *Telegraph*: 'if I starve the Tamils out, the Sinhala people will be happy'. When Jayewardene made the statement, the LTTE was not in *de-facto* control of Jaffna, but when Athulathmudali made his statement in 1987, it had control of Jaffna and some other parts of the North (Venkatramani, 1987). Thus, if in 1983 making the Tamils starve was for the Jayewardene regime a way of making the race/species that the state managed/fostered happy, in 1987 it was also about producing two effects of battle – making the 'enemy' race/species submit and isolate it from the 'bad' species that sought to establish a state for the 'enemy' race/species. The Sri Lankan state was making use of these biopolitical dynamics of economic embargo in 1987. But Sri Lanka's use of economic embargo throughout the 1990s and up to the 2002 ceasefire went beyond these biopolitical aspects and produced further effects of battle.

Whilst the economic embargo brought severe hardships to the poor sections of the Northern Tamil community, it also temporarily provided an opportunity for many Tamil businessmen, who had long remained accustomed to *laissez faire* economic practices since British colonial rule, to increase their profits by hoarding restricted goods and then selling them at a later date for a higher price. The LTTE intervened by making hoarding a punishable crime (*Liberation Tigers*, 1992: 12). The LTTE's Tamil Eelam Police confiscated hoarded goods and then sold them at a lower price to the people (*Liberation Tigers*, 1992: 12). Whilst praising traders who adhered to its anti-hoarding policies as 'patriots', the LTTE accused businessmen whom it caught hoarding of having been engaged in acts 'inimical to the people' and 'the [freedom] struggle' (*Liberation Tigers*, 1992: 12). Though these actions of the LTTE helped the poor sections of the Northern Tamil society, it pitted the entrepreneur classes against it.

The hostility of the Northern traders towards the LTTE increased as it imposed taxes on them to increase its revenues (see Sarvananthan, 2007b: 46). On the one hand, the Sri Lankan government's economic embargo curtailed the Northern traders' ability to continue trade in the way they had done prior to its imposition, thus sharply hitting their profits. However, having already been prevented from hoarding goods by the LTTE and thereby being denied of the opportunity to increase their profits in accordance with *laissez faire* economic practices, traders found it unacceptable that the remaining profits they were able to make were being diminished by the LTTE's taxes. The price controls the LTTE imposed in its territories on the sale of essential goods also made it impossible for traders to pass on the costs of those taxes to the consumers.

Meanwhile, the ban imposed on cement and iron, whilst affecting the civilians, also hit the LTTE. It found it difficult to construct camps for its fighting formations, house its injured cadres and set up its administrative offices, except by smuggling limited quantities of cement and iron from the government-controlled territories and South India. With the Indian navy imposing a blockade on the LTTE following the assassination of the former Indian Prime Minister Rajiv Gandhi in 1991, this became increasingly difficult. This obstacle, however, was overcome with the LTTE's political party, PFLT, led by Mathaya taking over lands and buildings belonging to people who had gone abroad with their families but had entrusted them for care to their relatives (*Liberation Tigers*, 1991a: 9). The LTTE's official organ justified the PFLT's decision by claiming that going abroad was 'an unpatriotic act' and pledged to return the lands to their rightful owners upon their return (*Liberation Tigers*, 1991a: 9). Those houses were also used to house some of the refugees (*Liberation Tigers*, 1991a: 9). These actions, not only angered those who went abroad without selling their lands, but also their relatives who wanted to use them but could not do so due to the actions of the PFLT.

When the hardships caused by the economic embargo worsened, many youth opted to go abroad. This further affected the LTTE's ability to continue recruitment. It therefore imposed a regime of permit system, making it difficult for the youth to leave its areas. This 'came into conflict with the aspirations of parents who wanted their children to escape from the conditions of war and to seek greener pastures abroad' (Balasingham, 2001: 274–275).

The economic blockade can also be said to have exacerbated the leadership crisis in the LTTE. Mathaya's autocratic style of running the LTTE's civil administration caused much resentment among the people (Balasingham, 2001: 297). His clientist approach transformed the PFLT into a 'corrupt institution promoting the interests of a few individuals who were loyal to him' (Balasingham, 2001: 297). Mathaya's short-sighted public statements also alienated him from the people. Speaking at an economic conference held at Jaffna University in June 1991, Mathaya suggested that the food crisis caused by the economic embargo could be countered by people not relying on commodities from outside the LTTE-held territories: 'We should produce whatever we need. *We should only eat food that grows in our land*' [emphasis added] (1991 cited in *Liberation Tigers*, 1991b: 3). As the leadership crisis within the LTTE worsened, in March 1993 Pirapaharan disbanded the PFLT and sacked Mathaya from his top post, deputy leader of the movement. A month later, Mathaya was arrested by the LTTE and later executed on 'charges of conspiracy to eliminate the LTTE leadership' (Balasingham, 2001: 296–298).

In biopolitical terms, Sri Lanka's economic blockade can thus be said to have produced four effects of battle: polarising the Tamil community in the LTTE-held territories on the basis of the rich (the businessmen and the professionals) and the poor, thereby weakening the Tamil secessionist spirit among the former group; weakening the LTTE's ability to raise funds and recruit for its fighting formations in its territories, thus transforming it from a popular mandated state-in-making to a non-democratic *de-facto* state in crisis; making many of Jaffna's upper and middle classes come to the conclusion that living in a Tamil state for which they voted for in the general election of 1977 was not conducive for furthering their economic interests; and causing the voluntary exodus of Tamils to foreign, especially Western, countries, thereby reducing the Tamil population on the island.

With the collapse of peace talks with the LTTE in April 1995, exploiting the effects of battle caused by the economic embargo, the Kumaratunga regime prepared to launch a series of major offensive operations to capture the Jaffna peninsula. The LTTE attempted to prevent the impending fall of Jaffna by undertaking a massive recruitment and fundraising drive. The modernisation of armed forces undertaken by the Kumaratunga regime coupled with the recruitment of more troops during peace negotiations, the effects of the 5-year-long economic embargo, the losses the LTTE sustained on the battlefield before Kumaratunga assumed power, and the effects of the leadership crisis caused by the Mathaya episode, had all tilted the military balance in Sri Lanka's favour. The LTTE's peace negotiations with the Kumaratunga regime, though short lived, also led to the upper and middle classes in Jaffna initially developing high hopes that a political solution to the conflict would soon be found, especially given Kumaratunga's statements at public forums that she was committed to peace. This could be said to have also had an effect on the LTTE's ability to recruit for its fighting formations because remaining LTTE supporters within those classes would have had no reason to join its military wing; in a time of peace, especially with prospects for a political solution looking so bright, it would have initially seemed imprudent for LTTE supporters to join an armed struggle that seemed to be on its wane. The haste with which Pirapaharan withdrew from peace talks in April 1995 showed he feared that unless he could prove to the Tamils that Kumaratunga had no plans for a political solution, but was intending to pursue a military solution, he would not be able to enhance the LTTE's manpower.

It was against this backdrop that after direct talks with the Kumaratunga regime collapsed in April 1995 the LTTE launched a massive fundraising and recruitment drive. An analysis of LTTE's official publications at that time reveal the desperation of the movement in seeking to increase its manpower and firepower, and thereby prevent the impending fall of Jaffna. Though around 800,000 Tamils lived in the Jaffna peninsula at that time, the LTTE struggled to increase the strengths of its fighting formations. In May 1995, the LTTE's official organ urged at least 5,000 Tamil youth in the North to enlist in the movement, claiming that if it was able to increase the strength of its fighting formations by another 5,000 cadres, it would be able to overrun all of the military bases in the North (*Liberation Tigers*, 1995a: 6). Yet, to its dismay, the LTTE could not increase its manpower. In September 1995, as the Sri Lankan military launched the last of the series of limited offensive operations to capture Jaffna, setting the scene for the final military push, the LTTE urged the people to donate money so that it could procure military equipment for defence against the forthcoming offensive by the Sri Lanka military (*Liberation Tigers*, 1995b: 4). For the first time revealing its annual military expenditures to amount to 1.8 billion rupees, as opposed to Sri Lanka's then defence expenditure of 40 billion rupees, the LTTE claimed that if it was able to double its annual military expenditure to 3.6 billion rupees, it would be able minimise its manpower losses, and move the struggle forward (*Liberation Tigers*, 1995b: 4).

An analysis of these statements against the backdrop of the fall of Jaffna city in December 1995, followed by the fall of the entire Jaffna peninsula in April 1996 to the Sri Lankan military reveals that despite the use of audio, video and print media and grass root level propaganda, the LTTE was neither able to come anywhere close to its target of 5,000 new recruits, nor the additional 1.8 billion rupees of funds it sought to increase its firepower. Though Jaffna Tamils did join the LTTE and contribute funds, the vast majority of them seemed to have not been convinced that risking their money by donating to the LTTE, or their lives by joining its military wing, would make life better for them. The LTTE made repeated claims throughout 1995 that unless the people of Jaffna helped to increase its manpower and firepower, the fall of Jaffna to the Sri Lankan military could not be prevented; it even warned the Jaffna Tamils that if the military was able to take control of the peninsula, they may face the fate of a large number of Eastern Tamils massacred by the state's military and paramilitary forces (*Liberation Tigers*, 1995c: 7). Yet, having undergone so much hardship for 5 years as a result of Sri Lanka's tough regime of economic embargo, it seems that the upper and middle classes of Jaffna were not convinced that they would prosper by continuing to live under LTTE's control. The LTTE's taxation and the way it sought to deal with the crisis caused by the economic embargo may have compounded this feeling. Those who were optimistic that Kumaratunga would deliver a political solution could not be convinced that Sri Lanka would pursue a military solution and bring misery to their lives. Even the atrocities of the Sri Lankan security forces in the East in the early part of the 1990s were seen as the legacies of the former President Premadasa. President Kumaratunga, however, was seen to belong to an entirely different political spectrum.

In sum, the tough regime of economic embargoes imposed by Premadasa following the resumption of armed hostilities in June 1990, and continued by Kumaratunga, seemed to have borne fruit to the state by April 1996. Sri Lanka's biopolitics that manifested through the economic embargo had eventually starved the LTTE of manpower and firepower, forcing it to abandon the populous Jaffna peninsula. In other words, through the economic embargo, Sri Lanka managed to drive a wedge between the 'bad' species (the LTTE) and a sizeable portion of the 'enemy' race/species (the Tamils). The success of the economic embargoes may have been the reason behind Kumaratunga's decision to enforce it on the LTTE-controlled Vanni region, until the 2002 ceasefire.

Though the LTTE managed to overrun a major military complex at the gates of the Jaffna peninsula in April 2000, and 2 months later came close to retaking Jaffna city and the entire southern and southeastern parts of the Jaffna peninsula, manpower and firepower shortages forced it to pull back. Thus, by the time of the ceasefire of February 2002, the LTTE had under its control only a land strip in the southeastern coast of the peninsula and some areas adjoining the gateway to the peninsula.

Nonetheless, the loss of Jaffna allowed the LTTE to consolidate its military forces in the Vanni region. With a population of around 450,000 Tamils, many of whom were either farmers, peasants or fishermen, who formed its support base, it was not difficult for the LTTE to sustain its manpower and face the Sri Lankan military in the region. The LTTE's ability to tap into the financial resources of the Tamil Diaspora following the fall of Jaffna also meant that it was able to compensate for the financial loses it incurred after losing the Jaffna peninsula. With a strong financial base in the Tamil Diaspora, the LTTE did not also have to impose heavy taxes on the traders of Vanni, or impose enforced funds/loan contributions on the local upper and middle classes. Also, learning from the state-building experiments in Jaffna, the LTTE made efforts to ensure that its civil administration was rooted in a commitment 'to the rights, welfare and development of the Tamil community' (Stokke, 2006: 1024). This ranged from undertaking humanitarian relief activities, to providing primary healthcare and preschool services (Stokke, 2006: 1029–1031). These also helped to solidify the support of the families of LTTE members, who also benefited from these services.

Yet, despite the humiliating failures of the military operations to capture the Vanni region in the late 1990s, Sri Lanka was not prepared to allow the Vanni region to remain permanently under the LTTE's control. Therefore, in the post-2002 ceasefire period, as part of its biopolitics of securing the Sinhala Buddhist ethnocratic state order, Sri Lanka used diplomacy in the space of 'peace' to weaken the LTTE before resuming military offensives in July 2006. The next chapter will explore these aspects.

References

Abadi, J. (2004) *Israel's Quest for Recognition and Acceptance in Asia*. London: Frank Cass Publishers.

Ali, A. (1997) 'The Muslim Factor in Sri Lankan Ethnic Crisis', *Journal of Muslim Minority Affairs*, 17(2), pp. 253–267.

Amnesty International (1990) *Sri Lanka: Briefing*. London: Amnesty International.

Amnesty International (1991) *Sri Lanka: Summary of Human Rights Concerns During 1990*. London: Amnesty International.

Amnesty International (1992) *Sri Lanka: Deliberate Killings of Muslim and Tamil Villagers in Polonnaruwa*. London: Amnesty International.

Ariyanetthiran, P. (2015) *"Expulsion of Northern Muslims Wasn't Ethnic Cleansing," Says Ex-TNA MP*. Available at: http://www.newindianexpress.com/world/Expulsion-of-Northern-Muslims-Wasn%E2%80%99t-Ethnic-Cleansing-Says-Ex-TNA-MP/2015/11/04/article3113324.ece (Accessed: 6 November 2015).

Asian Tribune (2007) 'Militant Wahabism Beats Other Islamic Fundamentalists in Sri Lanka'. Available at: http://www.asiantribune.com/index.php?q=node/7156 (Accessed: 10 June 2015).

Balachandran, P.K. (2007) *Rise of Wahabism in Eastern Sri Lanka*. Available at: http://www.hindustantimes.com/world/rise-of-wahabism-in-eastern-sri-lanka/story-AJuCl7hu8Dt2bEvky3FarO.html (Accessed: 18 February 2012).

Balasingham, A. (1995) Interviewed by A.S.Pannerselvan for *Outlook*, 8 November. Available at: http://www.outlookindia.com/magazine/story/we-did-not-kill-rajiv-gandhi/200167 (Accessed: 10 January 2016).

Balasingham, A.A. (2001) *The Will to Freedom: An Inside View of Tamil Resistance*. London: Fairmax Publishing.

Balasingham, A. (2004) *War and Peace: Armed Struggle and Peace Efforts of Liberation Tigers*. London: Fairmax Publishing.

Colvin, M. (2001) *The Shot Hit Me. Blood Poured from My Eye – I Felt a Profound Sadness that I Was Going to Die*. Available at: http://www.mariecolvincenter.org/?page_id=931 (Accessed: 3 January 2016).

Erimalai (1991a) 'A Noble Journey in the Direction of Dawn, Part III', April, pp. 8–9.

Erimalai (1991b) 'A Noble Journey in the Direction of Dawn, Part VI', July, pp. 8–9.

Erimalai (1991c) 'Kittu Answers Questions', January, pp. 24–25.

Foucault, M. (2004) *"Society Must Be Defended": Lectures at the College de France, 1975–76*. Translated by David Macey. London: Penguin Books.

Hoole, R. (2001) *Massacres of Muslims and What It Means for the Tamils*. Available at: http://www.uthr.org/Rajan/muslims.htm (Accessed: 10 February 2016).

Human Rights Watch (2013) *Sri Lanka: Probe into LTTE Crimes Should Start with Karuna*. Available at: https://www.hrw.org/news/2013/03/28/sri-lanka-probe-ltte-crimes-should-start-karuna (Accessed: 30 March 2013).

Imtiyaz, A.R.M. and Iqbal M.C.M. (2011) 'The Displaced Northern Muslims of Sri Lanka: Special Problems and the Future', *Journal of Asian and African Studies*, 46(4) pp. 375–389.

Janani, J.T. (2008) 'The Blind Spot in Genocide Theory', *Tamil Guardian*, 4 June, pp. 9 and 19.

Jayaram, P. (2013) *The Many Balachandrans of Jaffna*. Available at: http://www.thehindu.com/opinion/op-ed/the-many-balachandrans-of-jaffna/article4573887.ece (Accessed: 30 October 2014).

Jeyaraj, D.B.S. (2002) *A Face-Saving Manoeuvre*. Available at: http://www.frontline.in/static/html/fl1917/19170600.htm (Accessed: 7 January 2016).

Jeyaraj, D.B.S. (2005) *Fifteenth Anniversary of Muslim Expulsion from Jaffna*. Available at: http://www.thesundayleader.lk/archive/20051030/issues.htm#Fifteenth4 (Accessed: 7 June 2015).

Johansson, A. (2012) 'Sri Lanka Muslim Congress' Rise to Power', *Religionsvetenskaplig internettidskrift*, 2(13), pp. 1–6.

Kumaratunga, C. (2001) Interviewed by Tim Sebastian for *Hard Talk*, *BBC*, 3 November.

Liberation Tigers (1986) 'Islamic Tamils under the Grip of Racism', November, p. 5.

Liberation Tigers (1990) 'A Crisis Caused by the Muslims', October-November, pp. 1 and 11.

Liberation Tigers (1991a) 'We Are Taking Charge of Properties of those Who Have Left for Abroad, This Is Not Appropriation', February–March, p. 9.

Liberation Tigers (1991b) 'A Strong Economic Foundation Is Essential for Creating a Separate State', June, p. 3.

Liberation Tigers (1992) 'Hoarding – An Anti-People's Act', August–September, p. 12.
Liberation Tigers (1995a) 'Life Depends on Strength', May, pp. 5–6.
Liberation Tigers (1995b) 'Blood Donation Will Save Lives: Financial Donations Will Save a Nation', September, p. 4.
Liberation Tigers (1995c) 'Only the People Who Are Brave Enough to Fight Would Be Able to Live Freely', May, pp. 7–8.
LTTE (1985) *Socialist Tamil Eelam*. Madras: LTTE.
Lunstead, J. (2004) *Source Report on Muslim Militancy in Sri Lanka*. Available at: https://wikileaks.org/plusd/cables/04COLOMBO950_a.html (Accessed: 10 March 2016).
Mahendirarajah, K. (1990) 'Let Us Share the Hardships', *Liberation Tigers*, October–November, p. 5.
McGirk, T. (1994) *Out of Sri Lanka: Journey to a Land without Toilet Paper*. Available at: http://www.independent.co.uk/news/world/out-of-sri-lanka-journey-to-a-land-without-toilet-paper-1401702.html (Accessed: 10 January 2015).
Menon, R. (1990) *Communal Carnage: LTTE May Be Behind Massacre of Muslims*. Available at: http://indiatoday.intoday.in/story/ltte-suspected-behind-massacre-of-muslims-in-sri-lanka/1/315556.html (Accessed: 19 October 2015).
Nanjappa, V. (2016) *Is the ISIS Threat Catching Up to Sri Lanka?* Available at: http://www.slguardian.org/2016/02/is-the-isis-threat-catching-up-to-sri-lanka/ (Accessed: 5 February 2016).
Nuhuman, M.A. (1998) 'Ethnic Identity: Religious Fundamentalism and Muslim Women in Sri Lanka', *Women Living under Muslim Laws*, 21(September), pp. 1–15.
Perera, E.W. (1915) *Memorandum upon Recent Disturbances in Ceylon*. London: Edward Hughes & Co.
Pirapaharan, V. (1994) Interviewed by Anandhi Sooriyapragasam for *BBC Tamil Service*, 13 September.
Ponnambalam, S. (1983) *Sri Lanka: The National Question and the Tamil Liberation Struggle*. London: Zed Books and Tamil Information Centre. Available at: http://tamilnation.co/books/Eelam/satchi.htm (Accessed: 10 June 2015).
Ramanathan, P. (1916) *Riots and Martial Law in Ceylon, 1915*. London: St.Martin's Press.
Ranawana, A. (2000) *Caught in Limbo: In Jaffna's Uneasy Peace, No One Dares to Put Any Trust in the Future*. Available at: http://edition.cnn.com/ASIANOW/asiaweek/97/1107/nat3.html (Accessed: 12 April 2014).
Rudrakumaran, V. (1992) *The Tamils' Quest for Statehood: In the Context of the Birth of New States in the Former Soviet Union and Yugoslavia*. Camberley: International Federation of Tamils.
Sarvananthan, M. (2007a) 'In Pursuit of a Mythical State of Tamil Eelam: A Rejoinder to Kristian Stokke', *Third World Quarterly*, 28(6), pp. 1185–1195.
Sarvananthan, M. (2007b) *Economy of the Conflict Region in Sri Lanka: From Embargo to Repression*. Washington: East-West Center.
Shaheeb, A.M. (2012) Interview to *Muslim CN*, 8 August. Available at: https://www.youtube.com/watch?v=rJPEW2rS44g (Accessed: 12 January 2016).
Sheriffdeen, S. (2014) *Kattankudy Mosque Massacre 3 Aug 1990*. Available at: https://www.youtube.com/watch?v=uBnTzM7JbMg (Accessed: 12 January 2016).
Sivaram, D. (1992) *LTTE's Eelam Project and the Muslim People*. Available at: http://tamilnation.co/forum/sivaram/921115muslims.htm (Accessed: 10 October 2014).
Stokke, K. (2006) 'Building the Tamil Eelam State: Emerging State Institutions and Forms of Governance in LTTE-controlled Areas in Sri Lanka', *Third World Quarterly*, 27(6), pp. 1021–1040.

The Sunday Times (2001) 'Peace Moves Stumble Amidst Tiger Build-up'. Available at: http://www.sundaytimes.lk/010408/sitrep.html (Accessed: 7 June 2014).

Tamilnet (2002) 'Pirapaharan to Meet Muslim Leaders'. Available at: https://www.tamilnet.com/art.html?catid=13&artid=6824 (Accessed: 8 January 2016).

Tissainayagam, J.S. (2014) 'LTTE: Sri Lanka's Scapegoat for Its Own Terror', *Foreign Policy*, June 23. Available at: http://foreignpolicy.com/2014/06/23/ltte-sri-lankas-scapegoat-for-its-own-terror/ (Accessed: 30 June 2014).

TULF (1977) 'General Election Manifesto'. Available at: http://www.sangam.org/FB_HIST_DOCS/TULFManifesto77.htm (Accessed: 17 January 2017).

UTHR-J (1990a) *Report No 4: The War of June 1990*. Colombo: UTHR-J.

UTHR-J (1990b) *Report No 5, August: A Bloody Stalemate*. Colombo: UTHR-J.

UTHR-J (1991) *Report No 7: The Clash of Ideologies and the Continuing Tragedy in the Batticaloa and Amparai Districts*. Colombo: UTHR-J.

Venkatramani, S.H. (1987) *Bearing the Blockade*. Available at: http://indiatoday.intoday.in/story/sri-lankan-president-jayewardene-is-trying-to-fool-everybody-ltte-leader/1/336680.html (Accessed: 12 June 2015).

Weerasekara, M.H. (2014) *"The Mutual Respect and Support", The Anagarika's Close Ties With a Great Tamil Leader*. Available at: http://www.island.lk/index.php?page_cat=article-details&page=article-details&code_title=110276 (Accessed: 14 September 2014).

Wilson, J.A. (1974) *Politics in Sri Lanka, 1947–1973*. London: Palgrave Macmillan.

World Socialist Web Site (2002) *A First-hand Report of Life in LTTE-held Areas of Sri Lanka*. Available at: http://www.wsws.org/en/articles/2002/06/sri-j26.html (Accessed: 22 May 2014).

5 War through 'peace'

Numerous studies have been conducted on Sri Lanka's military victory over the LTTE in May 2009. Almost all of them attribute Sri Lanka's success to the determination of the regime of the former President Mahinda Rajapaksa to defeat the LTTE (see, for example Moorcraft, 2012: 165; Layton, 2015). Barely a week after declaring victory over the LTTE, in an interview with BBC, Gotabaya Rajapaksa (2009), Sri Lanka's then defence secretary and the brother of Mahinda Rajapaksa, claimed that the state was able to defeat the LTTE because there 'was a clear aim and mandate from the political level to the official level and to the military level to destroy the LTTE at any cost'. This implied that Sri Lanka failed to defeat the LTTE during the presidencies of Mahinda Rajapaksa's predecessors because there was no clear mandate for the LTTE's destruction; they were not prepared to bear the costs, ranging from the loss of lives and international backlash to the drain on the island's economy.

It is true that under Mahinda Rajapaksa's leadership of the state, Sri Lanka was ruthless in its prosecution of the military offensives against the LTTE, and dismissed the mass demonstrations and cries of distress from hundreds of thousands of Tamils in the Diaspora, and the Tamils of the neighbouring Indian state of Tamil Nadu. It also ignored the concerns expressed by international human rights groups over the loss of lives and violations of international human rights and humanitarian law, resisted international ostracism and criticism from Western political leaders and diplomats, all anxious about mounting Tamil civilian casualties and silenced critics from amongst the Sinhalese, until the state's military had achieved victory over the LTTE.

However, an important factor that has been overlooked by many commentators is that since the signing of the Norwegian-sponsored ceasefire agreement with the LTTE in February 2002 to the resumption of full-scale armed hostilities in July 2006, Sri Lanka's successive governments used 'peace' as a means of waging war against the LTTE. Before Mahinda Rajapaksa assumed power in November 2005, a war through 'peace' was waged by the regimes of Ranil Wickremesinghe and Chandrika Kumaratunga. Though the Rajapasksa regime also continued this war for a few months into Mahinda Rajapaksa's presidency, it was only after it was confident that the LTTE had been defeated at 'peace' that it launched military offensives. Thus, contrary to the claims of some strategic scholars (see, for example Moorcraft, 2012: 165) that the LTTE was defeated because the Rajapaksa regime adapted Mao Tse-tung's theory of fighting 'with the political will to win', it was able to defeat the LTTE because it adhered to the ancient Chinese strategic thinker Sun Tzu's (1998: 28) suggestion that 'in war the victorious strategist only seeks battle after the battle has been won'.

This chapter develops a biopolitical account of such strategic position. It begins with an analysis of the efforts of the Kumaratunga regime before the 2002 ceasefire agreement to project to the Western liberal world that the LTTE constituted a 'bad' species that had to be eliminated. This is followed by an analysis of the use of diplomacy as war during the 'peace' process by the regimes of Wickremesinghe and Kumaratunga, followed by that of the Rajapaksa, to weaken the LTTE militarily, or in biopolitical terms, to produce an effect of battle. The final section explores Sri Lanka's strategy for defeating the LTTE militarily. It addresses the period commencing the resumption of full scale armed hostilities in July 2006 to the LTTE's military defeat in May 2009. This section is placed within this chapter because despite the resumption of full scale armed hostilities, neither the LTTE nor the Sri Lankan government immediately withdrew from the ceasefire agreement: both parties refrained from giving, as per Article 4.4 of the ceasefire agreement, the obligatory 14 days' notice required to withdraw from the ceasefire (see Balasingham, 2004: 499). This meant, in principle, a ceasefire (or 'peace') was in force for part of the time, but a full-scale armed conflict was going on. Armed hostilities can be said to have officially resumed only in January 2008, after the Sri Lankan government submitted the obligatory 14 days' notice to the Norwegians. However, the official withdrawal from the ceasefire did not see any fundamental strategic change in Sri Lanka's campaign for defeating the LTTE. In other words, there is no distinction in the strategy adopted by Sri Lanka during the period of 'peace' and following the official end of the ceasefire; 'peace' and the official declaration of the end of the ceasefire were a continuum in Sri Lanka's campaign to defeat the LTTE.

Joining the liberal bandwagon

As we saw in Chapter 3, couched within the political context of the Cold War, from 1977 to 1987, Sri Lanka, under President Jayewardene, sought to militarily defeat the LTTE and other Tamil militant groups with counter-insurgency support from the West. Jayewardene (1985) projected Sri Lanka as a liberal democracy under threat from LTTE and other Tamil militant 'Marxist' groups seeking to take over the entire state, establish a communist government on the island and then export a Marxist revolution to India. Jayewardene's propaganda against the backdrop of the West's struggle against the Soviet Union to contain global communist revolutions contributed to a large extent to the perception in the West that the armed Tamil secessionist movement was spearheading a communist revolution in South Asia (see Willis, 1987: 180). It also led to the US president Ronald Reagan (1984) denouncing the Tamil armed struggle as 'terrorism' and a 'cowardly form of barbarism'. The then UK Prime Minister Margaret Thatcher (1985) also came down hard on the armed Tamil secessionist movement, asserting that 'terrorism must never be seen to win' because there 'is a democracy in Sri Lanka'. However, as we saw in Chapter 3, the hostility shown by India towards Western interference in the conflicts in its neighbouring states only exacerbated the situation, culminating in India training, arming and financing the LTTE and other Tamil militants.

The warming of relations between India and the West in the post-Cold War period did not make matters any easier for Sri Lanka. Though the West continued to support Sri Lanka's efforts to militarily defeat the LTTE in the post-Cold War era, this was not unconditional; to avoid antagonising India, the West was careful that its actions did not create anxiety in New Delhi (Lunstead, 2007: 11). The realisation on the part of the West that the LTTE had no real commitment to Marxism (see Spain, 1987), followed by the collapse of the communist Soviet Union, also made it impossible for Sri Lanka to continue using the Marxist card. Unlike during the Cold War when the West gave the green light to Sri Lanka for the military defeat of the LTTE, in the early years of the post-Cold War period, it encouraged both parties to seek a negotiated political settlement. Some Western countries, including Norway, Britain and Australia even offered to mediate with the LTTE (*Liberation Tigers*, 1991: 1; Balasingham, 1994: 3; Sorbo et al., 2011: 29).

Kumaratunga, during her period of office from September 1994 to November 2005, can claim some credit as the first Sri Lankan leader to have turned the opinion of the West against the LTTE in the post-Cold War period. Kumaratunga initiated peace talks with the LTTE in September 1994, creating a favourable and upbeat impression locally, regionally and internationally. But significantly, after ascending to power, Kumaratunga further impressed the West by announcing neoliberal economic policies (Lunstead, 2007: 14). Her commitment to adhere to democratic norms also contributed to a perception that Kumaratunga was leading the country in the path of good governance (Shastri, 2004: 88).

Thus, when the LTTE hastily withdrew from peace talks and resumed the armed struggle in April 1995, accusing the Kumaratunga regime of using the space provided by the cessation of hostilities to 'expand and modernise' the armed forces and setup 'a peace trap for a long-term war' (see Balasingham, 2004: 197 and 200), it only turned the tide of Western opinion against the organisation. The international community, led by the West, unreservedly condemned the LTTE for sabotaging the peace effort (Balasingham, 2004: 195). The LTTE claimed that it 'had justifiable reasons and compulsions to withdraw from the negotiating table' (Balasingham, 2004: 195). In the LTTE's view, Kumaratunga's government was not acting in good faith and 'failed to fulfil its pledges and promises', leading to the 'talks dragging on for more than six months without direction and progress' (Balasingham, 2004: 195–196). The LTTE also accused the government of showing a merciless and uncompromising attitude towards 'the Tamil population suffering enormously under the economic blockade and other bans imposed' (Balasingham, 2004: 196).

A number of attacks, including suicidal attacks, the LTTE carried out on economic targets in Colombo in response to Sri Lanka's invasion of Jaffna city in December 1995, only served to isolate the organisation further from world opinion. The killing of Sinhala settlers and Muslims attributed to the LTTE in the East in the early 1990s, and the LTTE's handling of other Tamil militant groups and politicians opposed to it, had already created the impression in the West that it was a ruthless authoritarian organisation. It was against this backdrop the LTTE launched attacks in Colombo. A notable LTTE attack that brought displeasure to the West was the suicidal truck bomb attack that it carried out on the World Trade Centre in Colombo in January 1996. Though no foreign nationals were injured in the attack, the very fact that the LTTE attacked the nerve centre of Sri Lanka's economy that housed hundreds of foreign and local financial and banking institutions was sufficient for the West to be convinced that the LTTE was seeking to destabilise the island's open market economy by creating a climate of insecurity in Colombo. Another attack by the LTTE 3 months earlier in October 1995 in Colombo, as the Sri Lankan military closed on Jaffna city, brought destruction to Sri Lanka's oil reserves. In April 1996, as the Sri Lankan military brought under its control the entire Jaffna peninsula, the LTTE attacked Colombo Harbour, possibly with the objective of reducing the state's shipping revenue (*Liberation Tigers*, 1996: 1; Varatharajan, 1996: 3). The hostile environment these attacks created for investors only served to reinforce Kumaratunga's (2001) frequent claims that the LTTE was an obstacle to 'the forward march of the Sri Lankan nation'. Western opinion against the LTTE became even more hostile after September 1997 when the LTTE attacked a Chinese ship manned by the Sri Lankan navy carrying a consignment purchased by an American company. The attack prompted an unnamed Western diplomat (cited in Athas, 1997) to warn that his government may consider taking 'joint retaliatory measures' against the LTTE if threats to the West's commercial interests on the island persisted.

In March 1996, 2 months after the LTTE's suicidal truck bomb attack on Colombo's World Trade Centre, the Pentagon launched a military programme code named *Operation Balanced Style* to train the Sri Lankan military to fight the LTTE. Initially, as part of this programme, the US military commandos trained Sri Lankan soldiers in jungle warfare; the US Navy Seals also conducted 'a joint exercise off the high seas' (Jansz, 1997). In 1997, these were increased to seven training programmes involving both the US Green Berets and the Navy Seals (Jansz, 1997). These programmes, however, had little impact on the LTTE as it had, following its withdrawal from Jaffna, consolidated and strengthened its fighting formations by inducting conventional weapons, including artilleries brought from funds raised overseas.

In an attempt to convince the LTTE that it would face further international isolation if it continued its armed struggle, in October 1997, the US proscribed the LTTE as a foreign terrorist organisation. Nine years later, spelling out the rationale behind the proscription, a US ambassador stated: 'The goal is not to ban or not ban the LTTE. The goal is not to get or not get money to the LTTE. The goal is for the LTTE to enter the political process, to negotiate with the government' (Lunstead, 2006a). Again, like *Operation Balanced Style*, the US ban did not have a great impact on the LTTE's fighting capabilities because its support base in the US was small: the Tamil Diaspora in the US is small, meaning the funds the LTTE was able to raise there, compared to other Western countries, were meagre. Even the Sri Lankan Foreign Minister Lakshman Kadirgamar (1997 cited in Vittachi, 1997) admitted that though the ban was made by the world's superpower, it was only of psychological significance.

Regardless, in convincing the US to proscribe the LTTE, the Kumaratunga regime can be attributed with having set the stage for the LTTE's international isolation and thus its eventual military defeat. Almost 3-and-a-half years later in February 2001, heeding the US call, the UK proscribed the LTTE as a terrorist organisation. The UK's proscription, compared to that of the US, can be said to have had a significant impact on the LTTE's ability to continue the armed struggle.

Earlier in November 1999, 2 years after the US ban, using conventional weapons acquired through funds collected in Western countries (including the UK), the LTTE launched a series of offensive operations, retaking the entire Killinochi and Mullaithivu districts and large swathes of rural areas in Mannar and Vavuniya districts, all in the Vanni region. In April 2000, the LTTE overran the major military complex at the gateway to the Jaffna peninsula, and took control of its southeastern coast. The LTTE's offensive operations moved with such speed that by June 2000, the LTTE had encircled Jaffna city. Using urgent military supplies sent by Russia, China, India, Pakistan and Israel, Sri Lanka was able to prevent the fall of Jaffna city, and later in February 2001, push the LTTE back to Jaffna's southeastern coast; the US navy also sent a warship to the international waters close to Jaffna, expressing solidarity with the Sri Lankan state (see *The Sunday Times*, 2001). However, the offensive operations of the LTTE sent a clear signal to both Sri Lanka and the West. Symbolic Western action against the LTTE would have no real value: regardless of the psychological impact the US ban had on the LTTE, it could not prevent the LTTE from developing its conventional fighting capabilities.

It was against this backdrop that the UK proscribed the LTTE in February 2001. A former LTTE overseas official told the author during an interview in October 2009 that the British ban had a significant impact on the ability of the LTTE to tap into the financial resources of the UK-based Tamil Diaspora, the second largest of the Tamil Diaspora, and thus its ability to engage in conventional offensive operations. This was apparent from the failure of the LTTE to launch any conventional offensive operations in 2001. In that year, the LTTE was only able to launch suicidal commando raids and engage in defensive operations.

The US-led GWoT following the Islamist terror attacks of 9/11 on the World Trade Centre in New York and the Pentagon can also be said to have had an impact on the ability of the LTTE to launch conventional offensive operations. In the words of Selvarajah Pathmanathan (2010), alias KP, the former head of LTTE's international arms procurement and shipping network, the GWoT had a major impact on the LTTE's overseas operations: 'Within 24 hours, the international community led by Western powers moved against all armed groups causing immense damage to our operations'. An aide to Pathmanathan told the author in an interview in March 2014 that fearing US reprisals, even arms dealers aligned with the North Korean government temporarily cut off ties with Pathmanathan.

Already a part of the liberal bandwagon, Sri Lanka tried to capitalise on the GWoT. Speculation was rife in Colombo that the GWoT was to be extended to the LTTE (Kleinfeld, 2004: 121). The LTTE theoretician Balasingham, then based in London, tried to save the LTTE from coming under the military radius of the US by condemning the terrorist attacks of 9/11 as 'a colossal human tragedy' and a 'brutal crime' (2001 cited in *Tamilnet*, 2001). His condemnation seemed to have worked. As the LTTE was already engaged in talks with the Norwegians on a ceasefire, and the Kumaratunga regime had shown its inability to defeat the LTTE on the battlefield, it seemed the US wanted to give the LTTE more time to give up its secessionist armed struggle through political negotiations. Thus, dismissing speculations that the GWoT was to be extended to the LTTE, the US embassy in Colombo announced: 'There is a distinction between the LTTE and the terrorists in the Middle East. So the US has not changed its stand in calling on the Sri Lankan Government to go for peace talks' (2001 cited in de Silva, 2001).

This did not mean that the West was prepared to adopt a lenient stance towards the LTTE. In an attempt to push the LTTE towards the negotiating table, Canada (which had the largest Tamil Diaspora) and Australia joined forces with the US and UK. Unlike the US and UK, Canada and Australia did not proscribe the LTTE as a terrorist organisation following 9/11, but imposed severe restrictions on the LTTE's ability to raise funds on their soil.

The collapse of Kumaratunga's coalition government in October 2001 led to her rival Wickremesinghe winning the general election 2 months later, with the pledge to 'open dialogue with the LTTE' and 'set up an Interim Council in the North and East for a limited duration' (United National Party, 2001). Whilst Kumaratunga in her capacity as President continued to remain the head of state, having secured the parliamentary majority required to form a new government, her rival Wickremesinghe assumed the office of Prime Minister. The stalemate on the battle front, the deterioration of Vanni region's economy and the danger that it faced in becoming a target in the GWoT contributed to the LTTE opting to negotiate with Sri Lanka through the Norwegians, culminating in the ceasefire agreement of February 2002.

By advocating neoliberal economic policies and making a commitment to uphold liberal democratic principles, Kumaratunga succeeded in making Sri Lanka a part of the post-Cold War liberal bandwagon. In doing so, she also succeeded in projecting the LTTE as a 'bad' species. As we saw earlier, the attacks the LTTE carried out on economic targets in Colombo only served to strengthen this perception. However, Kumaratunga's failure to defeat the LTTE militarily, which in turn had an impact on her ability to implement the neoliberal economic policies that she advocated, meant that she was, in the eyes of the West, no longer fit to lead the country in the direction of becoming a neoliberal economic success story.

However, Kumaratunga's rival Wickremesinghe, who was more enthused about transforming Sri Lanka into a vibrant open market economy than the former, emerged as the West's favourite in leading the country in the neoliberal direction (Lunstead, 2007: 27).

LTTE leader Pirapaharan's (2001) annual policy address a week before the December 2001 general election urging Sinhala voters to elect 'forces that seek peace' (implying Wickremesinghe) and reject those 'committed to militarism and war' (meaning Kumaratunga and her allies), can also be said to have convinced the West that Wickremesinghe was better poised to reach a political settlement with the LTTE. In his policy address, Pirapaharan also expressed his willingness to 'negotiate with the Sri Lankan government on a political framework that would satisfy the basic political aspirations of the Tamil people' (Pirapaharan, 2001). In other words, Pirapaharan seemed to have signalled that he felt comfortable dealing with Wickremesinghe. The LTTE's engagements with the Norwegians for a political settlement, coupled with these conciliatory signals from Pirapaharan, seems to have convinced the West that the LTTE could be disciplined through political negotiations to renounce its secessionist armed struggle, eventually leading to it transforming into a 'good' species and part of the global liberal order. This was evident from an interview given by Ashley Wills (2002), the US ambassador to Sri Lanka, after the 2002 ceasefire agreement was signed, wherein he opined that the LTTE seemed 'to have reached the conclusion that they will do a better job of representing the interests of the Tamil people by pursuing a peaceful solution rather than by continuing the so-called armed struggle'. Wills even stated that the US government had a 'fervent hope' that political negotiations between the Wickremesinghe regime and the LTTE would lead to the latter realising 'that the Tamils can have protection and respect in a United Sri Lanka' (Wills, 2002).

Tilting the military balance

A biopolitical analysis of the way the Wickremesinghe regime engaged in the 'peace' process indicates that its primary objective was to militarily weaken the LTTE through 'peace', eventually leading to its disarmament. Wickremesinghe seemed to have had calculated that if his government engaged in the 'peace' process with a strategy of war, it would be able to produce the effects of battle that his predecessors earlier sought to produce through military action. Wickremesinghe's strategy for the 'peace' process can thus be summarised in the following terms: preventing the LTTE from returning to war or make the return to war costly by creating an international safety net made up of international powers; strengthening the Sri Lankan military by enhancing its manpower and firepower, and upgrading its military strategies and tactics; curtailing the LTTE's ability to engage in conventional warfare in the future by interdicting its arms supplies at sea with the support of international powers; weakening the fighting spirit of LTTE cadres and their supporters by exposing them to the economic benefits of the 'peace' process through the lifting of the economic embargo; and preventing the LTTE from taking control of parts of the North and East that it had lost in previous years to the state by delaying the withdrawal of troops from occupied private and public lands. Though this strategy was never openly spelled out at the time of the 2002 ceasefire, it became apparent as political negotiations between both parties progressed.

From the outset, the Norwegian-facilitated 'peace' process had been an internationalised one. Though it was Norway that negotiated the ceasefire agreement with the LTTE and the Wickremesinghe regime, other international powers, especially the West and India, worked behind the scene to ensure that it came into force, to be followed by political negotiations.

Before the February 2001 ban, Britain complemented Norway's facilitatory role in the 'peace' process by interacting with the LTTE's Balasingham in London and Sri Lankan government officials in Colombo. Britain continued this role even after the proscription of the LTTE in February 2001, though no longer in an official capacity. This unofficial facilitatory role of Britain involved the allowing of Balasingham, a British citizen, to engage with the Norwegians and other Western diplomats in his capacity as the LTTE's chief negotiator and political strategist, despite the LTTE being proscribed in the UK as a terrorist organisation. In the words of Clare Short (2008 cited in Saunders, 2009: 12–13), the Secretary of State for International Development in Tony Blair's government, Balasingham was allowed to use the UK soil to advance the 'peace' process because the UK government 'realised that he was the most likely person' who was capable of persuading Pirapaharan 'to reduce his demands for a completely independent state'. Three months before the February 2001 ban, Britain's Foreign Office Minister Peter Hain spelled out the type of political solution that the LTTE should pursue. In a speech delivered in Colombo on 24 November 2000, Hain (2000) announced that 'whilst a Tamil Kingdom constitutionally split from the rest of the island will not receive recognition by Europe, the USA or indeed India', the LTTE's quest for 'self-determination and control over most if not all the key policies affecting daily life' of the Tamils 'would be supported by the international community'.

As well as repeatedly stressing that the conflict in Sri Lanka could not be resolved through military means, a year before the 2002 ceasefire, the US also hinted that it was backing Norway's facilitatory efforts by commending the latter and spelling out the framework of the political solution that it expected the LTTE and the Tamil people to accept (see Wills, 2001). In a speech in Jaffna in March 2001, whilst rejecting the idea of an independent Tamil state, the US Ambassador Wills announced that the US expected the future political solution to be one that treated the Tamil people 'equally, respectfully and with dignity within a democratic Sri Lankan state' (Wills, 2001).

When the ceasefire agreement was eventually signed in February 2002, Britain and the US were some of the first few countries to welcome it. Hailing the ceasefire agreement, Richard Boucher (2002 cited in Jaysinghe, 2002), then the spokesperson at the US Department of State and later the Assistant Secretary of State for South and Central Asia, made it a point to emphasise that the international community expected the 'peace' talks to lead to the LTTE ending its secessionist armed struggle: 'A political solution to this conflict in the context of an undivided Sri Lanka would be welcomed by the international community'. Though the British statement was different in content, it also hailed the ceasefire agreement. The British Foreign Office Minister Ben Bradshaw stated that his government hoped 'that all parties build on this agreement and continue to make progress towards a negotiated settlement that meets the aspirations of all communities in Sri Lanka' (2002 cited in *The Island*, 2002). Similar sentiments were also expressed by India

(*Tamilnet*, 2002), which had largely adopted a hands-off policy in the conflict following the assassination of Rajiv Gandhi in 1991, attributed to the LTTE.

The internationalisation of the 'peace' process was also evident from the way that Norway kept the US, Britain and India informed of developments. Every time the Norwegians made a visit to Colombo, Killinochi (the LTTE's administrative capital) and London (where Balasingham was based), they also visited New Delhi and Washington. In an interview with the author in September 2011, Suthaharan Nadarajah, an academic who acted as a resource person in the LTTE's negotiating team, suggested that in making trips around the world every time they visited Sri Lanka, the Norwegians demonstrated to the belligerents that their role in the conflict had the backing of the world's superpower, and they were keeping India informed of their moves.

The formation of an international ceasefire monitoring mechanism made up of former military officials from Norway and other Scandinavian countries, including those that were part of the EU, also internationalised the 'peace' process further. As well as monitoring and issuing reports on ceasefire violations, the ceasefire monitors also made it a point to stress to the LTTE that it had no right to use the ceasefire to strengthen its military forces. When there was speculation during the ceasefire that the LTTE was trying to develop an air wing, Hagrup Haukland (2005 cited in *Tamilnet*, 2005a), the head of international ceasefire monitors announced that while the Sri Lankan government 'had the legitimate responsibility for the defence of Sri Lanka and all of Sri Lanka, its land, sea and air', the LTTE could not stake similar claims as it was 'recognised only in so far as the ethnic conflict and the peace process'.

Wickremesinghe's efforts to form an international coalition to corner the LTTE received a boost when he visited the White House on 24 July 2002 and met President George W. Bush. In a televised address after returning from Washington, Wickremesinghe (2002 cited in *Zee News*, 2002) claimed that by obtaining the backing of Bush for his 'peace' initiative, he had set up an 'international safety net' for the 'peace' process. Wickremesinghe also announced: 'I have managed to secure US support towards improving our defence and intelligence set-up' (2002 cited in *Zee News*, 2002). In making these statements, Wickremesinghe hinted that the US, which had so far played a behind the scene role in the Norwegian facilitated 'peace' process, was now poised to play the role of the guarantor of the process, supported by other international powers. He also hinted that the US, by helping to improve Sri Lanka's defence and intelligence apparatuses, would help to tilt the military balance in the state's favour, thereby preventing the LTTE from returning to war or making the return to war costly. Four years later, when the prospects of LTTE returning to war seemed high, a US Ambassador echoed Wickremesinghe's sentiments: 'If the LTTE chooses to abandon peace, however, we want it to be clear, they will face a stronger, more capable and more determined Sri Lankan military. We want the cost of a return to war to be high' (2006 cited in Lunstead, 2007: 37).

This international safety net was formalised in June 2003 through the setting up of a loose body made up of international powers at a donor conference held in

Tokyo. Made up of the US, the EU, Norway and Japan, this body of international powers came to be known as the Tokyo Co-chairs. Though India refrained from becoming a part of this group, it signalled support for its formation by sending high ranking diplomats to attend the Tokyo Donor Conference. At the conference, the Tokyo Co-chairs outlined a road map for the 'peace' process, which included the LTTE disarming and accepting a federal political solution (see Ministry of Foreign Affairs Japan, 2003). Though the US had already made this call during another donor conference held in Oslo in November 2002 (see Armitage, 2002), this was the first time that it was joined by the EU, Norway and Japan. It was a clear signal that Wickremesinghe had scored a major victory in his diplomatic offensive to corner the LTTE.

By proscribing the LTTE in October 1997, in biopolitical terms the US could be said to have launched a war, parallel to that of Sri Lanka, against the LTTE on the diplomatic, legal and financial fronts. The US proscription sought to produce two effects of battle: militarily weakening the LTTE; and forcing it into a state of submission. In February 2001, Britain joined this war, followed by Canada and Australia in September that year. The formation of the Tokyo Co-chairs signalled that the EU, Norway and Japan had also joined this war on the diplomatic front. Already, the EU and Norway, being part of the international body of ceasefire monitors that monitored the ceasefire, were engaged in creating an effect of battle by trying to persuade the LTTE that it had no right to strengthen itself. By joining the Tokyo Co-chairs in June 2003, both the EU and Norway signalled that they stood by Wickremesinghe's efforts, and those of the US and other Western countries, to disarm the LTTE through 'peace'.

Back home, Wickremesinghe initiated a US-backed programme to strengthen the Sri Lankan military and the state's intelligence apparatus, as promised in July 2002 following his meeting with Bush. In late September 2002, 2 weeks after the LTTE and the Sri Lankan government formally began political negotiations in Thailand, a team of military officials from the 'US Pacific Command visited Sri Lanka and spent several weeks examining the entire Sri Lankan military', preparing a report on where its 'weaknesses were and how it could best address them' (Lunstead, 2007: 18). As well as being made up of high ranking officials from the US army, navy and air force, the team also included those specialising in special warfare, surface special warfare, aviation operations, aviation special operations, counter-terrorism, counter-insurgency, intelligence, counter-insurgency intelligence and psychological warfare (Athas, 2003). The key advice provided by the US military team was to enhance Sri Lanka's deep-sea fighting capabilities to interdict the LTTE's arm shipments (Moorcraft, 2012: 110). The US military team recommended that the Sri Lankan air force enhance its night fighting capabilities by upgrading with avionics and guided weapons (Moorcraft, 2012: 110). It also recommended the purchasing of more fighter jets from its ally Israel, rather than from Russia (Moorcraft, 2012: 110). The Americans also suggested the use of cluster bombs against the LTTE (Moorcraft, 2012: 110). In an attempt to demonstrate its 'commitment to strengthening the Sri Lankan armed forces', the US also enrolled Sri Lankan onto its Foreign Military Financing programme, thus providing grants for the purchasing of US military equipment (Lunstead, 2007: 17). In June 2004, America donated a large ship, the US Coast Guard Cutter 'Courageous', which after being transformed into a warship, boosted the Sri Lankan navy's deep-sea fighting capabilities against the Sea Tigers, the LTTE's naval wing (Lunstead, 2007: 17).

Heeding US advice, the Sri Lankan navy also set up an unofficial cordon around the Northern and Eastern seas, sinking two LTTE ships in international waters in March and June 2003. A medium-sized armed LTTE vessel was also sunk in the Northern waters (Balasingham, 2004: 419 and 423). Though the LTTE registered strong protests against the sinking and claimed that they were commercial and fishing vessels, these were of no avail because the LTTE could not prove that they were engaged in fishing or commercial operations.

Unlike Kumaratunga who, during the 1994–1995 peace talks, partially relaxed the economic embargo but refused to lift it fully, Wickremesinghe lifted it completely. Though this allowed the LTTE to increase its revenues, thereby assisting it to develop and expand its *de-facto* state apparatus, it also had a negative impact on the fighting spirit of its members and supporters. Food and other commodities were no longer scarce as a result of the lifting of the embargo. A number of exiled LTTE cadres told the author during interviews in 2015 that many of the LTTE cadres made use of the opportunity provided by the ceasefire to get married. This meant that new houses had to be constructed for them, as well as for senior cadres already married and with children, as opposed to the LTTE housing the majority of its bachelor and single woman cadres in large military bases. Lured by the comfortable life of their school day friends who had refrained from joining the armed struggle and instead went abroad seeking better opportunities, a large number of LTTE's fighting cadres began leaving the movement upon completing the compulsory 7 years of service. Many female LTTE cadres who earlier played frontline roles in its military also returned home, after marriage, to traditional roles allocated to women in Tamil society, i.e., cooking, house-keeping, looking after their husbands and bearing children. These led to the depletion of the LTTE's manpower.

The lifting of the economic embargo also affected the LTTE's ability to compensate for its manpower losses by recruiting new cadres from its support base in Vanni and other areas of the North and East; with the return of normalcy, many of them saw no need for the resumption of the armed struggle. Thus, in February 2003, in a work penned in the LTTE's official organ under the pseudonym Viyasan, Puthuvai Ratnathurai (2003a: 16), the head of LTTE's cultural affairs wing, lamented that the younger generations of Vanni were behaving as if there would be no war in the future. Four months later, as there was no progress in political negotiations, Ratnathurai (2003b: 16) chastised the Tamils for being overwhelmed by the economic benefits of 'peace', and warned that if the LTTE was weakened militarily, the Tamil land would be occupied by their enemies.

The high level of international involvement in the 'peace' process also made the cost of returning to war very high for the LTTE, at least in the eyes of the general Tamil public. In particular, the US invasion of Iraq in 2003 made many Tamils doubt whether the LTTE would ever risk returning to war. Considering Wickremesinghe's closeness to the US, some Tamils even suggested to the author during the 'peace' process that Pirapaharan was likely to face the fate of Sadam Hussein if he ever returned to war.

The increase in LTTE's revenues during the 'peace' process through the taxes it levied on local traders and the funds it raised abroad seemed to have had no value in strategic terms. With the Sri Lankan navy sinking the LTTE's vessels, it became virtually impossible for the LTTE to bring in arms shipments. Thus, the revenues it generated during the 'peace' process could not be translated into tangible military assets.

Taking advantage of the international safety net, the Wickremesinghe regime also refused to honour some of its obligations in the 2002 ceasefire agreement. One of those was the withdrawal of troops from private lands, places of worship and schools (Balasingham, 2004: 493–495). Sarath Fonseka (2003 cited in Balasingham, 2004: 409), the commander of the Sri Lankan army, announced that his forces would be withdrawn from occupied public and private lands only after the LTTE agreed to 'disarm its cadres and decommission of its long range weapons'. Though Articles 2.2 to 2.4 of the 2002 ceasefire agreement stipulated troop withdrawal from those places, neither Norway nor other Western powers made any effort to prevail on the Wickremesinghe regime to honour its obligations (for the full version of the ceasefire agreement, see Balasingham, 2004: 491–501). This underscored the fact that Wickremesinghe's diplomatic offensive against the LTTE at the international level had reached the stage in which the West had become completely supportive of his efforts to prevent the LTTE from obtaining any strategic advantages through the 'peace' process.

The LTTE's 'peace' strategy

When the ceasefire agreement was signed in 2002, the LTTE's strategy seemed to be obtaining international legitimacy for its *de-facto* state by taking advantage of Wickremesinghe's promise to establish an interim administration for the North and East; showing the international community that its armed struggle had been a legitimate one in accordance with the principles of the right to self-determination as enunciated in the UN Charter; exploring a political solution for the regional autonomy of the North and East; developing its conventional fighting capabilities so that in the event that Sri Lanka refuses to grant a political solution, resume the armed struggle to establish a Tamil state. This strategy can be inferred from an analysis of Balasingham's work, *War and Peace*, published in 2004, two interviews he gave to a Colombo weekly in November 2002 and March 2003, and Pirapaharan's annual policy address of November 2002 (see Balasingham, 2002; 2003; 2004: 366 and 383; Pirapaharan, 2002).

When the Wickremesinghe regime retracted from its election promise to set up an interim administration at the first round of political negotiations held in Thailand in September 2002 citing constitutional impediments, and instead suggested the creation of a 'pre-interim provisional mechanism with limited powers to undertake humanitarian and reconstruction activities', Pirapaharan initially showed flexibility by accepting such a proposal (Balasingham, 2004: 383 and 385). Though Pirapaharan was not happy with the Wickremesinghe regime's suggestion, he accepted Balasingham's advice that they 'should impress upon the international community that the LTTE was genuine and serious in pursuit of peace and that the Tamil people had urgent humanitarian needs' by showing flexibility (Balasingham, 2004: 385). He even made appointments to the sub-committees created as part of the pre-interim mechanism (see Balasingham, 2004: 389).

Two months later, Pirapaharan (2002) announced in his annual policy address of November 2002 that he was 'prepared to consider favourably a political framework that offers substantial regional autonomy and self-determination' for the North and East. A week later, during the third round of political negotiations held in Oslo, the LTTE and the Sri Lankan government agreed to explore a federal political solution (Balasingham, 2004: 403). This was followed by Pirapaharan forming a political affairs committee to explore federal models in Europe (Balasingham, 2003). A federal political solution, as the alternative to outright secession, seemed to have formed the LTTE's official policy since the time of negotiations with the Kumaratunga regime in 1995. In February 1995, the LTTE urged the Kumaratunga regime to 'present a proposal for a federal solution encompassing the North and East' that would 'give the Tamils regional autonomy' (see *Liberation Tigers*, 1995: 1; Balasingham, 1995). A month later, during a meeting with Western diplomats in Jaffna, Balasingham (1995 cited in Schaffer, 1995) announced that the LTTE was willing to consider a federal solution modelled on 'the American or Australian systems'. Eight years later in March 2003, in an interview with the Colombo weekly *The Sunday Leader*, Balasingham went on to spell out the federal political solution that the LTTE was willing to consider:

> Within a federal autonomy there will be regional courts for the Tamils, regional police for the Tamils and regional administration for the Tamils. The north and east will become a federal unit where the Tamils will have their own administration, own judicial system, own police, which is linked to the rest of Sri Lanka and where you will have the centre and regions sharing power. This is what we mean.
>
> (Balasingham, 2003)

In another interview with the same weekly earlier in November 2002, Balasingham (2002) stated that the LTTE expected 'a security system for the Tamil people' even in 'a federal system', so that there will be 'a military force' to 'protect life and interest' of the Tamils.

However, in April 2003, there was a marked shift in the LTTE's strategy for engaging in the 'peace' process. In April 2003, in the run up to the Tokyo Donor Conference, America held a preliminary donor conference in Washington. Citing the ban on the LTTE, the US refused to invite its representatives to the donor conference. Protesting against the exclusion, the LTTE announced that it was suspending political negotiations until Sri Lanka implemented the ceasefire agreement fully. The LTTE also announced that it would be boycotting the Tokyo Donor Conference. In the words of Balasingham: 'Marginalisation from the [Washington] meeting, Mr Pirapaharan felt, was a humiliation, totally unacceptable to an organisation representing the Tamil people and seeking to enjoy equal status as a party in negotiations' (2004: 430–431). Pirapaharan also demanded the Wickremesinghe regime fulfil its election promise of setting up an interim administration for the North and East. A senior LTTE official told the author during an interview in 2009 that Pirapaharan's renewed his demand for an interim administration following the advice of the LTTE's US based legal advisor Rudrakumaran that the US and the rest of the international community would not consider such a demand to be a hardline approach because they were instrumental in creating a similar mechanism in South Sudan. Balasingham's decision, citing ill health, to stay away from Pirapaharan's discussions with Western diplomats on an interim administration in May 2003 suggests that he was reluctant to engage in the 'peace' process along this line. Though Balasingham echoed Pirapaharan's demand for an interim administration in the letters he wrote to the Sri Lankan government and the Norwegians in May and June 2003 (see Balasingham, 2004: 446–458), his absence in the process for formulating the LTTE's proposals for an interim administration, which was led by his deputy in the LTTE's negotiating team and the head of political wing, S. P. Thamilchelvan (assisted by Rudrakumaran), created speculations that he may have been sidelined by Pirapaharan (Athas, 2003). The US Ambassador Lunstead (2003), in a cable sent to the State Department in Washington in August 2003, which was later released by WikiLeaks, expressed grave concerns about Balasingham's absence: 'If the experienced Balasingham remains out of the picture, it could represent a set-back for the peace process'.

An analysis of Lunstead's cable reveals that there was much confusion within the Western diplomatic community and among Tamil parliamentarians as to what may have happened to Balasingham. British diplomats in Colombo suggested that Balasingham, who had 3 years earlier undergone a kidney transplant in Oslo, was ill (Lunstead, 2003). However, British intelligence sources claimed that whilst keeping away from the LTTE's formulating process for a proposal on an interim administration, Balasingham had made personal trips outside the UK, meaning he was not really ill (Lunstead, 2003). Suresh Premachandran, a Tamil parliamentarian told US diplomats that Pirapaharan and Balasingham 'had had a bit of falling out over participation at the Tokyo donors conference' (Lunstead, 2003). Premachandran claimed that 'Balasingham had wanted the LTTE to go, but Prabhakaran had ordered the LTTE to boycott the June 2003 conference' (Lunstead, 2003). However, Kjersti Tromsdahl, the political officer at the Norwegian Embassy in Colombo told US diplomats: 'Balasingham appeared to be pacing himself, preparing for possible talks with the Sri Lankan government later this year [2003]' (Lunstead, 2003). Whatever the truth, Balasingham returned to forefront of the 'peace' process in November 2003 after the LTTE's interim administration proposals were rejected by Kumaratunga, in her capacity as the head of state, who also, citing the LTTE's proposals, took over the country's, defence, interior and financial ministries from Wickremesinghe. Following Balasingham's return,

Pirapaharan (2003) also softened his stance on the interim administration, claiming that the LTTE renewed its demand for an interim administration because it was 'not feasible to find a permanent solution to the Tamil national conflict immediately within a short period' of time.

Regardless, the shift in the LTTE's strategy in April 2003 to demand an interim administration, as opposed to its readiness earlier to explore a federal political solution, and its decision to boycott the Tokyo Donor Conference can be said to have made the West, especially the US, develop suspicions about its intentions in engaging in the 'peace' process and its willingness to compromise for a political solution instead of outright secession. In a cable sent to the US State Department in Washington in November 2003, Lunstead's deputy James Entwistle (2003) suggested that the future of the 'peace' process seemed to hinge on the ability of the LTTE to compromise and give up its strategy of 'all or nothing'. It can also be said that the shift in the LTTE's strategy made the West conclude that unless there was concerted diplomatic pressure on the LTTE, it may even return to war. This was reflected in a cable sent by Lunstead (2006b) to the US State Department 3 years later, shortly after the resumption of direct negotiations between the LTTE and the Sri Lankan government in February 2006, wherein he claimed: 'If our interlocutors [the Norwegians] are correct, international pressure played a key role in convincing the Tigers to return to the table'.

The LTTE's uncompromising position on the interim administration and its decision to boycott the Tokyo Donor Conference could also be attributed to the influence of the Tamil military analyst Sivaram (2004), who, once a merciless critic of the LTTE (see Chapter 4), had transformed from the late 1990s into a diehard LTTE supporter, becoming the editor of the pro-LTTE website *Tamilnet* and praising Pirapaharan as 'the chief political strategist of the Tamils'. Sivaram scoffed at the idea of the US helping Sri Lanka to defeat the LTTE if the latter returned to war. In an article written in September 2002, 3 weeks before the team from the US Pacific Command visited Sri Lanka, Sivaram (2002) argued: 'The LTTE is no Taliban. It is easily the most ferocious and resiliently compact conventional fighting force in the world today'. Sivaram even went to extent of allaying fears on the part of the LTTE and its supporters that the closeness of the US with Sri Lanka in the post-2002 ceasefire period was not intended to strengthen the Sri Lankan state militarily but instead 'aimed at critically enhancing the capabilities of the US Navy and Air Force to project power in South Asia, Central Asia and the Arabian Sea' (Sivaram, 2002). In another article, Sivaram (2003a) claimed that the international community can do nothing to prevent the LTTE from returning to war because the LTTE had 'proven capability to wage conventional and guerrilla war with limited supplies'. For Sivaram, the only option that the international community had for preventing the LTTE from returning to war was to 'hope' that it 'may remain locked in the talks for a long time' (Sivaram, 2003a).

Sivaram also took several hits at Balasingham for agreeing to explore a federal political solution. In an article published in the early part of April 2003, shortly before the LTTE withdrew from political negotiations, Sivaram (2003b) argued that by falling 'for federalism', the LTTE (read: Balasingham) had allowed 'the

US-British coalition' to successfully drive 'a wedge between the Tamil population and the very political basis of the LTTE's armed forces'. When the LTTE boycotted the Tokyo Donor Conference, however, Sivaram (2003c) praised the LTTE. He even suggested that had the LTTE's peace delegation attended the Tokyo Donor Conference, 'their mere presence plus the customary political pleasantries by Mr. Balasingham would have helped the Sri Lankan state to bury the stark truth about the Sinhala polity's constitutional intransigence even deeper into the quicksand of political obfuscation' (Sivaram, 2003c). Toeing the line of Rudrakumaran, whom he had in the early 1990s chastised for his position on the Muslim question, Sivaram also claimed that the LTTE's proposals for an interim administration were 'modelled on the Machakos Protocol', that led to an interim administration being set up for South Sudan with the backing of the US, UK, the EU and India (Sivaram, 2004). In Sivaram's (2004) opinion, the LTTE's proposals for an interim administration formed the basis of the 'concepts and structures of final solution', as opposed to the federal political solution envisaged by Balasingham in which powers were to be shared between the centre and the regional government for the North and East.

The influence of Sivaram on the LTTE's post-April 2003 strategy was evident from the condolence statement issued by Pirapaharan following the former's assassination in April 2005 by suspected Sri Lankan paramilitary operatives. In his statement, Pirapaharan (2005: 14) bestowed Sivaram with the title *Maamanithar*, meaning the 'Great Human Being', and praised him for having worked 'relentlessly to create political awareness among the Tamils' and thereby 'strengthening the Tamil nationalist spirit'. The LTTE's official organ also praised Sivaram, claiming that his 'hard hitting' words exposed 'Sinhala chauvinism' and became 'wakeup calls for the Tamils' (*Liberation Tigers*, 2005: 14).

Though the LTTE's post-April 2003 strategy helped to project itself among its cadres and supporters as an organisation committed to the goal of establishing a Tamil state, it also strengthened Wickremesinghe's diplomatic offensive to isolate it at the international level. This was evident from the response of the US to the LTTE's proposals for an interim administration. The LTTE's proposals, among other controversial demands, demanded the Sri Lankan state to transfer all the powers of governance that it had been exercising in the North and East to the proposed LTTE-dominated interim administration (Balasingham, 2004: 508). Commenting on these demands, Richard Armitage (2003 cited in *The Island*, 2003), the US Deputy Secretary of State, warned that the LTTE's proposals went 'outside the bounds of what was envisioned in Oslo [federalism] and Tokyo [the LTTE's disarmament]'.

In February 2004, Kumaratunga sacked Wickremesinghe's government and in the subsequent election held in April that year, her coalition returned to power. This resulted in a further setback for resuming political negotiations, with Kumaratunga refusing to talk to the LTTE on the basis of its proposals for an interim administration. The elections coincided with the LTTE's Eastern military commander Karuna's split from the LTTE. Taking advantage of the split, Kumaratunga accommodated Karuna and his loyalists in the state's paramilitary forces, providing logistical and financial support to Karuna's men to destabilise the LTTE-controlled areas in the East and assassinate LTTE leaders. The West, however, refrained from prevailing on Kumaratunga to return to talks or disband the Karuna Group. It seemed that the West was prepared to allow the Kumaratunga regime to militarily weaken the LTTE through the Karuna Group before prevailing on it to return to political negotiations.

The LTTE's strategy in countering Kumaratunga's proxy war isolated it further at the international level. Had the LTTE confined its strategy to the Karuna Group, it may have avoided the wrath of the West. However, its decision to carry out attacks on the Sri Lankan military using its own paramilitary force, the *Makkal Padai*, and the killing of its political opponents, especially members of anti-LTTE groups aligned to the state, while the ceasefire agreement was in force, only served to isolate it further. The proxy war between the LTTE and the Kumaratunga regime culminated in the killing of Sri Lanka's Foreign Minister Lakshman Kadirgamar in August 2005. Though the LTTE denied involvement in the killing, the West was not prepared to believe it was not responsible for the act (Peterson, 2005). Following Kadirgamar's killing, the Norwegian Foreign Minister Jan Peterson sent a toughly worded letter to Pirapaharan, warning him of international backlash:

> The killings and counter-killings over the last few months have been watched with mounting concern by Norway and the international community. Along with the continued recruitment of children to the LTTE, this has created distrust about the LTTE's intentions as regards the peace process.
>
> The assassination of Foreign Minister Kadirgamar has exacerbated the situation. It is not up to Norway to draw conclusions about the criminal investigations now under way in Colombo, or on any other judicial matter in relation with the killings. However, public perception both in Sri Lanka and internationally is that the LTTE is responsible. This public perception is a political reality.
>
> The LTTE needs to respond to this situation in a way that demonstrates continued commitment to the peace process. I see it as my obligation to make clear to you the political choice now facing the LTTE. If the LTTE does not take a positive step forward at this critical juncture, the international reaction could be severe.
>
> (Peterson, 2005)

Whilst the foreign minister of India and high-ranking Western diplomats attended Kadirgamar's funeral to express solidarity with the Sri Lankan state, the EU announced that it was imposing a travel ban on the LTTE in Europe (European Union-UN, 2005). The EU also announced that it was 'actively considering the formal listing of the LTTE as a terrorist organisation'. It was a warning that the West's war on the LTTE on the legal and financial fronts was being expanded from North America, Australia and the UK to mainland Europe.

Another political blunder the LTTE committed was the way it handled the controversy over the issue of child soldiers. For the LTTE, child soldiers were not a controversial phenomenon. Pirapaharan himself became a militant at the age of 15, joining the Tamil Student Federation in 1970. He became a wanted figure by the Sri Lankan police at the age of 16, before founding the Tamil New Tigers a year later at the age of 17 (Balasingham, 2004: 25). The LTTE's political wing leader Thamilchelvan also joined the LTTE at the age of 16 in 1984. Thus, in the 1980s and the early 1990s, it was not an unusual sight to see in the LTTE-held areas Tamil teenagers carrying assault rifles or playing the role of military commanders. However, with the international community adopting from the mid-1990s onwards an increasingly hostile position on the issue of child soldier, the LTTE came under pressure to end child recruitment. In May 1998, Olara Ottunu, the UN's Special Envoy for Children in Armed Conflicts, visited Vanni and held talks with Balasingham and Thamilchelvan to end child recruitment (*Tamilnet*, 1998). In February 2002, as the LTTE signed the ceasefire agreement with the Sri Lankan government, the *Optional Protocol to the Convention on the Rights of the Child on the Involvement of Children in Armed Conflict* also came into force, with Article 4 of the Protocol strictly prohibiting armed groups from recruiting or using 'in hostilities persons under the age of 18 years' (UN, 2002). This increased international pressure on the LTTE to refrain from recruiting anyone under the age of 18 years, resulting in Balasingham (2003 cited in Macan-Markar, 2003) announcing in January 2003: 'We will make a pledge to the United Nations that child recruitment will never take place'. Balasingham understood the implications of the LTTE contravening international norms.

However, with Balasingham's influence within the LTTE waning from April 2003 onwards, the LTTE adopted a confrontationist course with the UN on the question of child soldiers. In February 2007, whilst making a pledge that it would not recruit anyone under the age of 17, the LTTE announced that it would not adhere to Article 4 of the Optional Protocol until all states agreed to recruit individuals over the age of 18 (see *Tamilnet*, 2007). Two years before the announcement, the LTTE's legal advisor Rudrakumaran (2005: 83) argued that the LTTE did not have to adhere to the Optional Protocol. He even went on to suggest that if the LTTE adhered to the Optional Protocol, it would be in Sri Lanka's favour: 'There is no provision in the Optional Protocol for a national liberation movement and/or a *de-facto* government like the LTTE. Application of the Optional Protocol, which has not yet become customary international law, will favour the Sri Lankan state against the LTTE' (Rudrakumaran, 2005: 83). This confrontationist position adopted by the LTTE only served to isolate it further at the international level.

The LTTE antagonised the West further by enforcing a boycott of the November 2005 presidential election in the North and East, which led to the pro-Western Wickremesinghe losing the election and his statist rival Mahinda Rajapaksa becoming the head of state. In his election manifesto *Mahinda Chintana*, Rajapaksa (2005: 34) announced that he would overturn a number of key free market policies that his predecessors, commencing with Jayewardene, brought into force on the island. Rajapaksa also promised to formulate a 'national economic policy' by 'integrating the positive attributes of free market with domestic aspirations in order to ensure a modern and balanced approach where domestic enterprises can be supported while encouraging foreign investments' (Rajapaksa, 2005: 39). These announcements signified a marked shift from his predecessor Kumaratunga and rival Wickremesinghe's free market economic policies. Given Rajapaksa's hardline position on the Tamil national question, had the 2.5 million Tamils been allowed to vote, many would have voted for the pro-Western Wickremesinghe. The LTTE's enforced boycott prevented this from happening, with Rajapaksa winning with a narrow margin of 180,786 votes (*Tamilnet*, 2005b). The West was outraged. The US and the EU condemned the LTTE (*The Sunday Times*, 2005).

The LTTE's decision to engineer Wickremesinghe's defeat can partly be attributed to a statement made by one of his aides during the election campaign that he had engineered Karuna's split and created conditions for US and Indian troops to join the war to defeat the LTTE in the event that it returned to war (*Uthayan*, 2005: 1 and 16). It could also be attributed to the LTTE's calculation that if the pro-Western Wickremesinghe lost the election, the international safety net he created during the 'peace' process would crumble because the statist Rajapaksa was not close to the West. This was, however, not what actually happened.

Due to international pressure, both the LTTE and the Rajapaksa regime held direct talks in Switzerland in February 2006. However, the proxy war escalated with killings and counter-killings by both parties even after direct talks. In response, in April 2006, the Canadian government proscribed the LTTE as a terrorist organisation, claiming that its action had been 'long overdue' (cited in *Tamil Week*, 2006). A month later, the EU followed suit. Two months before the EU ban, both India and the US reached an agreement that there should be 'greater international cooperation on interdicting' the LTTE's 'fundraising and weapons procurement' (Lunstead, 2006c). In the words of Amandeep Singh Gill (2006 cited in Lunstead, 2006c), the first secretary of the Indian High Commission in Colombo, the international community had to act beyond the mere proscriptions of the LTTE because the 'Tigers have calculated that the [Tokyo] Co-chairs and the rest of the international community may "fire paper missiles" at them but will do nothing that will really hurt LTTE interests'.

Commenting on the EU ban, Balasingham (2006a) warned that '[d]iscredited, humiliated and globally isolated by world governments, the LTTE leadership may stiffen its attitude and adopt a singular, individualistic approach, as if it is freed from the constraints of international norms and pressures'. This was exactly what happened. A week after the EU ban, during a meeting with the Norwegian's in Oslo, the LTTE delegation led by its political wing leader Thamilchelvan (2006 cited in The Royal Norwegian Government, 2006), assisted by its legal advisor Rudrakumaran, announced that the LTTE leadership was 'not ready to accept' ceasefire monitors 'from states which separately or by membership in international organisations have included the LTTE on lists for the application of specific measures to combat terrorism'. Thamilchelvan (2006 cited in *Tamilnet*, 2006a) also accused Norway and the international community of failing to prevail on the Rajapaksa regime to end violence.

As it became more apparent that the LTTE was to face complete international isolation, Balasingham made a final attempt to prevent India from also turning on the LTTE. In late June 2006, in an interview with the Indian television channel NDTV, Balasingham (2006b) expressed regret for the assassination of Rajiv Gandhi, stating 'it is a great tragedy, a monumental historical tragedy', and urged 'the government of India and people of India to be magnanimous to put the past behind and to approach the ethnic question in a different perspective'. Complementing the Indian Prime Minister Manmohan Singh for 'admonishing' the Rajapaksa government earlier for inflicting violence on the Tamil people and suggesting a 'form of regional autonomy for the Tamils', Balasingham suggested that India could act 'diplomatically and politically, persuading Sri Lanka and the LTTE to seek a negotiated settlement' (Balasingham, 2006b). The LTTE leadership in Vanni, however, seems to have had a different policy stance on the question of reconciling with India. In an interview also to NDTV a week after Balasingham's interview, when asked about the LTTE's position on Rajiv Gandhi's assassination, Thamilchelvan (2006a) claimed that 'as the LTTE was putting its energy in winning the Tamil struggle', it was 'not willing to dig into the past, evoke bitter memories, and create another controversial scenario'. When the NDTV journalist pressed him on the rationale behind Balasingham's decision to express regret over Rajiv Gandhi's assassination, Thamilchelvan went on to claim that the LTTE's 'national leadership' (meaning Pirapaharan) had stated its position on the assassination 'many years ago' (which was denial of involvement), and he was not willing to give any 'new interpretations' to it (Thamilchelvan, 2006a). Thamilchelvan even suggested that Balasingham's statement of regret was his personal opinion: 'If Anton Balasingham has told you [he regretted Rajiv Gandhi's assassination], then it is he who you should ask' (Thamilchelvan, 2006a). Following this, Balasingham disappeared from the Tamil political scene, and 6 months later died from cancer of the gall bladder.

Though Pirapaharan posthumously bestowed Balasingham with the title, *Voice of the Nation*, Thamilchelvan's statement 6 months earlier created the perception that Balasingham had fallen out with Pirapaharan on the question of reconciling with India over Rajiv Gandhi's assassination. In the diplomatic circles, though Balasingham was known to be a hardliner close to Pirapaharan, he was nevertheless regarded as a 'pragmatic hardliner' and an 'independent minded' person (Lunstead, 2003). Thamilchelvan, however, was largely seen to be lacking stature; he was seen to be 'a creature of Prabhakaran than an influential actor within the LTTE circles in his own right' (Lunstead, 2003). In other words, in the diplomatic circles, whilst Balasingham was understood to be someone who was capable of speaking both independently and on behalf of Pirapaharan, Thamilchelvan was largely seen to be the mouthpiece of Pirapaharan. It is therefore plausible that Indian policy makers would have taken into consideration Thamilchelvan's statement, rather than Balasingham's to be the official position of the LTTE leadership on the question of Rajiv Gandhi's assassination and India's future role in Sri Lanka.

The fact that Sri Lanka was able to openly launch offensive military operations against the LTTE without any opposition from India less than 3 weeks after Thamilchelvan's statement suggests that this may have been the case. In the words of the Sri Lankan military general Udaya Perera (2012: 47), who played a leading role in the military offensives against the LTTE, the Rajapaksa regime launched offensive military operations against the LTTE only after receiving the backing of India, the West and other members of the international community. Mahinda Rajapaksa even set up a high powered team to lobby India so that it would not intervene in the LTTE's favour (Perera, 2012: 47). The team was led by his brother and special emissary Basil Rajapaksa, and made up of his private secretary Lalith Weeratunga, his brother and defence secretary Gotabaya Rajapaksa (who acted as the *de-facto* defence minister) and the secretary to the foreign ministry (Perera, 2012: 47). In sum, the Rajapaksa regime openly launched military offensives against the LTTE only after the war launched by Wickremesinghe through 'peace' in 2002, and continued by Kumaratunga and briefly by Mahinda Rajapaksa himself, on the diplomatic front had been won, thus adhering to Tzu's (1998: 28) suggestion of seeking battle only after it is won.

When the 2002 ceasefire agreement was signed, the LTTE, partly as a result of Kumaratunga's diplomatic manoeuvres and partly as a result of the way it responded to her military offensives (by attacking Sri Lanka's economic targets), had emerged as a 'bad' species in the eyes of the West. Yet, instead of seeking to eliminate the LTTE as Kumaratunga wanted to do following 9/11, the West was prepared to biopolitically discipline it into a 'good' species through political negotiations: the West wanted the LTTE to be transformed into a political outfit by agreeing to disarm and accept a federal political solution. However, as the 'peace' processes proceeded, the LTTE's uncompromising stance on an interim administration with exclusive governing powers for the North and East, as opposed to its willingness in the early stages of political negotiations to explore a federal political solution that adhered to the principles of power sharing between the centre and the region, created the perception that it was not willing to settle for anything less than outright secession, and was using the space provided by 'peace' to prepare for another war to create an independent Tamil state. This in turn strengthened Wickremesinghe's diplomatic offensive to isolate the LTTE at the international level. The LTTE's response to Kumaratunga's use of Karuna to launch a proxy war, and the way it handled the controversy over the issue of child soldiers from April 2003 onwards, only strengthened the perception of the West that it was a 'bad' species that could not be disciplined into a 'good' species through political negotiations. The failure of the LTTE to capitalise on Balasingham's conciliatory gestures towards India whilst Sri Lanka set up a high powered team to lobby for India's support strengthened this perception. Thus when the Rajapaksa regime launched military offensives to annihilate the LTTE, in biopolitical terms it had become a species that the West and India felt could not be disciplined through 'peace'.

Vanquishing the 'enemy'

When Sri Lanka launched its military offensives in July 2006, between 550,000 and 600,000 Tamils remained in the LTTE-held territories: 150,000 in the East and between 400,000 and 450,000 in the Northern Vanni region. From the outset, one of Sri Lanka strategies for defeating the LTTE was to flush out the Tamil civilian population from its territories. This had political and military benefits for the state. At the political level, Sri Lanka could claim that the majority of Tamils who lived in the LTTE territories did so due to compulsion and crossed over to government-controlled areas when they were given the opportunity to do so. Flushing out the civilian population also had the potential to render the LTTE's *de-facto* state administration meaningless, as it would have no people to govern in the territories it controlled. At the military level, the absence of civilians in the LTTE-held territories had the potential to render it without a recruitment base, and thus its ability to increase its manpower.

For the LTTE, the civilians in its areas also formed the backbone of its logistical support units: their services were used by the LTTE to transport combat units, food and military supplies to and from the frontlines, construct bunkers both on the frontlines and rear bases, care for the injured fighters in hospitals and contribute dry rations (see UN, 2015: 129–132).

The LTTE also had auxiliary forces made up of civilians. An analysis of the LTTE's official lists of deceased combatants and the issues of its official organ *Liberation Tigers* reveal that it had at least six auxiliary units. Of these, *Ellai Padai* (the Border Force), *Kiramiya Padaiyani* (Village Defence Force) and *Makkal Padai* (People's Force) were made up of part-time volunteers; *Thamil Eela Thesiya Thunai Padai* (Tamil Eelam National Auxiliary Force) and *Thamil Eela Thesiya Iranuvam* (Tamil Eelam National Army) were made up of salaried combatants; and *Poruthavi Padai* (War Support Force) was made up of a mixture of part-time volunteers and conscripts. Whilst the *Thesiya Thunai Padai* was formed in the early 1990s to defend the border villages of the Vanni region, the *Ellai Padai* and *Kiramiya Padaiyani* were formed after the LTTE retreated from Jaffna and set up its bases in the Vanni region in late 1995/early 1996. These three auxiliary units helped the LTTE to compensate for the manpower shortages it faced in the late 1990s to counter Sri Lanka's offensives in Vanni. The other auxiliary units came into existence from mid-2005 onwards when the proxy war escalated. Though for the best part of the LTTE's existence its fighting formations, both regular and auxiliary, were made up of volunteers, with the resumption of hostilities it also resorted to conscriptions (see Ravi, 2006: 4; UN, 2015: 128).

All of these factors made it imperative for Sri Lanka to flush out the civilian population from the LTTE territories. As we will see, Sri Lanka used three tactics to realise this strategy: constantly bombard LTTE targets and civilian settlements, leading to death and injuries among LTTE cadres and civilians; curtail the flow of medicine needed to treat LTTE cadres and civilians injured in airstrikes and artillery attacks; starve LTTE cadres and the civilian population by limiting the flow of food. All these, Sri Lanka seems to have calculated, would make life untenable in the LTTE-controlled areas, thus making civilians flee towards government-held territories.

This implied, in biopolitical terms, Sri Lanka's classification, though not officially spelled out, of the civilian population living in LTTE areas into two categories: the 'bad' species and the 'submissive' species. Whilst, those who opted to remain in the LTTE-held territories or could not leave those areas were placed in the category of the 'bad' species whom the state could clump together with the LTTE as 'terrorists' and eliminate, others who opted to leave the LTTE-held areas and seek refuge in government-controlled territories were placed in the category of 'submissive' species who qualified for the right to live. Becoming a 'submissive' species did not mean that civilians who opted to leave the LTTE areas automatically qualified to become the 'good' species. As we will see in the next chapter, some of the Tamil who were placed in the category of the 'submissive' species, but later identified as the 'bad' species, that is 'terrorists' or 'terrorist sympathisers', were also eliminated by the state. This way, Sri Lanka's biopolitics can be said to have gone beyond the traditional binary division of populations as 'good' and 'bad'. In Sri Lanka's biopolitics, a new category, the 'submissive' species, emerged, oscillating between the 'good' and 'bad' species. The Rajapaksa regime can thus be said to have assumed that it had the exclusive right to exercise the power of death over the Tamils. That is, the 'right to *take* life or *let* live' [emphasis in original] (Foucault, 1998: 136) of the ancient sovereign power of life and death. It was not the question of fostering the lives of the Tamils: it was about deciding whether they should be eliminated or simply be allowed to live.

Sri Lanka tested its biopolitical strategy of flushing out the Tamil civilian population from the LTTE areas first in the coastal land strip of Muthur East/Vaharai in the Eastern Province, which had a population of between 40,000 to 50,000 Tamils. Claiming that it was launching a humanitarian operation to open the sluice gates of a river in the land strip blocked by the LTTE, from 26 July 2006 onwards, the Sri Lankan military constantly shelled and bombed LTTE targets, civilian settlements and the camps of the internally displaced persons (IDPs). When Human Rights Watch (2007: 42) demanded the Sri Lankan government explain why its armed forces were targeting civilians, the government claimed that it was carrying out the attacks in accordance with the laws of armed conflict to neutralise LTTE's artillery and mortar positions in the vicinity of the IDP camps. The Rajapaksa regime also blamed the LTTE for casualties sustained by civilians in shelling and aerial bombardments carried out by the state's armed forces, accusing the LTTE of using the IDPs as human shields to immunise from attacks (Human Rights Watch, 2007: 42). However, interviews conducted by Human Rights Watch among the IDPs revealed that though the LTTE had tried to prevent civilians from leaving its areas, and at some instances its fighters shot and wounded IDPs who tried to leave, it had not used them as human shields, 'that is, purposefully using civilians to render' its fighters immune from attack; there were also no LTTE heavy guns in the vicinity of the IDP camps (Human Rights Watch, 2007: 43).

Sri Lanka also placed restrictions on the flow of food and medicine to Muthur East/Vaharai land strip (Sampanthan, 2006; Human Rights Watch, 2007: 6). This led to the Tamil National Alliance (TNA), the largest Tamil political party, accusing the Sri Lankan government of attempting to 'use food as a weapon of war' (Sampanthan, 2006). The LTTE also accused the Sri Lankan government of creating a humanitarian catastrophe in the landstrip by blocking the flow of humanitarian aid (*Tamilnet*, 2006b). Sri Lanka, however, was not deterred. Even the LTTE's engagement in another round of 'peace' negotiations with the Sri Lankan government in Geneva in October 2006 seemed to have had no effect.

By then, the LTTE seemed to have realised that it had committed a political blunder by brushing-off Balasingham's conciliatory gestures towards India. In an interview with NDTV on 22 November 2006, Thamilchelvan (2006b) changed his earlier tone and urged India to support the Tamil secessionist struggle: 'We need the support of the Indian government and the people. They should recognise our struggle for liberation'. But it was no use. The damage had already been done (Thamilchelvan was killed in an airstrike by the Sri Lankan Air Force a year later). India was no longer prepared to undertake any intervention, even political, in the LTTE's favour. This became apparent from a public statement made in February 2009 by Pranab Mukherjee (cited in Guha, 2009), the then Indian foreign minister who later became the country's president: 'We have no sympathy for the LTTE, which is a terrorist organisation.'

Sri Lanka was thus able to aggressively pursue its military offensive to capture Muthur East/Vaharai. Sri Lanka knew the worst that the West and India would do was to issue statements of condemnation when casualties on the part of Tamil civilians mounted. When the Tokyo Co-chairs, a day before Thamilchelvan's plea to India, issued a statement (see US Department of State, 2006) condemning the Rajapaksa regime for firing into heavily populated areas of the Muthur East/Vaharai land strip and 'killing and wounding innocent civilians', it did not halt its attacks. Undeterred, the Rajapaksa regime continued 'its indiscriminate shelling and restrictions on humanitarian aid', eventually compelling all civilians to flee from the area (Human Rights Watch, 2007: 6). In the words of a UN official, the IDPs were 'starving and exhausted' by the time they reached government-controlled areas (Perera, 2007). With the exodus of the civilian population, the LTTE could not hold onto the land strip and was forced withdraw from the area. Thus, in January 2007, 6 months after armed hostilities resumed, Sri Lanka captured Muthur East/Vaharai.

Two months later, adopting the same strategy, Sri Lanka launched another military offensive to capture the last of the populated LTTE-controlled territories in the East, the Paduvankarai region (referred to by the Sri Lankan government in Sinhala as Thoppigala). Fearing that they may undergo the sufferings that their counterparts in Muthur East/Vaharai faced earlier, Tamil civilians in the Paduvankarai region began fleeing from the area immediately after Sri Lanka launched its offensives (see *BBC*, 2007). Though the Sri Lankan government initially claimed that there was no ground offensive and that the civilians were fleeing because they feared that the LTTE would use them as human shields, the IDPs claimed that they were escaping heavy artillery fire by the Sri Lankan military (*BBC*, 2007).

Though the Paduvankarai region was many times larger than the Muthur East/Vaharai land strip and had an approximate population of 100,000 Tamils, Sri Lanka's biopolitical strategy of dividing the Tamil population as 'bad' and 'submissive' on the basis of their decision to stay or leave LTTE-controlled territories made it easier for it to capture the region. Unlike the offensive on the land strip of Muthur

East/Vaharai, which lasted nearly 6 months, Sri Lanka's offensive on the Paduvankarai region lasted no more than 4 months. With the fall of the Paduvankarai region, the remaining LTTE pockets in the East also fell into state's hands.

Having successfully tried its biopolitical strategy in the East, Sri Lanka turned its attention to the Vanni region in the North. However, unlike in the East, in the Vanni region, it took almost 1-and-a-half years for Sri Lanka to successfully implement this strategy. This can be attributed to a number of factors. Unlike the land strip of Muthur East/Vaharai and the Paduvankarai region, Vanni was a much larger land mass made up of dense jungles and vast areas of agricultural lands. This meant that, with the exception of the urban areas, the 400,000 to 450,000 civilian population of the region was sparsely spread out, making it difficult for the Sri Lankan military to carry out mass-scale shelling. Sri Lanka could only carry out airstrikes on civilian settlements (and LTTE targets) and shell villages close to the frontlines. The presence of international aid agencies in the region also made it difficult for Sri Lanka to impose a complete humanitarian blockade. Though life for many civilians in the region became difficult following the resumption of hostilities, it was not completely untenable. Sri Lanka therefore turned its attention to pushing the LTTE and the Tamil civilian population of the Vanni region into a small land strip similar in size to that of Muthur East/Vaharai.

The LTTE tried to stall Sri Lanka's military offensives. The shortage of manpower and firepower, however, meant that it could not hold on to its frontlines for no more than 9 months. Facing the 200,000 strong Sri Lankan military, as opposed to the 120,000 troops that it faced before the 2002 ceasefire agreement, was no easy task for the LTTE (Perera, 2012: 53; Layton, 2015). In the words of a Sri Lanka military general Perera (2012: 51), between the years 2007 to 2009, the army 'raised 96 battalions, 28 brigades and 12 divisions'. The LTTE could not match this. Even after resorting to conscriptions, the LTTE was only able to increase its strength to an estimated 20,000 to 30,000 cadres (Layton, 2015).

This was also the case with the LTTE's firepower. The international safety net that Wickremesinghe created during the 'peace' process prevented the LTTE from bringing in fresh arms supplies from abroad. Between 2006 to 2007, with Indian and US intelligence, the Sri Lankan navy attacked and sunk eleven arm ships of the LTTE (Moorcraft, 2012: 59; Blake, 2006). Four of these ships were sunk 1,620 nautical miles southeast of Sri Lanka, off the coast of Indonesia and close to Australia's Cocos Islands (Moorcraft, 2012: 60). In the words of Sri Lanka's former Defence Secretary Gotabaya Rajapaksa: 'The Americans were very, very helpful. Most of the locations of these ships were given to us by the Americans' (2013).

Wickremesinghe's international safety net also tightened the noose on the LTTE's overseas fund raising and procurement activities. A series of raids and sting operations carried out by the FBI in collaboration with the Canadian authorities in August 2006 resulted in the arrest of a number LTTE activists, both in the US and Canada. Further arrests were also made in the following month in Singapore on the information provided by American law enforcement agencies. The majority of those arrested were accused of attempting to procure anti-aircraft missiles for the LTTE to cripple the Sri Lankan air force. After hostilities ended, the Sri Lankan air force commander Roshan Goonetilke was all praise for the actions of the US:

> They [the LTTE] had Stingers and SAM-7 *Strelas*. They also had SAM-14s and 16s and were trying to get the SAM-18s. A low-flying helicopter would have found it difficult to survive an 18. We are grateful to the US for stopping that procurement of SAM-18s.
>
> (2012 cited in Moorcraft, 2012: 70)

In 2007, when the LTTE launched airstrikes using light aircraft converted into bombers in Colombo, additional arrests were made in France, Australia and the UK. In June 2008, as the armed conflict intensified, further large-scale arrests of LTTE activists took place in Italy.

In October 2007, when an attack on an airbase in the Northwestern district of Anuradhapura by one of LTTE's suicidal commando units destroyed 70 percent of the Sri Lankan Air Force's airborne surveillance capacity, US defence contractors, with the blessings of the US embassy in Colombo, moved to replace most of them within a month (see Blake, 2007).

It was not only the US that helped Sri Lanka to enhance its firepower and surveillance capabilities. Canada and the UK also played their parts by selling/licensing military equipments to Sri Lanka (*Tamil Guardian*, 2007; *Tamilnet*, 2008; Prince, 2009).

India also played its part. Whilst working alongside the US to help Sri Lanka interdict the LTTE's arms shipments, India quietly gifted Russian made MI-17 helicopters to Sri Lanka (Gokhale, 2009 cited in *Times of India*, 2009). These 'played a major role in several daring missions launched by the Sri Lanka Air Force to rescue army's deep penetration units and injured soldiers from deep inside LTTE-held territory' (Gokhale, 2009 cited in *Times of India*, 2009).

Unable to cope with both manpower and firepower shortages, the LTTE was forced to abandon large swathes of territories in the Vanni region, losing its administrative capital Killinochi in January 2009. Within a month, the LTTE, and between 320,000 to 420,000 Tamil civilians who had not managed to flee to government-controlled areas or India, were pushed into a small land strip in the East of the Vanni region, more or less similar in size to the land strip of Muthur East/Vaharai. Sri Lanka was now poised to try the biopolitical strategy that it had earlier enforced in the East to flush out Tamil civilians.

As its military closed in on the LTTE, the Rajapaksa regime also adopted the tactic of manipulating the population figures of Vanni. This suggests that it may have calculated that it would not be able to flush out the entire civilian population of Vanni to its territories. Many civilians in Vanni had 'genuine fears about possible mistreatment' by the Sri Lankan military if they crossed over to government-controlled areas (Holmes, 2009). This may be due to their support for the LTTE whilst living under its *de-facto* state administration. Many civilians in Vanni were involved with the LTTE in some way or other: a large number of them were either immediate or extended family members of serving, former and deceased LTTE cadres; some were either immediate or extended family members of paid civilian officials of the LTTE (i.e., the Tamil Eelam Police or the Tamil Eelam Bank) or its auxiliary units; even those who had no interest in getting involved with the LTTE were compelled to obtain basic arms training as part of the LTTE's strategy of preparing for war. Given these factors, it may be possible that Sri Lanka calculated that only between 50,000 to 100,000 Tamil civilians in the Vanni region would constitute the 'submissive' species who would opt to leave. The rest, it seems, Sri Lanka deemed to be the 'bad' species whose elimination was acceptable.

In February 2009, senior Tamil civil servants working for the Sri Lankan government in the Vanni region asked the government to supply food to 320,000 people (UN, 2015: 192). The Sri Lankan Defence Secretary Gotabaya Rajapaksa, however, turned down the request, claiming that there were only 100,000 civilians living in LTTE-controlled areas of Vanni (see *Daily News*, 2009). A month earlier, the Sri Lankan President Mahinda Rajapaksa claimed that there were no more than 50,000 Tamil civilians remaining in the LTTE territories (Weiss, 2011: 178). These conflicting figures were, however, revised again in February 2009 to 70,000 by Sri Lanka's Foreign Minister Rohitha Bogollagama (Weiss, 2011: 179). The International Crimes Evidence Project (ICEP) (2014: v), which conducted extensive studies into Sri Lanka's conduct in the final stages of the armed conflict, has suggested that there are reasonable grounds to suspect that 'the Sri Lankan government deliberately understated the number of civilians in the conflict zone and the need for food and basic medical supplies'. Gordon Weiss (2011: 184), a UN official based in Colombo at that time, argued that 'the government knew that its own persistent reduction of population estimates were untrue'. In his view, the Sri Lankan government adopted 'a tactic of deliberate starvation' of the people of Vanni (Weiss, 2011: 184). According to the ICEP (2014: 98), which cited the figures of the UN agency, the World Food Programme (WFP), the amount of food provided to the people of Vanni by the government 'was approximately 2% of the amount required'.

Sri Lanka's action to limit food supplies had far-reaching consequences for the Vanni people. According to the UN (2015: 195), by May 2009, when the conflict ended, 'acute malnutrition had reached 35 per cent'. There were also cases of civilians starving to death (ICEP, 2014: v and 102; UN, 2015: 193). The food crisis worsened as a result of the Sri Lankan military's 'shelling of food distribution queues and storage places', which resulted in 'diminished stocks' (UN, 2015: 170 and 195). Despite facing the risk of being killed in shelling, many opted to queue in front of food centres to avoid death by starvation (UN, 2015: 170 and 195). In some cases, people even resorted to eating unknown plants, which made them ill (UN, 2015: 170 and 195).

'Tens of thousands' of Tamils were also killed by government shelling (UN, 2011: ii, 23–27 and 41; Macrae, 2013; Miliband, 2013). The vast majority of Tamil civilian casualties in the LTTE-held territories occurred in areas unilaterally designated by the Sri Lanka government as 'No Fire Zones' (NFZs). After the conclusion of the armed conflict, the British Channel 4 network broadcast a series of video evidence of the Sri Lankan military subjecting Tamil civilians in the NFZs to 'merciless, sustained shelling' (Macrae, 2013).

Though the Sri Lankan government repeatedly claimed that its objective in setting up the NFZs was to provide '"maximum safety for civilians" from the effects of hostilities', in reality, this was not what happened (UN, 2015: 224). Claiming that the LTTE was using the NFZs to position its military assets and cadres, the Sri Lankan government constantly shelled them (UN, 2015: 224–225). An investigation, largely based on witness testimonies, by the UN in 2014–2015 found that there was evidence to back Sri Lanka's claim that the LTTE had military assets and armed cadres within the NFZs (UN, 2015: 224–225). However, the UN also noted that the Sri Lankan government declared the NFZs without consulting the LTTE and in the 'areas where the LTTE military was already positioned' (UN, 2015: 224–225). Moreover, the UN also accused the Sri Lankan government of targeting the entire NFZs, including the civilians who had sought refuge there, as opposed to only targeting LTTE positions: 'The manner the attacks were carried out suggests that the security forces may have treated all of the NFZs as a single military objective' (UN, 2015: 225). As well as using artillery shells to hit the NFZs, the Sri Lankan security forces also followed a 'consistent practice' of firing multi-barrelled rocket launchers (MBRLs), which, as the UN pointed out, 'are area weapons not designed for hitting a point target, and cannot be precisely targeted at military objectives in densely populated areas' (UN, 2015: 225). The UN also noted that rocket propelled grenades (RPGs) were fired by the Sri Lankan security forces 'in an upward parabola to increase their range beyond their maximum effective range', thereby 'decreasing the accuracy of the weapon' and causing them to explode in densely populated areas (UN, 2015: 225).

Hospitals too were not excluded from targeting (UN, 2015: 145 and 152). The Sri Lankan government justified attacks on hospitals by accusing the LTTE of using them to position its armed cadres and weapons (UN, 2015: 153). The UN investigation found that by constructing 'military fortifications (mostly earthen bunds and trenches)' and positioning 'artillery and other weaponry close to, and sometimes adjacent to hospitals and the surrounding densely populated areas', the LTTE had 'failed to comply with its obligations to take all feasible precautionary measures to protect the civilian population from attacks' (UN, 2015: 153). However, the UN also noted that as the Sri Lankan military 'pushed LTTE and civilians into an ever shrinking area, the possibilities that the LTTE had for separating military objects away from medical facilities and other protected objects became more limited' (UN, 2015: 153). The UN also noted that there was no evidence to 'indicate that Government or other hospitals and ambulances were used by the LTTE for military purposes' (UN, 2015: 153). Medical personnel testified to the UN that 'there were no LTTE military installations placed inside the hospitals' and the that the LTTE generally respected rules imposed by doctors 'strictly prohibiting carrying of weapons inside hospitals' (UN, 2015: 153).

In February 2009, when an attack by the Sri Lankan military on a hospital functioning outside the NFZ briefly caused an international outcry, the Sri Lankan defence secretary announced: '[N]othing should exist beyond the No Fire

Zone ... No hospital should operate in the area, nothing should operate' (Rajapaksa, 2009 cited in UN, 2011: 26). When questioned about the proportionality of the attacks carried out by the Sri Lankan military, the Sri Lankan defence secretary argued: 'to crush the terrorists, there is nothing called unproportionate' (Rajapaksa, 2009 cited in UN, 2011: 26).

In biopolitical terms, this statement of Gotabaya Rajapaksa suggests that to qualify for the temporary right to live in the LTTE-held territories, Tamil civilians had to live in the NFZs, unilaterally determined by the Sri Lankan government. It did not matter whether these enclosures were capable of housing all of the civilian population of Vanni or had basic facilities, i.e., hospitals, sanitations and food. All that mattered was that if the Tamil civilians living in Vanni wanted to qualify for the temporary right to live, they had to be present within these enclosures. These enclosures were also not permanent: Sri Lanka regularly changed their locations as its military closed on the LTTE. This meant that people had to constantly be on the move if they were to qualify for the temporary right to live. Anyone who opted to remain outside those NFZs was deemed by the state to have automatically lost this right.

Sri Lanka's constant shelling of the NFZs also suggests this biopolitical qualification for the temporary right to live was also placed in a permanent state of exception. That is, qualifying for the temporary right to live did not entail an automatic qualification for this right to be guaranteed. The state reserved the right to kill even those who were granted the temporary right to live. In *The History of Sexuality: Volume 1*, in reference to the advent of nuclear weapons, which gave nuclear states 'the power to expose a whole population to death', Foucault (1998: 137) suggested that it represented 'the underside of the power to guarantee an individual's continued existence'. That is, for Foucault, the guarantee for the lives of populations in nuclear states or those vulnerable to nuclear attacks revolves around the guarantee of being exposed to death. This differed slightly in the case of the Tamil civilian population in the NFZs. The state's guarantee for the life of the population of the NFZs was not simply determined by its guarantee to expose them to death. It was also determined by the willingness of the people to expose their own lives and die. That is, those opting to seek refuge in the NFZs were not placed in a better position to live than their counterparts who willingly or unwillingly stayed outside them. In theory, those seeking refuge in the NFZs were safe. But in practice, they, like their counterparts outside the NFZs, were not safe. Both populations were exposed to death: their lives depended on the discretion of the state.

In the ancient sovereign power of death, which gave the sovereign the right to take people's lives or allow them to live, the individual remained a 'neutral' subject: he/she was 'neither dead nor alive' (Foucault, 2004: 240). In Sri Lanka's biopolitics, this was the case with the Tamil population that remained in the LTTE-held areas of Vanni, both within and outside the NFZs; it was especially the case with the real population of Vanni minus those deliberately understated to be living there by the government. For the Rajapaksa regime, every Tamil who lived in the LTTE-held areas outside its understated figure of 50,000 to 100,000 civilians simply did not exist. They were alive, but in the eyes of the government, they did not exist.

Casualties on the part of civilians mounted further as a result of Sri Lanka limiting the supply of medicines to Vanni East (UN, 2015: 227). Though the International Committee of the Red Cross (ICRC) managed to rescue a portion of those injured and take them to government-controlled areas by ships for further treatment, 'as a result of lack of medical care and medicine' in the LTTE-held Vanni East, many of the injured succumbed to their wounds (UN, 2015: 174). Sri Lanka, Weiss suggested, limited medical supplies because it 'apparently calculated that it was better to let civilians die through a lack of medicine rather than risk supplying the Tigers [the LTTE] with drugs' (Weiss, 2011: 184).

Sri Lanka began realising the dividends of it biopolitical strategy by late March 2009. With life becoming untenable in the LTTE-held Vanni East, many Tamil civilians opted to leave for government-controlled areas. For many civilians, risking prosecution for supporting the LTTE after reaching government-controlled areas was better than dying from shelling by the Sri Lankan military or starving to death. Many people were also not prepared to risk death in battle by being conscripted into the LTTE's fighting formations or to allow their young ones to face the same fate (see UN, 2015: 128–141). Despite the tough regime of the permit system the LTTE imposed on the movement of civilians out of its territories, many risked to defy it and cross over to government-controlled areas. The UN investigation found LTTE cadres manning frontlines guilty of shooting and injuring some of the fleeing civilians (UN, 2015: 182–183). An unnamed senior LTTE official told the ICEP that the LTTE did not have a top-down policy of shooting fleeing civilians, and Pirapaharan had even punished some of his cadres who shot at civilians; however, he conceded that blocking civilians who tried to leave LTTE areas without permits formed the LTTE's official policy (ICEP, 2014: 90–92).

The tensions between the LTTE and the Tamil civilians who wanted to leave its territories mounted as the Sri Lankan military closed in, with LTTE-held territories shrinking to a single coastal village of Mullivaikaal in Vanni East. By May 15, 2009, as the armed conflict reached its catastrophic climax, it was not only civilians who opted to leave the LTTE-held Mullivaikaal; even LTTE cadres opted to leave their weapons behind and flee with the civilians. Three days later, the Sri Lankan military captured Mullivaikaal, declaring military victory over the LTTE. With this, Sri Lanka took into its custody approximately 290,000 Tamils, including 11,696 surrendered LTTE combatants (UN, 2011: 37 and 46).

The UN suggested in 2011 that as many as 40,000 Tamil civilians may have been killed in the Vanni war (UN, 2011: 41). However, investigations by some Tamil civil society leaders suggest that as many as 146,679 Tamil were unaccounted for (either dead or missing) (see UN, 2012: 38). The lack of any comprehensive ground-based international judicial investigation means that it may take many years before an accurate figure on the civilian deaths in Vanni is reached.

The next chapter will explore Sri Lanka's biopolitics of ensuring that the 290,000 Tamils, including LTTE fighters, it took into custody were disciplined into a 'submissive' species and those it identified as the 'bad' species were eliminated to secure the ethnocratic state order.

References

Armitage, R. (2002) 'Remarks at Sri Lanka Donor Conference', *Sri Lanka Peace Process Support Meeting*. Oslo, 25 November. Available at: http://2001-2009.state.gov/s/d/former/armitage/remarks/2002/15483.htm (Accessed: 10 September 2012).

Athas, I. (1997) *LTTE Claims Ilmenite as Eelam Property*. Available at: http://sundaytimes.lk/970914/sitrep.html (Accessed: 18 September 2009).

Athas, I. (2003) *The Cover Up of a Tiger Build Up in Trincomalee*. Available at: http://www.sundaytimes.lk/030914/index.html (Accessed: 18 August 2009).

Balasingham, A. (1994) 'War and Peace', *Liberation Tigers*, March, pp. 3 and 7.

Balasingham, A. (1995) Interviewed by A.S.Pannerselvan for *Outlook*, 8 November. Available at: http://www.outlookindia.com/magazine/story/we-did-not-kill-rajiv-gandhi/200167 (Accessed: 10 January 2016).

Balasingham, A. (2002) Interviewed by Lasantha Wickrematunge for *The Sunday Leader*, 3 November. Available at: http://www.thesundayleader.lk/archive/20021103/interviews.htm (Accessed: 18 December 2012).

Balasingham, A. (2003) Interviewed by Frederica Jansz for *The Sunday Leader*, 16 March. Available at: http://www.thesundayleader.lk/archive/20030316/interviews.htm (Accessed: 18 December 2012).

Balasingham, A. (2004) *War and Peace: Armed Struggle and Peace Efforts of Liberation Tigers*. London: Fairmax Publishing.

Balasingham, A. (2006a) Interviewed by *The Sunday Times*, 4 June. Available at: http://www.sundaytimes.lk/060604/columns/sitrep.html (Accessed: 8 December 2015).

Balasingham, A. (2006b) Interviewed by Noopur Tiwari for *Talking Heads*, NDTV, 27 June.

BBC (2007) 'Thousands Flee Sri Lanka Fighting'. Available at: http://news.bbc.co.uk/1/hi/world/south_asia/6430907.stm (Accessed: 13 August 2013).

Blake, R.O. (2006) *Ambassador Briefs Indian High Commissioner on US-Sri Lanka Military Discussions*. Available at: http://wikileaks.org/cable/2006/12/06COLOMBO123.html (Accessed: 7 March 2012).

Blake, R.O. (2007) *Sri Lanka: Airbase Attack Results in Heavy Damage, New Security Procedure*. Available at: http://cables.mrkva.eu/cable.php?id=127767 (Accessed: 7 March 2012).

Daily News (2009) 'Tell the Whole Truth – Defence Secretary'. Available at: http://archives.dailynews.lk/2009/02/07/sec01.asp (Accessed: 11 May 2015).

de Silva, S. (2001) *US Excludes LTTE from Global War*. Available at: http://www.sundaytimes.lk/010923/ frontm.html#fLABEL1 (Accessed: 10 November 2009).

Entwistle, J. (2003) *LTTE Counterproposals on Interim Administration in North/East Generate Mixed Reaction*. Available at: http://cables.mrkva.eu/cable.php?id=118402 (Accessed: 9 July 2012).

European Union-UN (2005) *EU Presidency Declaration Condemning Actions of Tamil Tigers*. Available at: http://www.europa-eu-un.org/articles/en/article_5060_en.htm (Accessed: 27 August 2010).

Foucault, M. (1998) *The History of Sexuality: Volume 1: The Will to Knowledge*. Translated by Robert Hurley. London: Penguin Books (Original work published 1976).

Foucault, M. (2004) *"Society Must Be Defended": Lectures at the College de France, 1975–76*. Translated by David Macey. London: Penguin Books.

Guha, S. (2009) *Spare Lankan Tamil Civilians*. Available at: http://www.dnaindia.com/india/report-spare-lankan-tamil-civilians-1228942 (Accessed: 7 June 2014).

Hain, P. (2000) *Britain Ready to Help SL in any Possible Way – Peter Hain*. Available at: http://www.island.lk/2000/11/24/news06.html (Accessed: 15 August 2010).

Holmes, J. (2009) *Let Them Decide*. Available at: https://www.theguardian.com/commentisfree/2009/apr/08/tamil-protests-sri-lanka-john-holmes (Accessed: 12 May 2015).

Human Rights Watch (2007) *Sri Lanka: Return to War: Human Rights Under Siege*. New York: Human Rights Watch.

ICEP (2014) *Island of Impunity?* Sydney: Public Interest Advocacy Centre.

The Island (2002) 'UK on Peace Moves in Sri Lanka'. Available at: http://www.island.lk/2002/02/23/news05.html (Accessed: 1 July 2015).

The Island (2003) 'Bush Expresses Confidence over Ranil's Commitment to Peace'. Available at: http://www.island.lk/2003/11/10/news08.html (Accessed: 10 June 2010).

Jansz, F. (1997) *US Troops to Help Counter LTTE*. Available at: http://www.sundaytimes.lk/971012/frontm.html#LABEL1 (Accessed: 10 August 2010).

Jayewardene, J.R. (1985) Interviewed by *BBC*. Available at: https://www.youtube.com/watch?v=ZncOQfvtVcU (Accessed: 2 April 2012).

Jaysinghe, A. (2002) *Truce Gets Underway with Foreign Backing*. Available at: http://www.island.lk/2002/02/24/news03.html (Accessed: 1 July 2015).

Kleinfeld, M. (2004) 'Strategic Troping in Sri Lanka: September Eleventh and the Consolidation of Political Position', in Brun, D. (ed.), *11 September and Its Aftermath: The Geopolitics of Terror*. London: Frank Cass Publishers, pp. 54–84.

Kumaratunga, C. (2001) *The President's Address to the Nation Following the LTTE Attack on the International Airport and Air Force Base at Katunayake*. Available at: http://www.priu.gov.lk/execpres/speeches/2001/20010730LTTE_attack_on_the_Katunayake.html (Accessed: 10 October 2012).

Layton, P. (2015) 'How Sri Lanka Won the War: Lessons in Strategy from an Overlooked Victory', *The Diplomat*, 9 April. Available at: http://thediplomat.com/2015/04/how-sri-lanka-won-the-war/ (Accessed: 18 April 2015).

Liberation Tigers (1991) 'Will India's New Intervention Affect the Tamils?' January, p. 1.

Liberation Tigers (1995) 'What Kind of Solution Is the LTTE Expecting?' February, p. 1.

Liberation Tigers (1996) 'Black Tigers Carry Out Daring Raids on Colombo Harbour, Continuing Assaults on Sri Lanka's Strategic Economic Centres', April, p. 1.

Liberation Tigers (2005) 'The Great Human Being Who Loved the Tamil Nation More than His Own Life', April-May, p. 14.

Lunstead, J. (2003) *Tiger Political Chief Thamilchelvam's Steady Eclipse of Group's Longtime Spokesman*. Available at: http://cables.mrkva.eu/cable.php?id=10428 (Accessed: 2 August 2012).

Lunstead, J. (2006a) *US Ambassador Lunstead's Farewell Press Conference*. Available at: http://tamilweek.com/news-features/archives/458 (Accessed: 8 March 2013).

Lunstead, J. (2006b) *Sri Lankan Government Delegation Members' Perspective on Ceasefire Talks with LTTE*. Available at: http://cables.mrkva.eu/cable.php?id=54995 (Accessed: 22 October 2013).

Lunstead, J. (2006c) *Indians Still Hoping Geneva Talks Can Resume Under "Broader Agenda"*. Available at: http://www.thehindu.com/news/the-india-cables/the-cables/article1588862.ece (Accessed: 10 January 2012).

Lunstead, J. (2007) *The United States' Role in Sri Lanka's Peace Process*. Colombo: The Asia Foundation.

Macan-Markar, M. (2003) *Politics-Sri Lanka: Finally, Peace Talks to Tackle Human Rights*. Available at: http://www.ipsnews.net/2003/01/politics-sri-lanka-finally-peace-talks-to-tackle-human-rights/ (Accessed: 12 May 2015).

MacRae, C. (2013) *Sri Lanka: Slaughter in the No Fire Zone*. Available at: https://www.theguardian.com/world/2013/sep/03/sri-lanka-slaughter-no-fire-zone (Accessed: 4 September 2013).

Miliband, D. (2013) *Britain Must Stand Up for Human Rights in Sri Lanka*. Available at: https://www.theguardian.com/commentisfree/2013/mar/11/britain-human-rights-sri-lanka (Accessed: 15 March 2013).

Ministry of Foreign Affairs of Japan (2003) *Tokyo Declaration on Reconstruction and Development of Sri Lanka*. Available at: http://www.mofa.go.jp/region/asia-paci/srilanka/conf0306/declaration.html (Accessed: 7 October 2012).

Moorcraft, P. (2012) *Total Destruction of the Tamil Tigers: The Rare Victory of Sri Lanka's Long War*. South Yorkshire: Pen and Sword Books.

Pathmanathan, S. (2010) Interviewed by Shamindra Ferdinando for *The Island*, 29 July. Available at: http://www.island.lk/index.php?page_cat=article-details&page=article-details&code_title=3160 (Accessed: 2 August 2010).

Perera, S. (2007) *Sri Lanka: Some 5,000 Civilians Find Refuge in Batticaloa after Fleeing Coastal Strip*. Available at: http://www.unhcr.org/news/latest/2007/1/45b627eca/sri-lanka-5000-civilians-find-refuge-batticaloa-fleeing-coastal-strip.html (Accessed: 23 June 2013).

Perera, U. (2012) *Defeating Terrorism through a Politico-Military Strategy: The Sri Lankan Experience*. Published Masters Dissertation. Carlisle: United States Army College.

Peterson, J. (2005) *Sri Lanka: Norwegian Facilitators Send Letter to LTTE Leader Prabhakaran via London: GSL Asks EU to List LTTE as Terrorist Organization*. Available at: http://cables.mrkva.eu/cable.php?id=38758 (Accessed: 12 January 2012).

Pirapaharan, V. (2001) *LTTE Leader Makes Special Plea to the Sinhalese: "Reject Racist Forces, Offer Justice to the Tamils"*. Available at: http://www.tamilnet.com/art.html?catid=13&artid=6506 (Accessed: 13 May 2013).

Pirapaharan, V. (2002) *LTTE Leader Calls for Autonomy and Self-government for Tamil Homeland*. Available at: http://www.tamilnet.com/art.html?catid=13&artid=7902 (Accessed: 11 February 2015).

Pirapaharan, V. (2003) *Pirapaharan's Heroes' Day Address*. Available at: http://www.tamilnet.com/art.html?catid=13&artid=10554 (Accessed: 11 February 2015).

Pirapaharan, V. (2005) 'Statement', *Liberation Tigers*, April-May, p. 14.

Prince, R. (2009) *UK Arms Used Against Civilians in Sri Lanka and Gaza*. Available at: http://www.telegraph.co.uk/news/politics/6049670/UK-arms-used-against-civilians-in-Sri-Lanka-and-Gaza.html (Accessed: 10 September 2009).

Rajapaksa, M. (2005) *Mahinda Chintana: Towards a New Sri Lanka*. Colombo: SLFP.

Rajapaksa, G. (2009) Interviewed by Anbarasan Ethirajan for *BBC*, 22 May. Available at: http://news.bbc.co.uk/1/hi/world/south_asia/8063409.stm (Accessed: 10 August 2014).

Rajapaksa, G. (2013) Interviewed by Greg Sheridan for *The Australian*, 13 September. Available at: http://www.theaustralian.com.au/news/features/sri-lankas-path-to-peace/story-e6frg6z6-1226718017231 (Accessed: 13 September 2013).

Ratnathurai, P. (2003a) 'Be Proud of Wearing the Flower: Be Prepared to Head Towards Coronation', *Liberation Tigers*, January-February, p. 16.

Ratnathurai, P. (2003b) 'Our Time Is Drifting Away', *Liberation Tigers*, May-June, p. 16.

Ravi, S. (2006) 'Increasing Manpower for Liberation', *Liberation Tigers*, August/September, p. 4.

Reagan, R. (1984) *Remarks at the Welcoming Ceremony for President J.R. Jayewardene of Sri Lanka*. Available at: http://www.presidency.ucsb.edu/ws/?pid=40055 (Accessed: 10 November 2012).

The Royal Norwegian Government (2006) *Norway Writes to Rajapakse, Pirapaharan*. Available at: https://www.tamilnet.com/art.html?catid=13&artid=18443 (Accessed: 12 September 2012).

Rudrakumaran, V. (2005) 'Asymmetries in the Peace Process: The Liberation Tigers of Tamil Eelam', *Accord*, 16, pp. 80–83.

Sampanthan, R. (2006) *TNA Warns of "Imminent Humanitarian Disaster" in Vaharai*. Available at: https://www.tamilnet.com/art.html?catid=13&artid=20356 (Accessed: 23 June 2013).

Saunders, J. (2009) *Sentencing Remarks: Regina v Arunachalam Chrishanthakumar*. London: Merrill Legal Solutions.

Schaffer, T.C. (1995) *Journey to Jaffna: The LTTE View of the Peace Process; A First Hand Look*. Available at: http://cables.mrkva.eu/cable.php?id=718 (Accessed: 12 March 2012).

Shastri, A. (2004) 'An Open Economy in a Time of Intense Civil War: Sri Lanka, 1994–2000', in Winslow, D. and Woost, M.D. (eds.), *Economy, Culture, and Civil War in Sri Lanka*. Bloomington: Indiana University Press, pp. 73–92.

Sivaram, D. (2002) *International Safety Net – You Can't Have the Cake and Eat It*. Available at: http://www.tamilcanadian.com/article/1144 (Accessed: 10 March 2011).

Sivaram, D. (2003a) *Is International Military Support to Crush the LTTE Possible?* Available at: http://www.tamilcanadian.com/page.php?id=1564 (Accessed: 10 March 2011).

Sivaram, D. (2003b) *LTTE's Big Mistake: Falling Again for Federalism*. Available at: http://www.tamilcanadian.com/article/1720 (Accessed: 10 March 2011).

Sivaram, D. (2003c) *The Cost of the Unitary State's Internal Colonialism*. Available at: http://www.tamilcanadian.com/article/1867 (Accessed: 10 March 2011).

Sivaram, D. (2004) *ISGA Entails Concepts and Structures of Final Solution*. Available at: http://tamilnation.co/forum/sivaram/040804.htm (Accessed: 10 Mach 2011).

Sorbo, G., Goodhand, J., Klem, B., Nissen, A.E. and Selbervik, H. (2011) *Pawns of Peace: Evaluation of Norwegian Peace Efforts in Sri Lanka, 1997–2009*. Oslo: Norwegian Agency for Development Cooperation.

Spain, J.W. (1987) *Inside the LTTE: A Look at the Tigers' Command Structure and Regional Leaders*. Available at: http://cables.mrkva.eu/cable.php?id=151 (Accessed: 15 March 2012).

The Sunday Times (2001) 'How Jaffna Was Saved: The Battle of Jaffna – Final Part'. Available at: www.sundaytimes.lk/010429/spec.html (Accessed: 7 August 2010).

The Sunday Times (2005) 'Voter Intimidation: But No Repoll for NE'. Available at: http://sundaytimes.lk/051127/news/10.html (Accessed: 7 August 2010).

Tamil Guardian (2007) 'UK Arms Sales to Sri Lanka Match Tsunami Aid'. Available at: http://www.tamilguardian.com/article.asp?articleid=1217 (Accessed: 10 October 2012).

Tamilnet (1998) 'UN Official Meets LTTE Delegation'. Available at: https://www.tamilnet.com/art.html?catid=13&artid=1443 (Accessed: 12 May 2015).

Tamilnet (2001) 'LTTE Condemns Attack on US'. Available at: http://www.tamilnet.com/art.html?catid=13&artid=6318 (Accessed: 7 August 2010).

Tamilnet (2002) 'International Community Hails Permanent Ceasefire'. Available at: http://www.tamilnet.com/art.html?catid=13&artid=6730 (Accessed: 1 July 2015).

Tamilnet (2005a) 'Sri Lanka Can Arm But LTTE Cannot – SLMM Chief'. Available at: http://www.tamilnet.com/art.html?catid=13 &artid=15003 (Accessed: 7 August 2010).

Tamilnet (2005b) 'Rajapakse Wins Sri Lankan Presidency'. Available at: http://www.tamilnet.com/art.html?catid=13&artid=16364 (Accessed: 7 August 2010).

Tamilnet (2006a) 'Undue Emphasis on Direct Talks Sidelined Key Issues – Thamilchelvan'. Available at: https://www.tamilnet.com/art.html?catid=13&artid=18445 (Accessed: 12 September 2012).

Tamilnet (2006b) 'Colombo Ignoring Humanitarian Catastrophe'. Available at: https://www.tamilnet.com/art.html?catid=13&artid=20343 (Accessed: 23 June 2013).

Tamilnet (2007) 'LTTE Responds to UN Report on Children and Armed Conflict'. Available at: https://www.tamilnet.com/art.html?catid=13&artid=21246 (Accessed: 12 May 2015).

Tamilnet (2008) 'High-tech Canadian Radar Sold to Sri Lanka'. Available at: http://www.tamilnet.com/art.html?catid=13&artid=24450 (Accessed: 7 August 2010).

Tamil Week (2006) 'Canada's New Government Lists the LTTE as a Terrorist Organization'. http://tamilweek.com/news-features/archives/271 (Accessed: 20 August 2010).

Thamilchelvan, S.P. (2006a) Interviewed by Noopur Tiwari for *NDTV*, 8 July.

Thamilchelvan, S.P. (2006a) Interviewed by Rajesh Ramachandran for *NDTV*, 22 November.

Thatcher, M. (1985) *Press Conference in Sri Lanka*. Available at: http://www.margaretthatcher.org/document/106022 (Accessed: 13 September 2012).

Times of India (2009) 'India behind Lanka's Victory over LTTE: Book'. Available at: http://timesofindia.indiatimes.com/india/India-behind-Lankas-victory-over-LTTE-Book/articleshow/4924585.cms (Accessed: 16 July 2014).

Tzu, S. (1998) *The Art of War*. Gainesville: InstaBook Corporation.

UN (2002) *Optional Protocol to the Convention on the Rights of the Child on the Involvement of Children in Armed Conflict*. Available at: http://www.ohchr.org/EN/ProfessionalInterest/Pages/OPACCRC.aspx (Accessed: 12 May 2015).

UN (2011) *Report of the Secretary General's Panel of Experts on Accountability in Sri Lanka*. New York: UN.

UN (2012) *Report of the Secretary-General's Internal Review Panel on United Nations Action in Sri Lanka*. New York: UN.

UN (2015) *Report of the OHCHR Investigation on Sri Lanka (OISL)*. Geneva: Office of the UN High Commissioner for Human Rights.

United National Party (2001) *"We Will Open Dialogue with the LTTE" – UNP*. Available at: http://www.thesundayleader.lk/archive/20011111/issues.htm (Accessed: 10 August 2012).

US Department of State (2006) *Joint Statement by Co-Chairs of the Tokyo Donors Conference Regarding Violence in Sri Lanka*. Available at: https://2001-2009.state.gov/r/pa/prs/ps/2006/76478.htm (Accessed: 23 June 2013).

Uthayan (2005) 'Karuna Group Was Formed by Ranil – Boasts UNP MP Naveen: If Pirapa Prepares for War American and Indian Troops Will Fight Him', *Uthayan*, 7 November, p. 1 and 16.

Varatharajan, S. (1996) 'Attacks on the Financial City: The Crumbling Economy', *Liberation Tigers*, March, p. 3 and 6.

Vittachi, I. (1997) *LTTE Already Outlawed Here, Says FM*. Available at: http://www.sundaytimes.lk/971012/news2.html#5LABEL1 (Acccessed: 10 July 2010).

Weiss, G. (2011) *The Cage: The Fight for Sri Lanka and the Last Days of the Tamil Tigers*. London: The Bodley Head.

Willis, P. (1987) 'The Tamils: Recent Events in Sri Lanka', *Asian Affairs*, 18(2), pp. 176–180.

Wills, A. (2001) *Diverse People Can Come Together: Build One Nation – US Ambassador Wills*. Available at: http://www.island.lk/2001/03/09/news13.html (Accessed: 10 October 2011).

Wills, A. (2002) Interviewed by Lasantha Wickrematunge for *The Sunday Leader*, 23 June. Available at: http://www.thesundayleader.lk/archive/20020623/interviews.htm (Accessed: 10 July 2010).

Zee News (2002) 'US Backing Gives Global Safety Net for Peace Process: Ranil'. Available at: http://zeenews.india.com/news/south-asia/us-backing-gives-global-safety-net-for-peace-process-ranil_51355.html (Accessed: 5 July 2013).

6 Managing life in pain

On 19 May 2009, declaring victory over the LTTE, Sri Lankan President Mahinda Rajapaksa (2009a) told the parliament that no one had to tell his government how to look after the internally displaced persons (IDPs) from the Vanni region: 'We who are schooled in the Buddhist tradition of loving kindness and compassion, and nurtured in the Hindu, Islam and Christian traditions, do not need to be taught how we should treat and care for the innocent and helpless.' Having already subjected tens of thousands of Tamil civilians to merciless shelling and airstrikes, in the post-LTTE period, one would have expected the Rajapaksa regime to treat the Tamil IDPs in a compassionate manner. As the LTTE had already been vanquished, there would have seemed no reason why it should mistreat the Tamils.

However, despite numerous promises by the Rajapaksa regime that the IDPs would be resettled in their homes as quickly as possible, many tens of thousands of them were kept interned *en masse* in camps established by the government, with many only being allowed to return to their homes after 1 year (UN, 2015: 217–218). Some of the IDPs spent more than 3 years in Sri Lanka's internment camps (UN, 2015: 218). For over 6 months, the Rajapaksa regime also banned the IDPs from leaving the camps. Approximately ten IDPs had to share a small tent (UN, 2015: 215). Toilet facilities were inadequate and the displaced people had to wait in long queues to use the toilet (UN, 2015: 215). In some cases, only one toilet was allocated for forty-five people (UN, 2015: 213). Flash floods caused by monsoon rains also led to water mixed in latrine pits spilling over into IDP shelters (Human Rights Watch, 2009a; UN, 2015: 213). These conditions, coupled with the poor quality of food given to the IDPs, made many of them ill (UN, 2015: 213). Though some of the elderly IDPs were allowed to leave the camps and stay with their relatives after it came to the attention of the local district magistrate that at least five elderly persons were dying in the internment camps every day, this was not the case with other IDPs (UN, 2015: 214). Individuals identified as LTTE members were taken away from the camps by the Sri Lankan military. Sunil Abeyasekara (2009 cited in *BBC Sinhala Service*, 2009a), a prominent Sinhala human rights activist who received an international human rights award from the UN Secretary General Kofi Annan in 1999, accused the Sri Lankan security forces of abducting, on a daily basis, between twenty to thirty Tamil IDPs suspected of involvement with the LTTE and making many of them disappear.

Why did the Rajapaksa regime keep approximately 290,000 Tamils in a state of mass internment for many months? In an interview with the Indian daily, *The Hindu*, Mahinda Rajapaksa (2009b) suggested that the IDPs were being kept in closed camps because there were 'security concerns'. Rajapaksa also claimed that because every square centimetre in Vanni had been 'mined by the LTTE', it was not possible for the government to resettle the IDPs until demining was complete (Rajapaksa, 2009b). Though it was possible that the LTTE would have placed landmines in some of the areas in the Vanni region, especially in the former frontlines where heavy fighting took place, Rajapaksa's claim that the LTTE had mined every square centimetre was nothing more than an exaggeration given the impossibility of carrying out such a task on a large land mass the size of the Vanni region. The LTTE had neither the manpower nor landmines to lay them all over the Vanni region. Moreover, as Brad Adams (2009 cited in Human Rights Watch, 2009a), the Asia Director of Human Rights Watch, was to point out at that time, the presence of landmines was 'not a valid basis for keeping people locked up'. Even if the LTTE had mined the entire Vanni region as claimed by Rajapaksa, the Sri Lankan government could have allowed the IDPs the freedom of movement until the demining process was complete: they could have been given the freedom to temporarily stay in other parts of the country, especially with their relatives.

A biopolitical analysis of Sri Lanka's mass internment process shows that it had three objectives: to discipline the Vanni Tamils to the stage that they come to the conclusion that supporting Tamil secessionism in the future would be costly; identify and weed out LTTE members and supporters hiding among the IDPs so that they could be dealt in an appropriate manner, i.e., eliminated or disciplined like the IDPs; and secure the ethnocratic state order.

Camps and disciplinary power

In his analysis of the prison apparatus since the eighteenth century, Foucault (1991: 110 and 127) suggested that it has become the space where the criminal is detached from society and disciplined so that he/she may one day be returned to it as a 'good' member. Whilst the prison punishes the criminal by depriving him/her of liberty during the time they are interned there, it also acts like a military barrack, a strict school and a dark workshop that transforms him/her into an obedient member of society (Foucault, 1980: 40; 1991: 233). In other words, the prison, through its disciplinary mechanisms, helps to requalify the criminal as a 'good' member of society. Can the same be said of Sri Lanka's internment camps where approximately 290,000 Tamils who fled from the Vanni region were interned?

Sri Lanka first tested its mass internment process in March 2008, 15 months before the conclusion of the armed conflict, when it took into custody 400 Tamils who managed to leave the LTTE-held Vanni region. These IDPs were held in a newly constructed internment camp in Kalimoddai, Mannar, which Sri Lanka called a 'welfare centre' (Human Rights Watch, 2008). Though civil servants were tasked to provide for the needs of the IDPs held at the camp, the camp itself was managed by the Sri Lankan military (Human Rights Watch, 2008). A tough pass system was also imposed on the movement of civilians in and out of the camp, allowing only around thirty civilians to go out of the camp each day, with the condition that their family members acted as sureties to guarantee their return by evening (Human Rights Watch, 2008).

As more and more civilians began fleeing from the LTTE-held territories, the Sri Lankan government began constructing more and more internment camps like the one at Kalimoddai. In January 2009, it even announced that it was planning to intern up to 200,000 Tamils, whom it said it had expected to flee the Vanni region (UN, 2015: 208). This figure of 200,000 Tamils, as the UN has later pointed out, was in stark contrast to the government's deflated figure of 70,000 Tamils said to be living in the Vanni region (UN, 2015: 208). Sri Lanka also announced in January 2009 that it was planning to keep the IDPs in those internment camps for up to 3 years (UN, 2015: 208). By the time this announcement was made, the limited freedom of movement that was earlier granted to the IDPs at Kalimoddai and other internment camps was revoked. By July 2009, minus those identified as LTTE cadres, who had been taken to 'rehabilitation' centres, secret detention facilities and prisons run by the Sri Lankan government, 281,621 IDPs were kept in a state of mass internment in thirty camps (Human Rights Watch, 2009b). Many IDPs thus began to feel that they were being kept as prisoners. An IDP told the Human Rights Watch: 'The way I see it, we are not internally displaced persons, we are internally displaced prisoners' (Premkumar, 2009 cited in Human Rights Watch, 2009b). That is, the internment camps blurred the distinctions between displaced persons and displaced prisoners. It was not the very fact of being deprived of the freedom to move out of the internment camps that made the IDPs feel this way.

As Human Rights Watch (2009c: 32) has documented, the camps, other than having civilians, lacked any civilian characteristics. They were 'secured with coils of barbed wire, sandbags, and machine-gun nests' (Human Rights Watch, 2009c: 32). There was also 'a large military presence inside and around the camps' (Human Rights Watch, 2009c: 32). In other words, the internment camps resembled high security prisons. The only difference was that they did not house criminals but the IDPs. In February 2009, the Sri Lankan military spokesperson Brigadier General Udaya Nanayakara (2009 cited in Chamberlain, 2009) claimed: 'They [the internment camps] have barbed wire around them for the safety of the civilians. If the [Tamil Tigers] lob a grenade, a lot of people will be killed and we are responsible for their safety.' However, even after the LTTE was militarily defeated in May 2009, meaning that there were no LTTE cadres to lob grenades at the people as Nanayakara had suggested, a heavy military presence was maintained in the camps. At Menik Farm internment camp in Chettikulam, Vavuniya, the largest of the thirty internment camps constructed by the Rajapaksa regime, and made up of several zones, a second line of barbed wire was installed to 'ensure that outsiders cannot approach the people in the camp close enough to talk to them' (Human Rights Watch, 2009c: 33). Major General Kamal Gunaratne (2010 cited in UN, 2015: 209), who was responsible for the internment camps in the North, claimed in September 2010 that the freedom of movement of the IDPs was curtailed because the government wanted to identify the LTTE members, whom he claimed were 'dangerous IDPs' hiding among the IDPs: 'We had to keep them under certain movement restrictions for about two-three months because we knew that there was a huge amount of fighters who were hiding behind this population'.

This implied that, in biopolitical terms, in order to identify the 'bad' species, Sri Lanka felt that it was necessary to keep the entire 'submissive' species interned. Keeping the 'submissive' species in a state of internment was, for Sri Lanka, a tactic of compelling them to assist the state's efforts to weed out the 'bad' species hiding among them. Sri Lanka may have calculated that frustrated by the fact that they were being kept like prisoners because of the presence of LTTE members, the IDPs would resort to helping the military identify them.

In 'Society Must Be Defended', Foucault (2004: 29) suggested that the subjects of power are also 'always its relays'. A biopolitical analysis of Sri Lanka's tactic of keeping the IDPs in a state of mass internment to frustrate them so that they would be compelled to identify LTTE cadres demonstrates that whilst the state treated them as subjects of its power, it also used them as the relays of its objectives.

Military intelligence personal and the state's anti-LTTE Tamil paramilitaries implicated in atrocities (summary executions and enforced disappearances) against Tamil civilians in the past were deployed in the internment camps to identify LTTE cadres (Human Rights Watch, 2009c: 33). At night, it became a norm for the Sri Lanka military and counter-terrorism police to conduct 'interrogation inside the camps, summoning young men and women into their premises' (Human Rights Watch, 2009c: 33). These interrogations were not confined to simply questioning the suspects. It also involved torture.

Keeping the IDPs in a state of constant surveillance, turning them against hiding LTTE cadres, and using torture helped Sri Lanka to identify many of the members of the 'bad' species it sought to weed out from the 'submissive' species. As Human Rights Watch (2009b) has documented, several thousand IDPs were removed from those camps by the Sri Lankan military for alleged membership or support of the LTTE. Approximately 12,000 Tamils identified as LTTE cadres were taken into custody for 'rehabilitation', or to go through the judicial process (Bureau of the Commissioner General of Rehabilitation, 2013). In reality, not all of the 12,000 detainees were LTTE members. Conscripts who deserted from the LTTE, and those who worked for one day for the LTTE, were also placed in the category of LTTE members and taken into custody (UN, 2015:15).

In Middle Ages Europe, the body of the criminal, or the member of the 'bad' species in its contemporary sense, was treated as the king's property on which 'the sovereign left his mark and brought down the effects of his power' through the punishments he meted on him/her (Foucault, 1991: 109). In the biopolitics of many contemporary societies, where sovereignty has shifted from the prince to the social body, the body of the criminal becomes 'the property of society' for 'collective and useful appropriation'; that is the criminal's body is disciplined in prison so that it can become useful, i.e., capable of working for society after his requalification as a 'good' member (Foucault, 1991: 109). In other words, the body of the member of the 'bad' species is expected to become useful for the 'good' species after he/she requalifies as a member of the 'good' species. Sri Lanka claimed that its mission in weeding out individuals suspected of involvement with the LTTE and rehabilitating them was to 'disengage, de-radicalise, rehabilitate and reintegrate the misguided men/women and children, who were radicalised by the protracted armed conflict' and to transform them into 'useful citizens and productive members of society' (Bureau of the Commissioner General of Rehabilitation, 2013). A biopolitical analysis of Sri Lanka's action, however, shows that this had not always been the case.

In the ethnocratic biopolitics of the Sri Lankan state, the minimum qualification for an individual to become a 'good' species depends on his/her affiliation to the Sinhala Buddhist race/species, and this therefore automatically excludes the Tamils, unless of course the Sri Lankan state abandons its Sinhala Buddhist ethnocratic biopolitics and adopts a commitment to uphold the civil liberties and human rights to all of its populations. The state's possession of the bodies of the 'bad' and 'submissive' species, and its actions of subjecting them to disciplinary mechanisms may lead to them becoming useful for the 'good' species. However, this would not entail that they would become a part of, or be seen as, part of the 'good' species.

The treatment of the IDPs and suspected LTTE cadres in the internment camps also shows that the appropriation of the bodies of the 'bad' and 'submissive' species in Sri Lanka was similar to that of the prince in Middle Ages Europe taking possession of the body of the condemned man as a way of showing his presence and power. In Sri Lanka's case, it was the Sinhala Buddhist 'good' species who possessed the bodies of the 'bad' and 'submissive' species as a way of demonstrating their presence and power. The UN, the Human Rights Watch and other international human rights organisations have documented the systematic sexual abuse of Tamil women, and some men, by the Sri Lanka security forces, in the internment camps, 'rehabilitation' centres, prisons and at the frontlines.

In many of the internment camps, there were only open bathing points (UN, 2015: 125). Sri Lankan military personnel positioned themselves close to those bathing points and watched the women bathing (UN, 2015: 125). Women who resorted to bathing at night to avoid being watched were frequently taken away by Sri Lankan soldiers and raped (Human Rights Watch, 2013: 100). In some instances, Sri Lankan soldiers removed women from their tents at night, and the women returned later distressed and traumatised (UN, 2015: 125). An IDP testified to the UN how uniformed personnel pulled her and her friends from the food queue, dragged them off and they were 'violently raped, bitten, kicked and scratched' (UN, 2015: 125). Human Rights Watch (2013: 114) has also documented the statement of a woman who, along with six other young women, was forced to remain in a tent in one of Sri Lanka's internment camps in Chettikulam, where they were systematically raped by uniformed military personnel while they were interrogated late at night. Another young mother testified to the Human Rights Watch (2013: 102) that she was taken into custody by a senior Sri Lankan military commander holding the rank of Brigadier, and raped repeatedly for 3 months. During the rape, the officer burned her breasts and inner thighs with cigarettes. In the words of the UN (2015: 123), the purpose of the rape of Tamil women by the Sri Lanka military, apart from terrorising the women into providing information about the victims' involvement with the LTTE, was for 'sexual gratification, degradation and humiliation'. Whilst raping the Tamil women, Sri Lankan soldiers would shout abuses at them, calling them 'Tamil dogs' (UN, 2015: 123). The rape and sexual abuse of the female IDPs by Sri Lankan soldiers sent a message to the Tamil women that their bodies belonged to the Sinhala Buddhist sovereign, and can be used in any manner preferred by its agents – the state's security forces.

The idea that the bodies of all Tamils belonged to the state was already made clear to many of the IDPs upon reaching government-controlled areas from February 2009 onwards. In February 2009, a female LTTE suicidal cadre posing as an IDP, blew herself up at an IDP registration point manned by Sri Lankan soldiers (UN, 2015: 124). Following this incident, it became a practice for Sri Lankan soldiers to force Tamil women and girls, both the IDPs and surrendered LTTE cadres, to strip naked or partially naked at the frontlines (UN, 2015: 124). In some instances, females soldiers forced the IDPs to strip naked, and male soldiers videoed the women, and frequently inappropriately touched them and made sexual comments (UN, 2015: 124). Some women were dragged to the nearby bushes and raped (UN, 2015: 125), and some of them never returned, having been summarily executed by soldiers after being raped (UN, 2015: 125). In other cases, women were forced to strip in front of their children and grandchildren, walk naked in circles around soldiers, and then raped (Human Rights Watch, 2013: 106). A 50-year-old woman testified to Human Rights Watch how soldiers forced an unrelated girl and a boy to strip, ordered them to hug each other, and then summarily executed them in front of other IDPs (Human Rights Watch, 2013: 106). In the words of one woman who testified at the UN, she felt 'like a corpse' after being forced to strip (UN, 2015: 12).

The Hindu Tamil society in Sri Lanka is largely a conservative society, particularly in regards to its attitudes towards women. Women are expected to be modest and to dress accordingly. Sexual purity is an ideal, and any woman known to have had sex, even if it was due to rape, with anyone other than her husband, is open to social ostracism. Thus, through the forceful nakedness of women and rape by its soldiers, which was an open secret among the Tamil community on the island and abroad, the Sri Lankan state created conditions for many of the female IDPs from Vanni to be shunned by their own people upon being released from the internment camps. It is therefore not surprising that many female IDPs felt like corpses when made to strip or subjected to sexual abuse and rape. In biopolitical terms, for the state, the female IDPs who left LTTE-held areas were neither dead nor alive; they were neutral subjects whose bodies the Sri Lankan state could appropriate for the pleasure of its security forces, or to inscribe the power of the 'good' species it represented.

Apart from the physical and psychological trauma Sri Lanka's actions caused to the victims, it also sent a signal to all of the IDPs, and Tamils living in other parts of the island, that they would be punished in similar ways for supporting Tamil secessionism in the future. In other words, Sri Lanka used rape and sexual abuse as part of its disciplinary mechanisms; to discipline Tamils to abandon support for a future Tamil state. However, rape, sexual abuse and torture were not only used by the Sri Lankan state for disciplinary purposes; the abuses and violence were also used for the production of 'truth'.

Producing the 'truth'

As we in Chapter 3, the use of torture for the production of 'truth' as part of its biopolitics of securing the ethnocratic state order was not a new practice for the Sri Lankan state. It had used it since the late 1970s to produce the 'truth' on the Tamil militancy. In the post-LTTE period this practice was enhanced and broadened. Instead of being used against selected individuals, in the post-LTTE period torture was used *en masse* by the state. Rape was also made 'a key element of broader torture or ill treatment', targeting both Tamil men and women (Human Rights Watch, 2013: 29).

There were three types of 'truth' that Sri Lanka wanted to produce by keeping Tamil civilians and suspected LTTE cadres in a state of mass internment: the 'truth' about the LTTE – that is, its characteristics, its structures (both military and political), and the strategies, tactics and methods it used to wage the secessionist armed struggle and manage the populations in the areas it controlled; the 'truth' on the level of involvement of individuals in the LTTE; and a narrative of 'truth' that there were no civilian casualties in Sri Lanka's military offensives to recapture the Vanni region.

Malkanthi Hettiarachi (2013: 109), a clinical psychologist who supported Sri Lanka's 'rehabilitation' programme, claims that the 'law enforcement authorities and intelligence agencies categorised former insurgents based on the depth of involvement, period of involvement, and activities conducted during involvement'. Hettiarachi claims that surrendered LTTE cadres were 'labelled as high, medium, or low risk', on the basis of interviews and background information collected on them (Hettiarachi, 2013: 109). Neither Hettiarachchi nor any other Sri Lankan official engaged in the 'rehabilitation' process have elaborated how LTTE suspects were interviewed, or how background information on them were collected.

An analysis of the witness testimonies made by 'rehabilitated' LTTE cadres to the UN and Human Rights Watch, coupled with some of the interviews conducted by the author reveal the tactics and mechanisms used by the state to gather those information. Sri Lanka's internment camps, secret detention facilities, 'rehabilitation' centres and prisons functioned as its factories for producing the 'truth' (see Human Rights Watch, 2009c: 32; UN, 2015: 78–81).

In March 2016, the author interviewed two middle-ranking LTTE cadres and a civilian doctor, all of whom fled from the LTTE-held territories in the last days of the armed conflict. Of those, Navarathinarajah Navaranjan alias Uyartchi, served in the LTTE's medical unit as a doctor and treated a large number LTTE fighters, senior commanders and civilians. The other LTTE cadre, Kandasamy Raveendran alias Arunmaran, served in the LTTE's financial department. The civilian doctor, Thurairajah Varatharajah, who was on the payroll of the Sri Lankan government, frequently gave video interviews from the conflict zones to the local and international media on civilian deaths and injuries caused by shelling and airstrikes carried out by the state's military and the deaths caused by the state's denial of food and medicine. All of them were taken into custody by the Sri Lankan security forces.

Uyartchi told the author that he was arrested at the frontlines of the Sri Lankan military after being identified by a fellow IDP as a doctor. Initially, when Uyartchi walked towards the frontline, he was not mistreated. However, upon being identified as a doctor, he was, along with other medical personnel, beaten severely by soldiers. The Sri Lankan security forces harboured anger towards doctors and medical personnel for two reasons: saving the lives of many of the injured LTTE cadres and commanders; and giving video interviews to the media on civilian deaths and injuries. Whilst being held in an open space with civilians and other LTTE fighters, Uyartchi was identified as an LTTE doctor. Once again he was subjected to severe beatings by soldiers. He was then handcuffed and taken to Rambaikulam Girls' School, Vavuniya, where around 2,000 suspected LTTE cadres were being held.

According to Uyartchi, not all of those detained at Rambaikulam Girls' School were LTTE cadres. Some had left the LTTE 15 years before the conclusion of the armed conflict. Many had no links to the LTTE but were nevertheless classified as LTTE members. In Uyartchi's view, of the 2,000 detained, only 500 were LTTE cadres.

Uyartchi told the author that whilst being kept in detention, every day each LTTE suspect was given three water bottles, each filled with 1.5 litres of water. The suspects had to use the 4.5 litres of water for drinking, washing after excretion and for bathing. Whenever the suspects went to bathe, they would be beaten with broom sticks by soldiers guarding the bathing points. Suspects would often be taken into classrooms, stripped naked and beaten. Sometimes the suspects would be made to stand naked on their heads. At other times they would be suspended upside down from the ceiling by ropes. Torture of LTTE suspects included being beaten with wooden planks whilst being hung upside down. Uyartchi claimed that during torture, his toe nails were pulled out.

The torture persisted even after being transferred to other detention facilities, and the Boosa Prison in Galle. Sometimes, Uyartchi claimed, the suspects would be made to stand naked and polythene carrier bags soaked in petrol placed over their faces before being beaten. Iron chains and electric wires were used to beat the suspects. On other occasions, logs would be placed between tables and the suspects suspended on them tied to ropes. According to Uyartchi, most of the torture took place from midnight onwards. Interrogators would take suspects away to the torture cells and constantly beat them throughout the night, depriving them of sleep. They would only be allowed to return to their enclosures in the morning.

The interrogators, according to Uyartchi, had three objectives in torturing the suspects: to make them confess that they were LTTE cadres, and in the case of existing evidence or confession, to make them confess that they held the rank of a military commander within the LTTE; to force them to identify other LTTE cadres and military commanders; and to reveal information about any weapons and ammunitions buried by the LTTE at secret locations in Vanni. That is, the soldiers wanted to know the 'truth' about the number of 'bad' species hiding among the IDPs and to deny them the possibility of taking up weapons again on their release, if they were not made to disappear.

Uyartchi was constantly tortured to confess that he was an LTTE commander. His heavily built physical features made the interrogators suspect that he may have been an LTTE military commander and not a doctor. Uyartchi claimed that a junior LTTE cadre, who was suspected by his interrogators of being another LTTE commander, made a false confession to that effect in an attempt to avoid torture, and was later taken away by soldiers, never to return. Arunmaran told the author how a mid-ranking LTTE cadre by the name of Iniyavan identified him to the Sri Lankan military and urged him to also become a government informant, but later became a disappeared person. This implied that for Sri Lanka, managing life in pain was not only for the production of 'truth' on the 'bad' species and disciplining their members into a 'submissive' species, but also for eliminating some of those identified.

In many instances, torture caused permanent scars on the bodies of ex-LTTE cadres. As Human Rights Watch has documented, one method of torture resulted in devastating injuries to the victim. An LTTE medical worker narrated how Sri Lankan soldiers 'pushed a pipe into his anus' and 'then inserted a piece of barbed wire into the pipe' (Human Rights Watch, 2013: 93). After pulling out the pipe, leaving the barbed wire in the victim's anus, the soldiers then 'ripped out the piece of barbed wire' from the victim's 'anus causing him to pass out unconscious with pain' (Human Rights Watch, 2013: 93). In some cases, metal or wire was inserted into the male genital organ (UN, 2015: 121). In other instances, small metal balls were inserted inside the male genital organ (Human Rights Watch, 2013: 103). Sometimes, male genital organs were slammed in table drawers (UN, 2015: 121). Chili powder was also sprayed on both male and female genital organs (UN, 2015: 121) In some instances, female Sri Lankan security personnel were used to perpetrate sexual abuse and rape of male detainees (Human Rights Watch, 2013: 97). These methods of inflicting excruciating pain on detainees for the production of the 'truth', for Sri Lanka, inscribed permanent marks on the bodies of many of the detainees, reminding them that their bodies were possessions of the Sinhala Buddhist sovereign. The permanent marks that torture leaves on the bodies, and the minds, of individuals are, in Foucault's (1991: 34) view, intended to 'brand the victim with infamy'; these marks trace on the bodies and minds of the victims 'signs that must not be effaced'. They are permanent marks of the sovereign (Foucault, 1991: 34).

Hettiarachi (2013: 118) claims that Mahinda Rajapaksa initiated the 'rehabilitation' programme for LTTE cadres with a message to officials involved in the process: 'treat them as your own children'. In ancient Roman society, the doctrine of *patria protestas* granted the father the 'right to "dispose" of the life of his children and his slaves' (Foucault, 1998: 135). The witness testimonies on torture made by former LTTE cadres suggests that much of Sri Lanka's 'rehabilitation' programme was conducted in a similar manner. Either Rajapaksa had intended his officials to adopt the doctrine of *patria protestas* in rehabilitating surrendered LTTE cadres/suspects, or his officials interpreted his message in such terms.

However, not all LTTE cadres were tortured. An LTTE member who held senior positions within the movement in the 1980s and the early 1990s, told the author after his release in 2014 that he was not tortured in military custody. He claimed that though he was interrogated, because he told the interrogating officers the truth about his role in the LTTE and the officers knew that he had been sidelined by the LTTE leadership following the Mathaya episode in 1993, he was not physically tortured. The author was also able to meet a number of LTTE cadres who managed to escape from the internment camps by bribing military officials before they could be identified as combatants (these LTTE cadres, though willing to disclose what happened in the internment camps, asked the author to keep their names anonymous). They narrated how some of the soldiers and police officers showed compassion towards the IDPs, the other side of *patria protestas*. In some instances, the police officers cried when they saw Tamil civilians receiving treatment in government hospitals due to injuries sustained in shelling carried out by the military in Vanni. Some soldiers also expressed disbelief at seeing tens of thousands of Tamil civilians coming out of LTTE-held territories, because they had been told earlier by the government that only 'terrorists' and a few thousand civilians lived in the Vanni region. Regardless, these LTTE cadres also told the author that had they been identified as combatants, they may have faced the fate of their colleagues. This suggests that the fate of IDPs and LTTE cadres in the internment camps depended on the discretion of individual Sinhala Buddhist soldiers and police officers, or, as Dissanayake (1983) commented following the 1983 Black July mass violence: 'It is we [the Sinhala Buddhists] who can attack you and protect you.'

As well as using physical torture, the Sri Lankan security forces also used psychological torture on some detainees. Varatharajah, the civilian doctor interviewed by the author, was arrested by the Sri Lankan military in the last days of the armed conflict.

He was injured in Sri Lankan military's shelling, and was taken into custody on 15 May 2009 by soldiers who took control of the building in Mullivaikaal that he and his fellow doctors were staying in. Unlike Uyartchi, Varatharajah told the author that he was not beaten after being identified as a doctor, but briefly admitted to the nearby makeshift military hospital for treatment. He was then taken from the makeshift military hospital to a secret detention centre in Killinochi, the LTTE's former administrative capital. There, Varatharajah was locked up in a 7 feet long and 3 feet wide cage with space to stand or lie down only. Food would be passed through a small flap at the bottom of the cage. He was allowed to use the toilet and wash within a short period of time allocated daily for the purpose. He was kept isolated for 8 days, and given no further medical treatment. On the eighth day, the military commander in charge of the secret detention facility met Varatharajah and told him: 'You are lucky the war has ended. Otherwise it would be a different story.' Varatharajah believes that the tone of the military commander made him feel that he may have been summarily executed by the Sri Lankan military had the armed conflict not ended. Varatharajah was then taken to the infamous Fourth Floor, in Colombo, where once again he was locked in a cage.

Though Varatharajah was eventually taken to hospital for further treatment, whilst warded in hospital, the intelligence personnel continued to interrogate him. The interrogations lasted for 2 weeks, and most of the questions were centred on whether he had treated the LTTE leader Pirapaharan, and why he had given video interviews to the media about shelling by the Sri Lankan military. Although Varatharajah was not physically tortured at the Fourth Floor, he was warned that he would face the fate of other detainees if he did not tell the 'truth'. At one point, Varatharajah was told by a military intelligence officer that he faced the prospect of being detained for up to 5 years. In another instance, Varatharajah was told by the same officer that if he wanted to be released, he had to do something to please the Sri Lankan President Mahinda Rajapaksa and his brother, the Defence Secretary Gotabaya Rajapaksa. A few days later, the officer returned suggesting to Varatharajah that if he wanted to please the president and the defence secretary, he should give a public testimony, along with other civilian doctors at a press conference that the government was in the process of organising, that they had lied about the shelling by the Sri Lankan military. They also had to confess the 'truth' that there were 'zero civilian casualties', and hospitals were not targeted by the military. With the prospect of spending years in detention, Varatharajah and his colleagues retracted their previous media statements on the extent of casualties during the last stages of the armed conflict, and thus told the 'truth' that the Rajapaksa regime wanted the local and international media to hear.

A few days before the press conference, hinting that the civilian doctors' release depended on them facilitating the production of this narrative of 'truth', President Mahinda Rajapaksa (2009b) told an Indian daily: 'I told them to organise a press conference. Let the doctors come and say what they have to say'. Also present during the interview, the president's secretary Lalith Weeratunga (2009 cited in Rajapaksa, 2009b) added: 'They were lying through their teeth [about civilian casualties in the No Fire Zone]. And they are public servants, paid by the government. If they go scot-free, it will set a very bad precedent.'

Five years after his release, Varatharajah told the BBC, and later in March 2016 the author, that what he and his colleagues had initially said about civilian casualties whilst in Vanni were not exaggerations: 'Every day we received hundreds of casualties. I only told what actually happened on the ground. Tamil Tigers [the LTTE] neither forced us nor did we exaggerate casualty figures' (Varatharajah, 2014); the counter narrative of 'truth' of the events that the Tamil civilians were subjected to leading up to the end of the armed conflict.

For Sri Lanka, the retraction of the doctors' previous statements whilst in the zone of conflict was not only a public relations exercise intended to enhance the image of the state; it also represented the outcome of a battle for 'truth' that the state was engaged in. This was evident from the way that Sri Lanka's state media, the *Sunday Observer*, published the confessions of Varatharajah and his colleagues, with the headline: '*LTTE Propaganda Defeated, Truth Revealed*' (see Yatawara, 2009). For the state media, the doctors' retractions were the state's final victory in the battle for a narrative of 'truth' that no Tamil civilians were killed by its security forces in the final military offensives to vanquish the LTTE. In Middle Ages Europe, physical torture served as a ritual 'that "produced" truth' in the battle that the sovereign fought with the prisoner (Foucault, 1991: 41). Varatharajah's story reveals that in the ethnocratic biopolitics of the Sri Lankan state, psychological torture complemented physical torture and led the state to victory in its battle for a narrative of 'truth'.

Securing the ethnocratic state order

The legality of Sri Lanka's mass internment of the IDPs and suspected LTTE cadres and supporters came under fire from both local and international human rights groups. Human Rights Watch (2009d) accused Sri Lanka of acting unlawfully by detaining the IDPs *en masse*. Similar accusations were also levelled by Amnesty International (2009). Both groups also accused the Sri Lankan government of violating international human rights law (see Amnesty International, 2009: 6; Human Rights Watch, 2009d). In June 2009, challenging the legality of the mass internment, two petitions were filed in Sri Lanka's Supreme Court, first by the relatives of a group of interned IDPs, and the second by the Colombo-based think-tank, Centre for Policy Alternatives (CPA) (Wickremasinghe, 2009). However, Sri Lanka's politicised Supreme Court repeatedly postponed the hearing of the petitions; they were not taken up even after all of the IDPs had been released (UN, 2015: 209).

There is no doubt that Sri Lanka violated international human rights law by keeping the IDPs in a state of mass internment. The UN (2015: 229) has even suggested that Sri Lanka's actions 'may amount to discrimination under international human rights law, and, if established by a court of law, may amount to the crime against humanity of persecution'. But how correct is the claim that Sri Lanka also violated its domestic laws? An analysis of Sri Lanka's emergency legislation, the PSO, indicates that the mass internment of the IDPs may have not been in violation of the island-state's laws, as section 5 (2) of the Act allows for people to be detained in groups when a state of emergency is in operation; and during the period the IDPs were kept interned *en masse*, a state of emergency was in force.

The legal position of the IDPs, however, was set out, albeit unofficially, by Sarath N. Silva, Sri Lanka's Chief Justice at that time. A few days before his retirement, Silva (2009 cited in *BBC Sinhala Service*, 2009b) told a public gathering: 'They [the IDPs] live outside the protection of the law of the country'.

Silva's statement has been misinterpreted by many to imply that by keeping the IDPs in a state of mass internment, the Rajapaksa regime was not treating them 'according to the law of the land' (see, for example *BBC Sinhala Service*, 2009b). A biopolitical analysis of Silva's statement, however, shows that he was not challenging, but affirming the legality of Sri Lanka's actions; all of the internment camps functioned within the jurisdiction of Sri Lanka's laws, and therefore the laws of the land should have been extended to the interned population. How could the protection of law be denied to the IDPs? It could only be done by law itself denying this protection. In the case of the Vanni IDPs, section 5 (2) of the PSO can be said to have denied them the protection they were supposed to have been enjoying under Sri Lanka's ordinary laws. In other words, law was assisting the state in its endeavour of biopolitically disciplining the IDPs by denying them the protection that they would have usually enjoyed had they not constituted the 'bad' or 'submissive' species. This was what Silva implied by claiming that the Vanni IDPs did not have the protection of law.

Sri Lanka has, however, never been shy in publicly spelling out the legal basis of the mass detention of suspected LTTE cadres and putting them through its 'rehabilitation' programme: they were detained *en masse* pursuant to section 22 of the *Emergency (Miscellaneous Provisions and Powers) Regulations* No. 1 of 2005 (ER, 2005), a secondary legislation enacted under the PSO.

In 2013, the Sri Lankan government announced that approximately 12,000 former LTTE cadres who had gone through its 'rehabilitation' programme had been successfully reintegrated back into society (Bureau of the Commissioner General of Rehabilitation, 2013). The programme, it claimed, was 'guided by the Buddhist principles of forgiveness and compassion': Mahinda Rajapaksa foresaw that 'as the terrorists are human beings whose minds were distorted, and hence misguided', they could be reformed and 'rehabilitated to enlist their services as useful citizens of the country' (Bureau of the Commissioner General of Rehabilitation, 2013). But according to Uyartchi and Arunmaran, the two mid-ranking LTTE cadres interviewed by the author, rather than being allowed to study or undertake vocational training as part of 'rehabilitation', they were tortured and made to work for the Sri Lankan military. Similar testimonies have also been given by a number of LTTE cadres interviewed in 2012 as part of a human rights project undertaken by the University of Virginia (see McRaith, 2012: 28–29).

The most striking aspect of Sri Lanka's 'rehabilitation' programme was the detainees being ordered to salute, on a daily basis, Sri Lanka's national flag, which, as we saw earlier in Chapter 2, symbolises the supremacy of the Sinhala Buddhist race/species, and sing the national anthem in the Sinhala language. Both Uyartchi and Arunmaran claim that they were forced to learn the Sinhala language and memorise the national anthem in Sinhala. Some of the detainees who failed to sing the national anthem were made to 'kneel down under the scorching sun all day' (see Jeya, 2010 cited in Kyung, 2010). An ex-combatant who 'coughed while the anthem played' was kicked by soldiers (Jeya, 2010 cited in Kyung, 2010). As the BBC has documented, even teenagers identified as having been conscripted by the LTTE and put through the 'rehabilitation' programme were not spared (see Sackur, 2010). When Stephen Sackur of BBC asked in June 2010 whether the Sri Lankan government was reprogramming the Tamil teenagers by making them sing the Sri Lankan national anthem in the Sinhala language rather than Tamil, Brigadier Sudantha Ranasinghe (2010), the military officer in charge of rehabilitating them responded: 'I have never heard any country which has their national anthem sung in different languages. And what you witnessed this morning in this school is something which is done in every school in Sri Lanka.' Ranasinghe made the claim despite the existence of the Tamil version of Sri Lanka's national anthem; and this had been used for decades, and even during the armed conflict in government-controlled areas of the North and East. Six months later in December 2010, the Sri Lankan government officially banned the Tamil version of Sri Lanka's national anthem. Justifying the ban, President Mahinda Rajapaksa (2010 cited in *The Sunday Times*, 2010) claimed that it was necessary to make everyone 'think of Sri Lanka as one country'. In effect, Rajapaksa implied that it was only the Sinhala language that could symbolise the country. For Rajapaksa, other languages may exist as subordinate languages, but the Sinhala language would always reign over them.

However, the singing of the national anthem in Sinhala only was just one of the many measures taken to consolidate the Sinhala Buddhist ethnocratic state order. During the armed conflict, official road signs in the North and East were written in the Tamil language, followed by Sinhala and English. After the LTTE's defeat, these were rewritten with the Sinhala language first, followed by Tamil, and then the English words. To assert the dominance of Buddhism on the island, statues of Buddha were erected, and Buddhist temples built in predominantly Tamil-speaking areas, where there were virtually no Sinhala Buddhists, except newly inducted Sinhala soldiers and police officers. M. A. Sumanthiran (2012 cited in Majeed, 2012), a Tamil parliamentarian, accused Sri Lanka of undertaking a cultural intrusion in the Tamil areas. Sri Lanka also resumed its Sinhala colonisation programmes, leading to R. Sampanthan (2014 cited in *The Hindu*, 2014) another prominent Tamil parliamentarian, accusing the state of attempting to change the identity of the traditional Tamil areas.

In the post-LTTE period, Sri Lanka also sought to secure the ethnocratic state order by making a number of Tamils whom it considered to be attempting to revive the LTTE, or pose a challenge to the state's authority, disappear. Sinhala and Muslim journalists and human rights defenders were also not spared. Abductions in unmarked white vans manned by plain-clothed gunmen passing freely through military camps and police checkpoints became a norm (Haviland, 2012; *Channel 4*, 2013; UN, 2015: 74). In one case, a Tamil businessman, who filed a fundamental rights petition at Sri Lanka's Supreme Court after being tortured in police custody earlier, was abducted and made to disappear (Haviland, 2012). The bodies of some of the disappeared later emerged in public places (Haviland, 2012).

Though Sri Lanka consistently denied the existence of state-run death squads, at one point, when rumours spread that there were plans by human rights groups to launch mass scale street protests, an unnamed senior police officer told a local newspaper: 'we have arranged to bring tear gas, and we have plenty of white vans in Sri Lanka' (cited in Haviland, 2012). This is tantamount to an admission by a senior official representing the state that Sri Lanka had at its disposal both law and 'lawlessness' to deal with challenges to the ethnocratic state order that was being secured.

152 *Managing life in pain*

The idea that Sri Lanka had the legitimate right to use whatever means it required to secure the state order was openly mooted by the Defence Secretary Gotabaya Rajapaksa, as early as in 2007, when many Tamils in government-controlled areas suspected of involvement with the LTTE were abducted in white vans and made to disappear. In an interview with the BBC that year, Gotabaya Rajapaksa claimed that what his forces were doing was analogous to the covert counter-terrorist operations of the United States:

> All the militaries do covert operations. When the US does operations they say covert operations. When something is in Sri Lanka they call abductions. This is playing with the words. What I am saying is, if there is a terrorist group, why can't you do anything? It's not against a community . . . I'm talking about terrorists. Anything is fair.
>
> (2007)

In other words, for Gotabaya Rajapaksa, the state was entitled to do anything to eliminate the 'bad' species. It did not matter whether those identified as the 'bad' species should be given the chance to present their cases. All that mattered was that anyone deemed to constitute the 'bad' species had to be eliminated. The Rajapaksa regime had already demonstrated this policy at the conclusion of the armed conflict by killing or disappearing a number of high profile LTTE political officials who surrendered to the security forces (UN, 2015: 63–70). Even the LTTE leader's 12-year-old son Balachandran Pirapaharan was not spared; he was executed after surrendering to the Sri Lanka security forces (UN, 2015: 68).

But apart from getting rid of the 'bad' species, post-LTTE, the state also aimed to ensure that the 'submissive' species continued to remain in a state of submission. In the North, rehabilitated LTTE cadres and supporters were required to 'report regularly – normally on a weekly, fortnightly or monthly basis (depending on the decision of the area commander) – to a police or army base' (UN, 2015: 78). In some cases, the 'rehabilitees' were rearrested and tortured, including being subject to rape and sexual abuse (UN, 2015: 78). This implied that the state was convinced that in order to keep the 'submissive' species in a continued state of submission, it had to regularly inscribe in their bodies the mark of the sovereign: they had to be reminded that they always remained inferior to the sovereign.

The state also sought to showcase the power of the sovereign by introducing a new phenomenon known as the 'grease devils'. At night, men covering their bodies and clothes with grease roamed the Northern and Eastern Provinces and parts of the Northwestern Province where Tamils and Muslims remain the majority, randomly attacking men, sexually assaulting women and robbing houses (Haviland, 2011a). Though some Sinhala villages in the central and southern parts of the island were also targeted, most of the attacks took place in predominantly Tamil and Muslim areas, especially the North and East (US Department of State, 2012: 23). This led to a feeling of insecurity among the Tamil and Muslim people, with many, especially women and children, feeling 'afraid to walk at night' (Blake, 2011). In the words of the Human Rights Commission of Sri Lanka (HRCSL)

(2011), the constant appearance of the so-called grease devils in the North and East created a 'fear psychosis' among the women.

Many of those grease devils were seen by the locals to be entering military camps and police stations and disappearing (Haviland, 2011a). The police refused to register complaints made by the locals (HRCSL, 2011). In some cases, when the locals attempted to enter military camps and police stations to apprehend the grease devils, or attacked the security forces for protecting them, they were either shot or arrested (Haviland, 2011a; HRCSL, 2011). A large number of troops, and even battle tanks, were deployed in the areas where the locals clashed with the Sri Lanka security forces (Haviland, 2011a). During a meeting with the Muslim clergy in the East, Gotabaya Rajapaksa (2011 cited in Aneez and Sirilal, 2011) warned that anyone who attempted to attack the security forces over the grease devil issue would be treated as a terrorist: 'Surrounding military camps and attacking the forces are terrorist acts. Our forces are capable of facing any threat after facing a 30-year brutal terrorist war. So do not try to joke with the forces'. It seemed, for Gotabaya Rajapaksa, the 'submissive' species had to always remain in a submissive state. If violence was being inflicted on them, it was to test their submissiveness. Any attempt to resist the state would mean that they would automatically become the 'bad' species, against whom the full force of the sovereign would be unleashed.

The grease devils phenomenon signalled that Sri Lanka had extended its war to secure the Sinhala Buddhist ethnocratic state order to the island's Muslim population also. Sri Lanka wanted to ensure that not only the Tamils but also the Muslims remained in a submissive state. In September 2011, a few weeks after Gotabaya Rajapaksa warned the Muslims, an Islamic shrine in the North-central town of Anuradhapura was demolished by Sinhala Buddhist extremists led by a Buddhist monk, who claimed that the Islamic shrine was in a land given to the Buddhists 2,000 years ago (Haviland, 2011b). The demolishing of the shrine was followed by a spate of attacks on mosques. The Rajapaksa regime also facilitated the formation of an extremist Sinhala Buddhist organisation by the name of *Bodhu Bala Sena* (BBS), meaning the army of people's power. The group was led by Buddhist monks who openly incited hatred and violence against Muslims. Speaking at the inauguration event of the BBS, Gotabaya Rajapaksa (2013 cited in *BBC*, 2013) praised the role of the Buddhist monks during the armed conflict and openly extended the government's support for their activities: 'It is the monks who protect our country, religion and race. No one should doubt these clergy. We're here to give you encouragement'. After its inauguration, the BBS began holding rallies, inciting hatred against the Muslims (*BBC*, 2013), culminating in June 2014 in mass violence in the South-western town of Alutgama, where Muslim people, their homes and businesses were attacked (*BBC*, 2014). Three Muslims and a Tamil security guard working in a Muslim business were killed, with over eighty people sustaining injuries (Colombage, 2014). Though the human casualties on the part of the Muslims were low, the scale of destruction caused to their properties, and the behaviour of the security forces who refrained from arresting any of the Sinhala Buddhist extremists, were testimony to the fact that Sri Lanka was allowing the sovereign to directly assert its power. That is, after Black July 1983, the state was allowing 'lawlessness' to ensure the submissiveness of the Muslims.

Some Muslims retaliated by attacking the Sinhala Buddhists in the area, including the extremists. In response, the Sri Lankan President Mahinda Rajapaksa (2014 cited in *BBC*, 2014), who was away in Bolivia at that time, warned: 'The government will not allow anyone to take law into their hands'. There was nothing that even Muslim political leaders who held ministerial posts in the government could do. SLMC leader Hakeem (2014 cited in *BBC*, 2014), who held the portfolio of Justice Minister in the Rajapaksa government, could do nothing but only express outrage and say that he was 'ashamed' to be in the government.

In the post-LTTE period, Sri Lanka also considered the Sinhala Christian population a threat to the ethnocratic state order it was in the process of securing. Having harboured, since Portuguese colonial rule in the sixteenth century, animosity towards the Christian clergy engaged in converting the Sinhala Buddhists to Christianity, the Buddhist monks saw the post-armed conflict period as a great opportunity to target the Sinhala Christians. Many churches in the Sinhala areas came under attack from gangs of Sinhala Buddhist extremists led by Buddhist monks (UN, 2014: 6). Although the military was not involved in the attacks, the police in particular were complicit in the violence by refraining from taking action against the perpetrators (UN, 2014: 6). In August 2013, Navi Pillay (2013), the visiting UN High Commissioner for Human Rights, expressed concern at 'the lack of swift action against the perpetrators'. Pillay also expressed surprise at the government's efforts to downplay the atrocities (Pillay, 2013).

The popularity Mahinda Rajapaksa enjoyed among the Sinhala Buddhists after the military defeat of the LTTE suggested that his term in office would be long. However, when Maithripala Sirisena, a senior minister in the Rajapaksa government and a confidant of Kumaratunga, emerged as his main opponent in the presidential election of 8 January 2015, it became apparent that Rajapaksa's fall was imminent. Like Rajapaksa, Sirisena was also popular among the Sinhala Buddhists. However, for the Sinhala Buddhist electorate, when compared to the nepotic Rajapaksa, Sirisena, from a humble background, was better poised to serve their interests. Sirisena's role as the acting defence minister in the final stages of the armed conflict also enhanced his reputation among the Sinhala Buddhists. The fact that Sirisena remained in the country and oversaw the military defeat of the LTTE while Rajapaksa was away on a foreign tour in the last days of the armed conflict meant that he could stake a claim that he was the real leader who stayed with the armed forces, and led the state to victory. Field Marshall Fonseka, the commander of the Sri Lanka army in the last days of the armed conflict, also threw his weight behind Sirisena. Kumaratunga, who was remembered by the Sinhala Buddhist electorate for capturing the Jaffna peninsula from the LTTE in April 1996, also supported her confidante's bid for presidency. Wickremesinghe, also popular among the Sinhala Buddhists for successfully creating an international safety net of diplomacy, military expertise and material that laid the foundations for the military defeat of the LTTE, led Sirisena's election campaign, with the hope of becoming prime minister under Sirisena. The JVP, having shunned militant Marxism and emerging as the third-largest Sinhala Buddhist political party during Kumaratunga's presidency, and the Sinhala Buddhist ultranationalist party Jathika Hela Urumaya (JHU), both of which previously supported Rajapaksa, this time supported an alternative Sinhala Buddhist leadership led by Sirisena.

The majority of the Tamils, Muslims and the Sinhala Christians saw the January 2015 presidential election as a once in a life-time opportunity for ousting Rajapaksa from power. It did not matter to them whether Sirisena was close to the Sinhala Buddhist extremists, or the role he played in the final stages of the armed conflict. Thus, the political defeat of Rajapaksa at the ballot box in the January 2015 presidential election was not, as many Western leaders and diplomats (see, for example Biswal, 2016) would like to believe, the result of the people of Sri Lanka coming together to restore democracy by ousting a leader who was leading the country in an authoritarian direction, and replacing him with a leader who 'rejected the politics of fear and division and sought to bring the country together'. In fact, since assuming office, whilst promising to enact a new constitution devolving power to the Tamils and Muslims, Sirisena (2016) has also sought to assure the Sinhala Buddhists that the foremost place given to Buddhism since 1972 will not be compromised; implying that Sirisena, like his predecessors, is committed to securing the Sinhala Buddhist ethnocratic state order.

Thus, in biopolitical terms, the regime change of January 2015 can be summarised as follows: on the one hand, large sections of the 'good' species formed an alliance to bring to power a leader to better serve their interests; on the other hand, the 'submissive' species aligned themselves with the 'good' species to oust the leader who had inflicted on them untold sufferings and miseries.

References

Amnesty International (2009) *Unlock the Camps in Sri Lanka: Safety and Dignity for the Displaced Now*. London: Amnesty International.
Aneez, S. and Sirilal, R. (2011) *More than 100 Arrested in New Sri Lanka "Grease Devil" Clash*. Available at: http://uk.reuters.com/article/uk-srilanka-devils-idUKTRE77M4N620110823 (Accessed: 20 May 2015).
BBC (2013) 'The Hardline Buddhists Targeting Sri Lanka's Muslims'. Available at: http://www.bbc.co.uk/news/world-asia-21840600 (Accessed: 26 March 2013).
BBC (2014) 'Sri Lanka Muslims Killed in Alutgama Clashes With Buddhists'. Available at: http://www.bbc.co.uk/news/world-asia-27864716 (Accessed: 17 June 2014).
BBC Sinhala Service (2009a) 'Youth Disappear from IDP Camps'. Available at: http://www.bbc.com/sinhala/news/story/2009/06/090615_sunila_hooded.shtml (Accessed: 8 August 2013).
BBC Sinhala Service (2009b) '"IDPs Not Protected by Law" – CJ'. Available at: http://www.bbc.com/sinhala/news/story/2009/06/090604_ceejay.shtml (Accessed: 16 September 2014).
Biswal, N.D. (2016) *Remarks Introducing Sri Lankan Foreign Minister Mangala Samaraweera*. Available at: http://www.state.gov/p/sca/rls/rmks/2016/253743.htm (Accessed: 26 February 2016).
Blake, R.O. (2011) *Transcript of Press Conference by Assistant Secretary Robert O. Blake, Jr. at the American Center in Colombo*. Available at: https://srilanka.usembassy.gov/tr-14-2sept11.html (Accessed: 20 September 2011).

156 Managing life in pain

Bureau of the Commissioner General of Rehabilitation (2013) *Rehabilitation of Excombatants*. Available at: http://bcgr.gov.lk/history.php (Accessed: 5 February 2014).

Chamberlain, G. (2009) *Trapped Sri Lankans "Dying in Makeshift Hospital"*. Available at: https://www.theguardian.com/world/2009/feb/15/sri-lanka-tamil-tigers (Accessed: 17 May 2015).

Channel 4 (2013) 'Who Are Sri Lanka's Disappeared?' Available at: http://www.channel4.com/news/sri-lanka-disappeared-white-vans-missing-people-war-chogm (Accessed: 6 January 2015).

Colombage, D. (2014) *In Pictures: Sri Lanka Hit by Religious Riot*. Available at: http://www.aljazeera.com/indepth/inpictures/2014/06/pictures-sri-lanka-hit-religio-2014617112053394816.html (Accessed: 19 June 2014).

Dissanayake, G. (1983) 'Speech', *Executive Committee Meeting*. Lanka Jathika Estate Workers' Union, Colombo, 5 September.

Emergency Regulations No. 01 of 2005 (No. 1405/14). Colombo: Government of Sri Lanka. Available at: http://documents.gov.lk/Extgzt/2005/pdf/Aug/1405–14/1405–14e/e1.pdf (Accessed: 8 June 2011).

Foucault, M. (1980) *Power/Knowledge*. Translated by Colin Gordon, Leo Marshall, John Mepham, and Kate Soper. Harlow: Pearson Education.

Foucault, M. (1991) *Discipline and Punish: The Birth of the Prison*. Translated by Alan Sheridan. London: Penguin Books (Original work published 1975).

Foucault, M. (1998) *The History of Sexuality: Volume 1: The Will to Knowledge*. Translated by Robert Hurley. London: Penguin Books (Original work published 1976).

Foucault, M. (2004) *"Society Must Be Defended": Lectures at the College de France, 1975–76*. Translated by David Macey. London: Penguin Books.

Haviland, C. (2011a) *The Mystery of Sri Lanka's "Grease Devils"*. Available at: http://www.bbc.co.uk/news/world-south-asia-14673586 (Accessed: 30 August 2011).

Haviland, C. (2011b) *Sri Lanka Buddhist Monks Destroy Muslim Shrine*. Available at: http://www.bbc.co.uk/news/world-south-asia-14926002 (Accessed: 16 September 2011).

Haviland, C. (2012) *Sri Lanka's Sinister White Van Abductions*. Available at: http://www.bbc.co.uk/news/world-asia-17356575 (Accessed: 16 March 2014).

Hettiarachi, M. (2013) 'Sri Lanka's Rehabilitation Program', *PRISM*, 4(2), pp. 105–121.

The Hindu (2014) 'Sinhala Colonisation a Great Worry for Tamils'. Available at: http://www.thehindu.com/news/national/tamil-nadu/sinhala-colonisation-a-great-worry-for-tamils/article6358994.ece (Accessed: 30 August 2014).

HRCSL (2011) *HRCSL Report on Grease Yakkas*. Available at: http://hrcsl.lk/english/2011/09/29/media-communique-issued-by-the-human-rights-commission-of-sri-lanka/ (Accessed: 2 January 2015).

Human Rights Watch (2008) *Sri Lanka: End Internment of Displaced Persons*. Available at: https://www.hrw.org/news/2008/07/02/sri-lanka-end-internment-displaced-persons (Accessed: 28 May 2014).

Human Rights Watch (2009a) *Sri Lanka: World Leaders Should Demand End to Detention Camps*. Available at: https://www.hrw.org/news/2009/09/22/sri-lanka-world-leaders-should-demand-end-detention-camps (Accessed: 10 May 2014).

Human Rights Watch (2009b) *Sri Lanka: Free All Unlawfully Detained*. Available at: https://www.hrw.org/news/2009/11/24/sri-lanka-free-all-unlawfully-detained (Accessed: 10 May 2014).

Human Rights Watch (2009c) *War On the Displaced: Sri Lankan Army and LTTE Abuses Against Civilians in Vanni*. New York: Human Rights Watch.

Human Rights Watch (2009d) *Sri Lanka: End Illegal Detention of Displaced Population.* Available at: https://www.hrw.org/news/2009/06/11/sri-lanka-end-illegal-detention-displaced-population (Accessed: 23 June 2013).

Human Rights Watch (2013) *"We Will Teach You a Lesson": Sexual Violence against Tamils by Sri Lankan Security Forces.* New York: Human Rights Watch.

Kyung, L.Y. (2010) *Sri Lanka: Thousands of Tamils Still Detained, Torture Alleged.* Available at: https://www.greenleft.org.au/content/sri-lanka-thousands-tamils-still-detained-torture-alleged (Accessed: 2 November 2010).

Majeed, I. (2012) *Misguided Buddhist Zealots.* Available at: http://www.thesundayleader.lk/2012/02/05/misguided-buddhist-zealots/3/ (Accessed: 7 May 2015).

McRaith, C. (2012) *Arbitrary Detention in Post-Conflict Sri Lanka.* Virginia: University of Virginia.

Pillay, N. (2013) *Opening Remarks by UN High Commissioner for Human Rights Navi Pillay at a Press Conference during Her Mission to Sri Lanka Colombo, 31 August 2013.* Available at: http://www.ohchr.org/EN/NewsEvents/Pages/DisplayNews.aspx?NewsID=13673 (Accessed: 2 September 2014).

Public Security Ordinance: Ordinance No. 25 of 1947. Colombo: Government of Ceylon.

Rajapaksa, G. (2007) Interviewed by Roland Buerk for *BBC News Channel*, 12 June. Available at: http://news.bbc.co.uk/1/hi/world/south_asia/6745553.stm (Accessed: 10 July 2011).

Rajapaksa, M. (2009a) *This Victory Belongs to the People Lined Up behind the National Flag.* Available at: www.island.lk/2009/05/20/features4.html (Accessed: 17 July 2015).

Rajapaksa, M. (2009b) Interviewed by N.Ram for *The Hindu*, 6 July. Available at: http://www.thehindu.com/todays-paper/tp-opinion/i-want-to-resettle-these-people-as-soon-as-possible-rajapaksa/article221971.ece (Accessed: 13 May 2013).

Ranasinghe, S. (2010) Interviewed by Stephen Sackur for *Hardtalk, BBC*, 9 June. Available at: https://www.youtube.com/watch?v=4gXbFPoDWSI (Accessed: 12 September 2012).

Sackur, S. (2010) *A Sri Lankan Re-education for Tamil Child Soldiers.* Available at: http://news.bbc.co.uk/1/hi/8721974.stm (Accessed: 12 September 2012).

Sirisena, M. (2016) *Sirisena Orders Probe into Jaffna Shooting Incident.* Available at: http://www.thehindu.com/news/international/south-asia/buddhisms-position-in-sri-lanka-will-not-change-sirisena/article9256021.ece (Accessed: 22 October 2016).

The Sunday Times (2010) 'National Anthem Only in Sinhala; Tamil Version Out'. Available at: http://www.sundaytimes.lk/101212/News/nws_01.html (Accessed: 14 December 2010).

UN (2014) *Promoting Reconciliation and Accountability in Sri Lanka: Report of the Office of the United Nations High Commissioner for Human Rights.* Geneva: Office of the UN High Commissioner for Human Rights.

UN (2015) *Report of the OHCHR Investigation on Sri Lanka (OISL).* Geneva: Office of the UN High Commissioner for Human Rights.

US Department of State (2012) *Sri Lanka: Country Reports on Human Rights Practices for 2011.* Washington: US Department of State.

Varatharajah, T. (2014) Interview by Saroj Pathirana for *BBC*, 20 March. Available at: http://www.bbc.co.uk/news/world-asia-26670691 (Accessed: 10 June 2015).

Wickremasinghe, N. (2009) *Two Legal Cases Challenge Sri Lanka's Mass Detention of Tamil Civilians.* Available at: https://www.wsws.org/en/articles/2009/06/sldc-j19.html (Accessed: 10 July 2012).

Yatawara, D. (2009) *LTTE Propaganda Defeated: Truth Revealed.* Available at: http://www.sundayobserver.lk/2009/07/12/fea02.asp (Accessed: 8 June 2013).

Conclusion

Developing a biopolitical perspective on government and politics in Sri Lanka, this book has shown that though the island-state has institutions similar to those existing in Western liberal states and holds regular elections, these do not make it a democracy. In Sri Lanka's case, its elected legislature that allows it to stake a claim it is a democracy has also allowed it to exercise power in the same way that authoritarian states do. All of the discriminatory and draconian legislations that Sri Lanka has in place were enacted by its elected legislature. It is also Sri Lanka's elected legislature that accorded the foremost place to Buddhism and the pre-eminent position to the Sinhala language and renamed the island 'Sri Lanka' through the two republican constitutions of 1972 and 1978, thereby giving constitutional validity to the *Mahavamsa's* claim that the island is the holy land of the Sinhala Buddhists. In other words, the very institution developed by the English at the threshold of modernity to prevent the encroachment of the powers of the prince on their liberties and assert their rights has been used by Sri Lanka to transform into an ethnocracy and violate *en masse* the civil liberties and human rights of its non-Sinhala Buddhist populations and those of the Sinhala Buddhist Marxists who challenged the state.

Using the lens of biopolitics, this book has also shown that much of the violence inflicted on the Tamils and other sections of the island's population by the Sri Lankan security forces were pursuant to the powers vested on them by the state's emergency legislations, the PSO and the PTA. As we saw in Chapter 2 and Chapter 3, the mass violence unleashed by the Sinhala Buddhist extremists on the Tamils were not acts of lawlessness but those sanctioned by the state with the objective of asserting the supremacy of the sovereign and the laws enacted in its favour and the supremacy of the state.

Building on Foucault's reconceptualisation of the term 'war', the book was also able to highlight Sri Lanka's use of power relations in addition to military action to produce the effects of battle. Before the emergence of the Tamil armed struggle, Sri Lanka's war to biopolitically transform the island into an ethnocracy manifested through law and 'lawlessness'. With the emergence of the Tamil armed struggle in the 1970s and 1980s, the state's war to 'defend' the Sinhala Buddhist race/species that it managed/fostered and secure the ethnocratic state order expanded into the terror of law and military action, complemented by a reformed state of 'lawlessness'. In the 1990s, economy, in the form of an economic embargo on the LTTE-held territories of the North, became another means of producing the effects of battle for Sri Lanka. The state also aligned with Jihadi extremists to retake the Eastern Province, thereby revealing that exercising biopower along extreme ethnological lines does not constrain states from making tactical alliances with opposing extremist power complexes. Following the signing of the Norwegian-sponsored ceasefire agreement with the LTTE in February 2002, Sri Lanka used diplomacy, through the 'peace' process, to produce the effects of battle, thereby highlighting that 'peace' can also become a means of waging war.

The analysis in this book has also exposed how Sri Lanka's biopolitics of constructing and securing a Sinhala Buddhist ethnocratic state order, despite some of its productive dynamics for the Sinhala Buddhist people (the 'good' species), has largely remained tilted in favour of the power of death. Whilst taking measures to improve the lives of the 'good' species, postcolonial Ceylon/Sri Lanka has dedicated much of its energy to eliminating those whom it considered to constitute the 'bad' species or to belong to the 'enemy' race/species. As Chapter 6 has shown, in the post-LTTE period, even when the Tamils became a 'submissive' species, Sri Lanka continued to exercise the power of death over them, whilst at the same time targeting other 'submissive' species: the Muslims and the Sinhala Christians. This power of death, as we saw in Chapter 6, also manifested through disciplinary mechanisms, largely in the form of torture, sexual abuse and rape, allowing the state to keep the 'submissive' species in a state of submissiveness, and for the production of 'truth' on the LTTE and the scale of Tamil civilian casualties in the final stages of the armed conflict.

Since assuming office in January 2015, the regime of Sirisena–Wickremesinghe has, with the exception of isolated incidents of violence by the state's security forces, largely refrained from unleashing violence in its naked form on Sri Lanka's populations. Tamil nationalists, human rights defenders and civil society activists are able to stage street demonstrations, often criticising the government. Tamils are also able to hold private, and to some extent public, commemoration events for fallen LTTE fighters. Some of the lands previously occupied by the Sri Lankan military in the North and East have been released to their Tamil owners. A number of military personnel and paramilitary operatives long implicated in assassinating Tamil politicians and Sinhala journalists in the past have been arrested and remain in detention pending trial. Attacks on religious places, especially mosques and churches in the Sinhala areas have also decreased, though not ceased altogether. With some notable exceptions, mass-scale Sinhalisation programmes in the predominantly Tamil-speaking areas have also been put on hold. The ban on singing the Sri Lankan national anthem in Tamil has also been lifted.

The Sirisena–Wickremesinghe regime has also reversed the statist economic policies of the Rajapaksa regime and curbed some of the powers of the executive presidency, transferring them to the prime minister and the island's legislature.

This, however, does not give grounds for rejoicing that democracy would be restored in Sri Lanka soon or give sound reason to believe that the racial violence/

mass atrocities of the past will not occur again. Despite taking steps to repeal the PTA and replace it with another counter-terrorism legislation, the Sirisena–Wickremesinghe regime has not taken any steps to repeal the PSO, which allows the state to use draconian powers at times deemed to be of emergency. The power of Sri Lanka's legislature to enact further discriminatory and draconian legislations has also not changed. Moreover, there are no checks and balances to prevent the political monopoly of the Sinhala Buddhists in Sri Lanka's legislature.

As we saw in Chapter 6, since ascending to power, whilst promising to devolve power to the Tamils and Muslims, the Sirisena–Wickremesinghe regime has also sought to reassure the Sinhala Buddhists that the foremost place accorded to Buddhism in the island-state's constitution will not be compromised. This means that the ethnocratic character of Sri Lanka is unlikely to change, even if it is to devolve power to the Tamils and Muslims beyond the existing Provincial Council system and give force to the Tamil language provisions of the *Thirteenth Amendment*, discussed in Chapter 3.

Though the Sirisena–Wickremesinghe regime has promised to hold an internal investigation into the violation of international human rights and humanitarian law and the mass atrocities committed by the Sri Lankan security forces in the last stages of the armed conflict, it has remained vehemently opposed to any international judicial investigation. This may be attributed to the fact that such an investigation could implicate, on the basis of the chain of command, as well as former President Mahinda Rajapaksa and his Defence Secretary and brother Gotabaya Rajapaksa, the current President Sirisena, who was the acting defence minister, and his cabinet minister and former Army Commander Fonseka. Thus, the promise of the Sirisena–Wickremesinghe regime to investigate the mass atrocities of the past continues to remain an elusive one, leading to fears on the part of many Tamils that justice will never be served.

As we saw in the Introduction, a democracy, in its contemporary sense, is not simply a state that only upholds the will of the majority. Nor does a state qualify to be called a democracy simply because it holds periodic elections, upholds its laws and adheres to open market economic policies or because it maintains close ties with Western liberal states. Instead, a democracy is a state that is also capable of guaranteeing the civil liberties and human rights of all of its citizens, not simply that of the majority ethnic community that holds political monopoly. Sri Lanka has held periodic elections, and upheld the will of its majority community – the Sinhala Buddhists. Many of its actions, including the mass atrocities it perpetrated on the Tamils and other sections of its populations, were largely in accordance with the laws enacted by its legislature, or carried out for the purpose of upholding the state, the sovereign and laws enacted in its favour, though these were in contravention of international human rights and humanitarian law. With the exception of the period from 1956 to 1977, when the island-state was ruled by the statist regimes of the Bandaranaikes (see Chapter 2 and Chapter 3), and 2005 to 2014, when it was ruled by the statist Rajapaksa regime, for most of its postcolonial history, Ceylon/Sri Lanka has implemented *laissez faire* economic policies. If these characteristics allow Sri Lanka to stake a claim that it is a democracy, its ethnocratic biopolitics of violating *en masse* the civil liberties and human rights of its non-Sinhala Buddhist populations make it an ethnocracy.

For Sri Lanka to stake a claim to be a democracy, it needs, as a first step, to move beyond its Sinhala Buddhist ethnocratic biopolitics, and guarantee the civil liberties and human rights of all of its populations. For this to happen, it is imperative that Sri Lanka abandon the constitutional provisions that give foremost place to Buddhism and the pre-eminent position to the Sinhala language; replace the name 'Sri Lanka' and the sword-wielding lion flag surrounded by Indian fig leaves; and change the unitary character of the state. This way, it would be able to reflect the multiethnic and multicultural character of the island and its history. The repeal of all of its discriminatory and draconian legislations, including the *Sixth Amendment* to the constitution that criminalises non-violent secessionist demands, would assure the Tamils that they would be able to realise their political aspirations through democratic means, like the people of Quebec and Scotland. A reform of the legislature with entrenched provisions in the constitution to secure those reforms, and to ensure that no ethnic community on the island is able to monopolise governmental power, or enact legislations detriment to other ethnic communities, would also help build trust amongst the island's populations. Until such time, Sri Lanka will remain a democracy in name only.

Index

Abadi, J. 81, 98
Abeyasekara, S. 138
Agamben, G. 13–14, 24–5
Agathangelou, A.M. 7, 9
Ali, A. 75–9, 98
all-island sovereignty 60, 64, 69
Amnesty International 54–8, 62, 68–70, 98, 149, 155
Aneez, S. 153, 155
Annan, K. 138
Aradau, C. 5, 9, 11, 14–15, 25
Ariyanetthiran, P. 81, 98
Armitage, R. 111, 117, 132
Arunmaran 144, 146, 150
Aryan lion race, the 41–3
Ashraf, M.H.M. 82–3
Athas, I. 105, 111, 115, 132

Balachandran, P.K. 50, 70, 80, 99
Balasingham, A. 65, 70, 74, 84–5, 95, 99, 107, 113–14, 119, 121, 132
Bandaranaike, S.W.R.D. 29–31, 39, 65
bare life 13–14, 25
BBC Sinhala Service 138, 149, 155
BBC Tamil Service 82, 84, 100
BBS 153
biopolitics 11–16
Biswal, N.D. 1, 9, 155
Black July 64–5, 94, 147, 154
Blake, R.O. 126–7, 132, 152, 155
Blanke, T. 15, 25
Bloom, M.M. 28–44
Bogollagama, R. 128
Bose, S. 63, 71
Boulainvilliers, H. 17
British Empire, the 1, 7, 27, 36, 38–9, 47
British India 24, 77
Buddha 3, 32–3, 41, 43, 151

Buddhism 2–3, 32, 40–1, 43, 155, 158, 160–1
Bush, G.W. 1, 9, 110–11, 133

Ceylon (Constitution) Order in Council 1946 38–9, 41, 43–4
Ceylon Citizenship Act No.18 of 1948 28–9, 33, 39, 44, 46
Ceylon Independence Act 1947 43–4
Chacko, P. 66, 71
Chamberlain, G. 140, 156
Chandler, D. 4, 9
Chelvanayagam, S.J.V. 34, 40, 42, 49
Chilcott, D.J. 2, 9
civil liberties 1, 3, 142, 158, 160–1
Claiborne, W. 64, 71
Clausewitz, C. 16–18, 25
Cockburn, A. 38
Cohen, S.P. 66, 71
Coke, E. 17–18, 20, 25
Colombage, D. 153, 156
Colvin, M. 92, 99
The Constitution of the Democratic Socialist Republic of Sri Lanka 50, 64–5, 68, 71
The Constitution of the Republic of Sri Lanka 40–1, 43–5
Coomaraswamy, R. 38–9, 45
Court of Appeal Act No.44 of 1971 40, 45

David, S.A. 52, 71
Davy, J. 27, 45
de-facto state 74, 85, 96, 112–13, 119, 123, 127
Defence of Realm Act 1914 36
democracy 1, 27, 36, 44, 103–4, 155, 158–61
DeVotta, N. 2, 9, 66, 71
Dharmapala, A. 41, 45, 75, 77

Dillon, M. 15, 25
diplomacy 8, 17, 98, 103, 154, 159
diplomatic front, the 89, 111, 122
Dissanayaka, T.D.S.A. 51, 71
Dissanayake, G. 59, 63–4, 71, 147, 156
district quota 48–9, 65
Dixit, J.N. 65–6, 71
Doyle, M.W. 1, 9
Dunlap, C.J. 24–5
Dutch, the 2, 76
Dutthagamani 32

economic embargo 8, 75, 90–7, 108, 112, 159
economic front, the 88
economic inequalities 16, 39, 91
Edrisinha, R. 40, 45
Eelam 41
Ellalan 32
Emergency (Miscellaneous Provisions and Powers) Regulations No. 1 of 2005 150
emergency law 7, 18, 24, 35, 69, 149, 158; *see also* martial law
Emergency Powers Act 1920 36
Emergency Regulation 15A 54–6
Emergency Regulation 55 B-G 56
Entwistle, J. 116, 132
Escobar, A. 7–9
Eyre, E.J. 38, 45

federal political solution 111, 114, 116–17, 122
Fernando, J.L. 34, 45
Finlason, W.F. 36, 38, 45
Fonseka, S. 113, 154, 160
Forbes, J. 37–8, 45
Foucault, M. 2–7, 11–24
Fourth Floor, the 148
free trade *see* open market economic policies

The Gal Oya Development Board Act No.51 of 1949 33–4
Gandhi, I. 66–7, 71
Gandhi, M. 28
Gandhi, R. 68, 95, 110, 121
genocide 12, 15, 62, 72, 84, 99
Goodhand, J. 135
Goonetilke, R. 127
grease devils, the 152–3, 156
Green Berets, the 105
Guha, S. 125, 132
Gunaratne, K. 140
GWoT 5, 8, 106–7

Hain, P. 109, 133
Hakeem, R. 85, 154
Hamlyn, M. 63–4, 71
Haniffa, F. 40, 45, 50, 71
Hardt, M. 14–15, 25
Harris, N. 28–9, 37, 45, 48–9, 71
Haukland, H. 110
Haviland, C. 151–3, 156
Hettiarachi, M. 144, 146, 156
historico-political discourse 17–18
Hobbes, T. 19–20, 25
Holmes, J. 127, 133
home guards, the 34, 81
Homo Sacer 13–14, 25
Hoole, R. 52, 58–9, 71, 79, 81, 84, 99
Horowitz, D.L. 48, 71
human rights 1, 3, 86, 138, 142, 151, 158–61
Human Rights Watch 124, 139–44, 146, 149
Hunt, A. 22, 25
Huntington, S.P. 44, 46
Hussain, N. 24, 26
Hussein, S. 89, 113
Hyam, R. 7, 10

Ibralebbe v. R (1964) 43, 46
Imtiyaz, A.R.M. 85, 99
Indian troops, the 7–8, 68–70, 74–5, 79, 86–7, 94, 120
Indira Doctrine, the 66
Indo-Sri Lanka Accord 68
interim administration 113, 115–17, 122, 132
international safety net 108, 110, 113, 120, 126, 135, 154
internment camps 8, 138–44, 147, 149
IPKF *see* Indian troops, the
Iqbal, M.C.M. 85, 99
Islamic fundamentalism 80, 89–90

Janani, J.T. 62, 72, 94, 99
Jansz, F. 105, 132–3
Jayapalan, N. 66, 72
Jayaram, P 92, 99
Jayasuriya, M. 69, 72
Jayewardene regime, the 64, 66, 68, 78, 94
Jaysinghe, A. 109, 133
Jeyaraj, D.B.S. 80, 83–6, 99
Jihad Group 79–81, 83, 86–7, 89
Jihadists 8, 75, 80, 83, 87–90, 159
Johansson, A. 89, 99
Judicial Committee of the Privy Council, the 39–40, 43, 46

judicial prerogative, the 43
JVP 7–8, 37, 50–1, 65, 69–70, 90, 154

Kadirgamar, L. 106, 118
Kalbag, C. 63, 72
Kannangara, W. 60, 72
Kant, I. 20, 26
Kapferer, B. 61, 63, 72
Kapur, S.P. 66, 72
Karikalan, S. 82–3, 85
Karuna 81–3, 85–6, 89, 99, 117–18, 122, 136
Kemper, S. 2, 10, 27, 33, 46
Kennedy, D. 24, 26
Kittu 86, 99
Kleinfeld, M. 107, 133
Klem, B. 135
Kodeeswaran v Attorney General 1969 40, 46
Krishna, S. 65, 72
Kumaratunga regime, the 91, 93, 96, 103–4, 106–7, 114, 118
Kyung, L.Y. 150, 157

lawfare 24
lawlessness 30–6, 58–65
Layton, P. 102, 126, 133
Locke, J. 19–20, 26
Lokubandara, W.J.M. 60, 72
LTTE 4, 7–9, 49, 78–9
Lunstead, J. 89, 100, 104–5, 107, 110–12, 115–16, 120–1

Macan-Markar, M. 119, 133
McGirk, T. 91–2, 100
McGowan, W. 29, 37, 46
Machakos Protocol 117
MacRae, C. 128–9, 134
McRaith, C. 150, 157
Mahavamsa 3, 10, 29, 32–3, 41–3, 69, 158
Mahinda Chintana 119
Majeed, I. 151, 157
Mandelbaum, M. 1, 10
Marshall, H.H. 40, 46
martial law 18, 36–8, 45–6, 76, 100
Mathaya 79, 85–6, 95–6, 147
Mel, N. de 69, 71
Mendis, G.C. 39, 46
Menon, R. 82, 87, 100
Middle Ages Europe 3, 31, 48, 53–4, 141–2, 149
Miliband, D. 128, 134
Mobilisation of Supplementary Force Act No.40 of 1985 34, 46

Mohamed, M.H. 90
Moorcraft, P. 57, 72, 102–3, 111, 126–7, 134
Motor Transport Act No.48 of 1957 34, 46
Mukherjee, P. 125
Mullivaikaal 131, 147
Murray, N. 59–60, 62, 72
Muthur East 88, 124–7

Nadarajah, S. 3, 10, 110
Nadesan, S. 29–31, 42, 46
Nanayakara, U. 140
Nanjappa, V. 90, 100
Navy Seals 105
Neal, A.W. 5, 10
Negri, A. 14–15, 25
Neocleous, M. 5, 10, 18, 22–4, 26
Nissen, A.E. 135
No Fire Zones (NFZs) 128–30
Not kennt kein Gebot 31
Nuhuman, M.A. 75–8, 80, 100

Obama, B. 1, 10
Official Language Act No.33 of 1956 29–31, 34, 39–40
Old Park 51–2
open market economic policies 1, 105, 107, 160
Operation Balanced Style 105
Operation Victory Assured 75
Optional Protocol 119, 136
Ottunu, O. 119

Paduvankarai 88, 125–6
Paris, R. 1, 10
Pathmanathan, S. 106, 134
patria protestas 146–7
Pentagon 105–6
Perera, E.W. 76, 100
Perera, S. 125, 134
Perera, U. 121–2, 126, 134
Peterson, J. 118, 134
The Petition of Right 1627 17–18, 26
PFLT 79, 85, 95
Pieris, K. 42, 46
Pillay, N. 37, 47, 154, 157
Pirapaharan, V. 67, 84–7, 95–6, 107–9, 113–19, 121, 131
political monopoly 42, 160
politics of death *see thanatopolitics*
politics of life 13
Ponnambalam, S. 30–1, 34–5, 40, 46, 51, 72, 78
Portuguese, the 2, 27, 41, 154

power complexes 7–8, 12, 16, 50, 159
power of death, the 12, 14, 58, 63–4, 75, 124, 130
pre-interim mechanism 114
Premachandran, S. 115
Premadasa, R. 70, 89–90, 93, 97
Prevention of Terrorism (Temporary Provisions) Act No. 48 of 1979 *see* PTA
Prince, R. 127, 134
provincial council system 68, 160
PSO 35–7, 50–1, 54, 69, 149–50, 157–8, 160
PTA 50–2, 69, 158, 160
Public Security Ordinance No.25 of 1947 *see* PSO

qualified life 13

Rabinow, P. 13–14, 26
Rajapaksa regime, the 103, 120–2, 124–5, 127, 138–40, 148–9
Ramanathan, P. 36–7, 46, 76–7, 100
Ranasinghe, S. 150–1, 157
Ranawana, Arjuna 91–3, 100
Rao, V.P. 66, 72
Ravi, S. 123, 134
Reagan, R. 1, 10, 103, 134
regional autonomy 49, 113–14, 121; *see also* federal political solution
rehabilitation 64, 140–2, 144, 146–7, 150
Reid, J. 15, 25
reign of terror 38, 50, 59, 69–70
religio-cultural identity 79
Republic of Sri Lanka Act 1972 44, 46
right to kill, the 12, 14, 50, 130
Rose, G. 22, 26
Rose, N. 13–14, 26
Rossiter, C.L. 36, 46
Rousseau, J. 20, 26, 30–1, 46
Rudrakumaran, V. 84, 86, 100, 115, 117, 119–20, 135
R v. Hemapala (1963) 43, 46

Sackur, S. 150, 157
Said, E. 7, 10
Samarakkody, E. 59, 72
Sampanthan, R. 124, 135, 151
Saravanamuthu, S. 52–3
Sarvananthan, M. 74, 91, 94, 100
Satyendra, N. 30, 46
Saunders, J. 109, 135
Saxena, G.C. 67
scaffold service, the 22, 31, 58–9

Schaffer, T.C. 114, 135
secession 49–50, 58–9, 65, 114, 116, 122
Selbervik, H. 135
Selby, J. 6, 10
self-determination 49, 78, 109, 113–14
Selvakkumaran, N. 40, 45
Shaheeb, A.M. 82, 100
Shastri, A. 104, 135
Sheriffdeen, S. 81–2, 87, 100
Short, C. 109
Silva, K.M. de 28, 39, 45
Silva, N. de 107, 132
Sinhala Hamudawa 34–5
Sirilal, R. 153, 155
Sirisena, M. 1, 154–5, 157
Sirisena regime, the 159–60
Sivaram, D. 79, 83–4, 100, 116–17, 135
Sixth Amendment, the 64, 161
Snyder, J. 28, 46
social body, the 12, 17–18, 141
Sorbo, G. 104, 135
Soulbury, V. 39, 46
Soviet-type socialist states 15–16
Spain, J.W. 104, 135
Spieker, J. 11, 14, 18, 26
standardisation 48–9, 65, 78
state of emergency 36–7, 51, 149
state of exception, the 24–5, 130
state terror 44, 50
statist 1, 77, 119–20, 159–60
STF 57–8, 69, 81, 87
Stokke, K. 74, 98, 100
Stoler, A.L. 7, 10
strategy of power 11
Sufism 80
Sumanthiran, M.A. 151
sword-wielding lion, the 41–3, 161

tactics of battle 16
take life or let live 12, 124
Tambiah, S.J. 31–2, 37, 47, 51, 60–1, 63, 72
Tamil Diaspora, the 65, 98, 105–7
Tamil Eelam 49, 74, 85–6, 94, 100, 123, 128
Tamil Eelam Police 94, 128
Tamil homeland, the *see* Tamil-speaking areas
Tamil Language (Special Provision) Act No.28 of 1958 40, 47
Tamil Nadu 65, 67, 76, 102
Tamil-speaking areas 33–5, 37, 40, 69–70, 88, 159

Tamil state *see* Tamil Eelam
Taylor, M. 37–8, 47
terror of law, the 50–1, 69, 158
Thamil Arasu 36–7
Thamilchelvan, S.P. 115, 119–21, 125, 136
thanatopolitics 13
Tharmalingam, K.N. 33, 47
Thatcher, M. 1, 10, 103, 136
Thirteenth Amendment, the 68, 160
Tissainayagam, J.S. 80, 89–90, 101
Tokyo Co-Chairs, the 111, 120, 125
Tokyo Donor Conference 111, 114–17
Torrington, V. 36, 47
Trawick, M. 32, 47, 69, 73
Tromsdahl, K. 115
truth, the 3–4, 144–9
TULF, the 50, 78–9, 101
Tzu, S. 103, 122, 136

Udugampola 52
unitary state 3, 41, 32
universal franchise 1, 28
US Department of State, the 109, 115–16, 125, 136, 152, 157
UTHR-J 74, 79–87, 89–90, 101
Uyartchi 144–7, 150

Vaharai 88, 124–7
Vanni 75, 92–3, 126–31, 139–40, 143–4, 146–8
Varatharajah, T. 145, 147–8, 157
Varatharajan, S. 105, 136

Venkatramani, S.H. 94, 101
Vimalarajah, L. 3, 10
violence of law, the 7, 27, 37–8, 57
Vittachi, I. 106, 136
Vittachi, T. 30–1, 33–5, 47, 54, 73
Viyasan 112

Wahabism 80, 99
war 16–25
Weerasekara, M.H. 77, 101
Weeratunga, L. 122, 148
Weeratunge, T.I. 51
Weiss, G. 128, 131, 136
Weizman, E. 24, 26
Welhengama, G. 37, 47
Welikade Prison 52, 62
white vans 151–2
Wickham, G. 22, 25
Wickramasinghe, N. 28, 47, 51, 73
Wickremesinghe regime, the 103, 108, 113–15, 159–60
Wijaya 41–2
Wijemanne, A. 28, 47
Wijeratne, R. 82, 87
Willis, P. 103, 136
Wills, A. 108–9, 137
Wilson, J.A. 28–9, 39, 47–8, 61, 73, 76, 101
Wriggins, H. 28, 45

Yatawara, D. 149, 157
Yiftachel, O. 2, 10